ISRAEL AND THE NATIONS

ISRAEL AND THE NATIONS

from the Exodus to the Fall of the Second Temple

by

F. F. BRUCE

M.A.(Cantab.), D.D.(Aberd.)

Rylands Professor of Biblical Criticism and Exegesis
in the University of Manchester

with Thirty-Six Illustrations
and Three Maps

WILLIAM B. EERDMANS PUBLISHING COMPANY
GRAND RAPIDS, MICHIGAN

TO

FRED AND LENA ROSSETTER

SBN: 85364 093 9

Copyright © 1963 The Paternoster Press

Second Impression . . . May, 1965

Third Impression . . . March, 1968

Fourth Impression . . . January, 1972

Fifth Impression . . . February 1975

This Illustrated Edition . . . October 1969

PREFACE

THIS BOOK HAS ITS INCEPTION, NOT IN ANY INWARD URGE ON THE part of the author (who makes no claim to be a specialist in the greater part of the field which it attempts to cover), but in a request by a group of Scripture teachers for a handbook which might prove useful to them in their work. It is based on two courses of lectures – a shorter one sketching the story of Israel from the Exodus to the Babylonian Exile, and a longer and more detailed one from the Exile onwards. It can accordingly be charged with lopsidedness; but I have reflected that the period treated in greater detail is the period that is less well known to the majority of potential readers of the book, some of whom may therefore be not displeased to have the treatment proportioned thus.

The limited scale of treatment has dictated the complete or virtual exclusion of some important aspects of the history of Israel. While we cannot speak of the nation of Israel before the Exodus, Israel's history cannot be separated from its "prehistory" – the history of the patriarchal period. The Israelites never supposed that the God who delivered them from Egypt and brought them into covenant relationship with Himself was a God of whom no one had ever heard before: to them He was the God of their fathers, Abraham, Isaac and Jacob. The patriarchal period, however, constitutes a subject in itself, especially with the wealth of light that archaeological discovery has shed on it, and deserves separate treatment, by someone better versed in the history of the second millennium B.C. than the present writer.

Again, throughout this book Israel's religion is dealt with only incidentally, for all its centrality in the life and continuity of the nation. Israel's literary history receives even more cursory treatment. Each of these subjects also deserves a volume to itself. But what is given in the following pages may, I hope, serve in some sort as prolegomena to the volumes in the Paternoster Church History series.

Special thanks are due to Miss June S. Hogg, B.A., who typed out the whole work from a none too legible manuscript. I am further indebted for valuable comments to Mr. H. L. Ellison, B.D., B.A., who read the typescript, and the Rev. A. A. Anderson, B.D., B.A., who read the proofs; and – last but not least – to my wife, for help with proof-reading and the compilation of the index.

March, 1963   F.F.B.

PREFACE TO ILLUSTRATED EDITION

THE GENEROUS RECEPTION GIVEN TO THIS BOOK SINCE ITS FIRST appearance has been most gratifying to publishers and author alike. When my publishers suggested that the addition of illustrations would increase its usefulness, I readily agreed, and together we approached Mr. Alan Millard, Librarian of Tyndale House, Cambridge, who kindly undertook the selection and preparation of illustrations. The sound judgment and meticulous care with which he has carried this task through have given us much pleasure and earned our unstinted gratitude. Our sincere thanks must be expressed, too, for the kindness with which so many owners of photographs, in this country and overseas, have permitted their reproduction here; full and detailed acknowledgment is recorded in the letterpress accompanying the respective illustrations.

October, 1969   F.F.B.

CONTENTS

8 CONTENTS

LIST OF ILLUSTRATIONS

LIST OF MAPS

The maps indicate positions of places mentioned in the text, but omit relief features and numerous other places, for the sake of clarity.

INTRODUCTION

WHY SHOULD THERE BE SUCH DEEP AND WIDESPREAD INTEREST at this time of day in the early history of Israel? Why should schoolteachers in the English-speaking world find that the things that happened to that small nation in the last millennium B.C. are relevant to their task of educating young people in the last half-century of the second millennium A.D.? Why Israel? Why not her kinsfolk and neighbours – the Edomites, Moabites and Ammonites, for example?

The answer to this question can be found nowhere but in the distinctive features of Israel's religion. There was something about it that was unparalleled in the surrounding world. An Assyrian king might try to discourage any resistance on the part of the Israelites by pointing to the uselessness of the gods of greater and more powerful states which he had overthrown. "Where are the gods of Hamath and Arpad?" he asked. A most pertinent question, which might well be repeated today. Where, indeed, are they? And how does it come about that the God of Israel continues to be worshipped by millions of people in every one of the earth's continents? The Israelites had their own explanation. As they considered their experience of the God of their fathers, they affirmed: "He has not dealt thus with any other nation." Their affirmation is vindicated by the course of their history.

Yet Israel's national history was not lived out in isolation from other peoples. The Israelites were surrounded by nations greater and mightier than themselves, who impinged upon the life of Israel at innumerable points. It is in the varied response to the challenge presented by these other nations, Asian, African and European, that Israel's own nationhood acquires its special character. Hence the subject of this book is not *Israel* in isolation but *Israel and the Nations*.

For much of the period covered in this work, our most important primary sources are the books of the Hebrew Bible, which Christians call the Old Testament. In these books the story of Israel is told as "sacred history". That is to say, the narrators' interest was not so much in political developments as in the dealings of the God of Israel with His people. They retain their religious value to this day both for the Jewish people and for the Christian church.

Yet, while these books have come down to us as Holy Scripture, they are historical source-documents of first-rate worth. The chapters which follow are not concerned with them as canonical writings, but as material for constructing a political narrative. Other source-material has also been laid under contribution, for which no canonical claims have been made – the writings of secular historians, and the inscriptions of ancient cultures contemporary with the life of Israel in the period under review. These last-named documents have come to light as a result of the archaeological research carried out in the Near East for well over a century and a half. Their discovery has enabled us to appreciate, in a way previously impossible, how remarkably faithful is the historical outline preserved in the Hebrew Bible, from the age of the patriarchs to the Macedonian supremacy.

But to our tale.

CHAPTER I

ISRAEL'S BEGINNINGS

(*c.* 1300—1100 B.C.)

THE EARLIEST REFERENCE TO THE ISRAELITES IN ANY RECORD OUTSIDE the Old Testament occurs in an inscription on a pillar set up about 1220 B.C. by Merneptah, king of Egypt, to celebrate several victories won in the course of his reign. Among other claims to have conquered neighbouring peoples, he boasts:

> Israel is desolate; it has no seed left.[1]

From the way in which "Israel" is written in this inscription, it appears that Israel was not yet a settled nation; the inscription will therefore have to be dated within a generation or two after the departure of the Israelites from Egypt. If Merneptah's claim had been well founded, there would be no story of Israel to tell. But ancient commanders, like their more recent successors, were prone at times to overestimate the scale of their victories; Israel was not so completely desolate, so utterly bereft of all hope of posterity, as Merneptah claimed.[2]

We cannot be sure if the desolation of Israel to which King Merneptah refers corresponds to any occasion mentioned in the Israelites' own records. It is just conceivable that it is the only official Egyptian account of the circumstances attending their crossing of the "Red Sea",[3] although the context suggests rather that Israel had already entered Canaan.

At any rate, the departure of the people of Israel from Egypt marks their birth as a nation. Some generations previously their ancestors, members of a pastoral clan, had gone down from Canaan to Egypt in time of famine and settled in the Wadi Tumilat. The early kings of Dynasty XIX, Seti I and Rameses II (*c.* 1300—1225 B.C.) drafted them

---

[1] *Cf. DOTT*, pp. 137 ff.

[2] Rather less than four centuries later we find a similarly exaggerated claim on the victory monument set up by King Mesha of Moab: "Israel utterly perished for ever" (see p. 48).

[3] More properly "the Sea of Reeds" (Heb. *yam suph*), a name applied to the Gulfs of Suez and Aqaba. Another suggested correlation of Merneptah's claim with the biblical record is that which connects it with the disaster suffered by Israel at Hormah in the Negev (Num. 14:45).

13

in large numbers into forced labour gangs for the building of fortified cities on the north-eastern frontier of Egypt. They rapidly lost their former manner of life and were in danger of forgetting the faith of their fathers. A few generations more, and they would have been assimilated to their depressed fellow-serfs of Egyptian origin. Their ancestral faith, however, was rekindled by Moses, a man of their own race. This Moses had been brought up, through a strange combination of events, at the Egyptian court; but eventually had to flee for his life to North-West Arabia when he was caught espousing the cause of his enslaved kinsmen. In North-West Arabia he became allied by marriage with a priestly family of the Kenite tribe, and in a vision he received a command from the God whom Israel's ancestors had worshipped to return to Egypt and lead his brethren out to the place where the vision appeared to him. The land of Canaan, he was told, had been divinely promised to these ancestors, and their God had not forgotten His promise nor had He failed to observe the affliction of their children. He was about to redeem His promise, and in token of His purpose He made Himself known to Moses by the name Yahweh – a name by which the patriarchs had not worshipped Him, but which expressed His character as a covenant-keeping God. Moses therefore returned to Egypt, and led his people out of that land into the wilderness of North-West Arabia amid a series of natural phenomena in which could be traced the directing power of the patriarchs' God, intervening for the deliverance of their descendants. And indeed, these phenomena were such as Moses in the ordinary way could neither have foreseen nor controlled; yet their occurrence just at that time confirmed the directions given to him in his vision and rendered possible Israel's escape from Egypt in the way in which Moses assured them it would happen.

Moses, in fact, was the first and greatest of the long succession of prophets whose influence upon the religious life of Israel was in the long run so decisive – men who spoke in the name of Israel's God and interpreted the events of the past, present and future in terms of His revealed character and will. But no prophet's influence was so determinative of the national life as was that of Moses – so much so that it has been well said that if he did not exist, he would have to be invented to account for the rise and progress of the nation of Israel. The plagues which afflicted the Egyptians on the eve of Israel's departure from their land; the recession of the waters of the Yam Suph – a northerly extension of the Gulf of Suez – which took place in a moment of desperate need and enabled them to cross when they were hard pursued by the Egyptian chariotry and hemmed in by hills to the north and south; the pillar of cloud by day and fire by night which led them to their rendezvous with God; the awe-inspiring phenomena which they saw and heard as they approached the sacred mountain: all these were interpreted to them by Moses as revelations of the power of their God acting for them in deliverance and providence.

The band of Egyptian chariotry which pursued the departing Israelites to prevent their escape from Egypt was caught and over-whelmed when the Yam Suph returned to its normal limits, and the Israelites, after exulting in this fresh display of Yahweh's care for them, trekked eastwards by "the way of the wilderness of the Yam Suph" across the head of the Gulf of Aqaba until they reached the sacred mountain variously called Horeb or Sinai. Here, near the place where Moses had received his first commission from Yahweh, the people solemnly undertook to keep the covenant into which Yahweh had brought them with Himself; He would be their God (as He had already shown Himself to be), and they would be His people. The basis of the covenant was an early form of the Ten Commandments or "Ten Words" in which Yahweh made known His will for His people. The preamble to the "Ten Words" clearly identified the God who thus declared His will for them: "I am Yahweh your God, who brought you out of the land of Egypt, out of the house of bondage."[1] The God who had done that for them, to whose power and mercy thus displayed they owed their existence as a people, might well be accepted as their God: there was none like Him among the gods – "majestic in holiness, terrible in glorious deeds, doing wonders."[2] Well might they bow to His exclusive terms, "You shall have no other gods before me",[3] for what other god was worthy to be mentioned alongside Yahweh?

In paying Him worship they were to make no attempt to represent His likeness by means of an image; they were to treat His name with the reverence which was His due, they were to reserve for Him every seventh day; and in thought and word and deed they were to treat one another in a manner befitting the covenant which bound them all together. They were to regard themselves as a holy people – i.e. a people set apart for Yahweh – but Yahweh was a God who was not only incomparably powerful, but also incomparably righteous, merciful and true to His pledged word; and therefore men and women who were holy to Him, reserved for Him, must reproduce these qualities in their own life and conduct.

This attitude we may call practical monotheism. Whether other gods – the vanquished gods of Egypt or the gods of the Canaanites or of other nations – might have some sort of existence was not a question about which either Moses or his followers were likely to trouble themselves: their business was to worship Yahweh their God and serve Him alone.

Moses has ever been looked upon as the first and greatest lawgiver of

[1] Ex. 20:2.   [2] Ex. 15:11.   [3] Ex. 20:3.

the Israelites. In his own person he combined the functions of prophet and priest and king; he judged their lawsuits and taught them the principles of their religious duty, not only in the details of sacrificial worship but in many aspects of ordinary life as well. No matter in how many parallel or successive recensions his laws might be preserved and from time to time repromulgated, no matter how they might be expanded and applied to changing conditions of life, in written form or in oral tradition, Israel's law would never cease to be known as the law of Moses. Rightly so: for the principles laid down in his time, before the settlement in Canaan, remained the principles of Israel's law for all centuries to come.

The Mosaic legislation is divided on grounds of style and content into two readily distinguishable groups of laws. There are the case-laws or "judgments", cast in such a form as "If a man do so-and-so, he shall pay so much"; and there are the statutes, expressed in categorical or "apodictic" form: "Thou shalt (or shalt not) do so-and-so" or "Whosoever does so-and-so shall surely die". When these Old Testament laws are compared with other ancient Near Eastern law-codes, it is to the former group, the case-laws, that parallels are found. This is the form, for example, in which the laws of the Babylonian king Hammurabi (1728—1686 B.C.) are cast, like the laws of still earlier codes in that part of the world. But the categorical type of statute-law, with its distinct religious note, is (as law) distinctively Israelite, though it has, strikingly enough, affinities with the form in which international treaties were cast in those days, especially treaties between a superior power and vassal states.[1]

The undisciplined body of slaves which left Egypt under the guidance of Moses had to spend a generation in the wilderness before a nation could be fashioned to invade the land of Canaan as conquerors and settlers. Some who did attempt to raid the Negev within a year from their leaving Egypt met with a costly repulse and were not disposed to repeat the experiment. A considerable part of the time that elapsed between the solemn events at Sinai-Horeb and the large-scale entry into Canaan was spent in the oasis of Kadesh, to the south of the Negev. Another name given to this place is En-Mishpat, "the spring of judgment", which may enshrine a tradition that here judgment was pronounced as the Israelites submitted their cases for the adjudication of Moses and his assessors. As for the name Kadesh, it simply means "sanctuary"; the fuller form Kadesh-barnea distinguishes it from other sanctuaries. This suggests that even before the settlement in Canaan the Israelites consisted of a number of tribes united in part by a common ancestry but much more so by common participation in the covenant with Yahweh. The outward and visible sign of their

[1] *Cf.* G. E. Mendenhall, *Law and Covenant in Israel and the Ancient Near East* (1955).

covenant-unity was the sacred chest, the ark of testimony, constructed by Moses, housed in a tent-shrine. The tribes thus formed what in Greek history is known as an amphictyonic league, a group of states or tribes sharing a common sanctuary which served as the focus of their federation. A tent-shrine was conveniently movable, and very suitable for a community that was so frequently on the march. Into the covenant-bond other groups might enter: in particular we know of nomad communities of the Negev such as the Kenites (to whom Moses' wife belonged), the Kenizzites and the Jerahmeelites who now or later allied themselves with the members of the tribe of Judah and ultimately appear to have been largely incorporated in that tribe. Closely related to these nomadic groups was another called the Amalekites, and the bitter feud which Israel pursued against these from generation to generation can best be explained if they were guilty of some breach of covenant. Alliance with such nomad groups was a very different thing from alliance with the settled agricultural population of Canaan, with its seducing fertility ritual so menacing to the essential features of the pure Yahweh-worship which Israel learned in the wilderness. Even before they entered Canaan the Israelites were strictly forbidden to make common cause with its inhabitants.

There was some infiltration from the south into the central Negev, with which the tribe of Judah had an earlier connection; but the route followed by the main body when they left Kadesh led them south and east of the Dead Sea, where they skirted the territories of their kinsfolk of Edom, Moab and Ammon, who had recently organized themselves as settled kingdoms. While they made no attack on these kindred groups, the Israelites acted quite differently towards two other kingdoms which lay farther north in Transjordan – the Amorite kingdoms of Sihon in Heshbon and his northern neighbour Og in Bashan. They entered the realms of Sihon and Og as hostile invaders, overwhelmed their forces, and occupied their territory (the territory which became the tribal heritage of Reuben, Gad and Eastern Manasseh). Part at least of the Israelite community had thus adopted a settled agricultural way of life before the crossing of the Jordan, and when Moses is represented as giving them there in Transjordan in codified form the judgments and statutes which they were to observe in their new habitat, those which imply an agricultural way of life need not be regarded as anachronistic.

There in Transjordan Moses died, after he had commissioned his aide-de-camp, the Ephraimite Joshua, to be his successor and lead the people into Canaan proper. Joshua led them over Jordan in circumstances which impressed themselves on the national memory alongside the circumstances of their departure from Egypt. If, when Israel went out of Egypt, "the sea looked and fled", as a later poet wrote, when they came into Canaan "Jordan turned back."[1] The Old Testament record attributes the drying up of the river to a landslide at Adam (modern Ed-Damiyeh), some fifteen miles north of the place where Jordan runs into the Dead Sea; but the fact of its occurrence just at this time was evidence to them that the God of their fathers who had brought them safely out of Egypt was now bringing them safely into Canaan. The collapse of the walls around the citadel of Jericho, which lay two miles west of the place where they crossed the river, was no doubt caused by the same seismic action as had brought about the landslide at Ed-Damiyeh; to the Israelites it brought further confirmation of the directing power of Yahweh. Jericho, by the collapse of its walls, lay defenceless before them; as the firstfruits of their conquests in Canaan it was solemnly "devoted" to Yahweh with all that was in it. The imperishable wealth in the citadel was set aside to the service of Yahweh's sanctuary; the rest was consumed in a gigantic holocaust.[2] The "devotion" of Jericho, together with the solemn ritual that preceded the assault, as described in the book of Joshua, indicates that the Israelites were engaged in a holy war; the engagements in which they took part both east and west of Jordan were known as the "wars of Yahweh" and celebrated as such in sacred song.

From Jericho they pressed into the heart of the country, taking one citadel after another, for the news of the fall of Jericho had struck terror into the hearts of many Canaanite garrisons. At one time they could have called upon Egypt for help, but Egypt was entering on a period of decline and was unable to make effective the control she had formerly claimed over Central Canaan. Only along the western coastal strip as far north as the Pass of Megiddo did Egypt still exercise some measure of control, and even there the Philistine settlement on the Mediterranean seaboard was soon to form a barrier against the extension of Egyptian power.

A coalition of five military governors of Canaanite citadels attempted to bar the Israelites from turning south from Gibeon and the other cities of the Hivite tetrapolis in the central hill-country, which had submitted to them as subject-allies; but it was completely defeated, and the road to the south lay open to the invaders. They were unable to operate in the plains and valleys, where the chariot-forces of the Canaanite citadels were too formidable for them to face; but before long they dominated and occupied the hill-country of the centre and south, and also the Galilaean uplands, north of the Plain of Jezreel. The decisive stroke in the conquest of the north was the storming of

---

[1] Ps. 114:3.

[2] The destruction of Late Bronze Age Jericho is very difficult to date archaeologically, owing to the considerable erosion of the site during the 400 years that elapsed before the building of Iron Age Jericho (I Kings 16:34). See K. M. Kenyon, *Archaeology in the Holy Land* (1960), pp. 209 ff.

the great city of Hazor, formerly "the head of all those kingdoms."[1]
Hazor is but one of several sites, laid bare by archaeological excavation
in recent years, of citadels which fell shortly before 1200 B.C., to be
rebuilt some decades later with thinner walls and a lower standard of
material culture.

The tribes who settled in the north were divided from their fellows
in Central Canaan by a Canaanite chain of fortified positions strung
along the Plain of Jezreel, from the Mediterranean coast to the Jordan;
the central tribes, in their turn, were cut off even more effectually
from contact with Judah farther south by the stronghold of Jerusalem
which remained a Canaanite enclave for a further two centuries.

On one notable occasion, the northern and central blocks joined
forces in an uprising against the military governors of the Plain of
Jezreel,[2] who were steadily reducing them to serfdom; and their
united rising was crowned with success at the Battle of Kishon (c. 1125
B.C.) when a sudden downpour flooded the torrent-bed and put the
horses and chariots of the Canaanites out of action. The light-armed
Israelites swept down upon them and routed them. The impetus to
united action on this occasion came not from the Israelite commander
Barak but from the prophetess Deborah, to whom at her headquarters
in the hill country of Ephraim the tribesmen went up to have judgment pronounced in their disputes. It was at her instance that the
message was sped throughout the tribes, calling them together for this
holy war – "to the aid of Yahweh against the mighty" – as we are told
in the ancient triumph song in celebration of the victory, preserved
in Judges 5. The tribes that failed to respond are reproached, but
nothing is said of a summons going to Judah; Judah was too completely
cut off from the tribesmen of the centre and north.

When the tribes of Israel remembered their covenant-bond, on an
occasion like this, their united strength enabled them to repel their foes.
But such united action, even on a smaller scale, was rare. When the
danger which caused them to call upon the God of the covenant
receded, the tendency was strong to slip back into conformity with
the way of life of their Canaanite neighbours, to intermarry with them,
to imitate their fertility rites in order to secure regular rainfall and good
crops, and to think of Yahweh rather as a ba'al or fertility-god than
as the God who had delivered them from Egypt and made His nature
and will known to them in the wilderness. The bond which united
them to their fellow-Israelites was thus weakened, and they became
an easy prey to their enemies. It was not only Canaanite cities in the
land itself that tried to reduce them to serfdom; from time to time they
suffered from incursions from beyond Jordan, by their own kinsmen
of Moab and Ammon and Edom, and more disastrously by the

[1] Josh. 11:10.   [2] Led by Sisera (see p. 21).

beduin from remoter parts of Arabia, who, mounted on camels, raided their territory year by year at harvest time and destroyed their crops. These "Midianites" or "Ishmaelites", as they are called in the biblical record, would have made life impossible for the Israelites, had they not been rallied by a leader from the tribe of Manasseh, Gideon by name, who led a small and mobile band against the invaders, took them by surprise, pursued them across Jordan and wrought great havoc in their ranks. The grateful tribesmen invited Gideon to become their king and found a hereditary monarchy, but he refused: such a monarchy, on the pattern of the monarchies which governed Israel's neighbours, was too much out of keeping, in his judgment, with the ideals which they had learned in the wilderness. Let Yahweh alone be acknowledged as King in Israel; let Him use as His agents not one particular family but the man whom from time to time He might choose and endow with special powers to rule His people and defend their cause.[1]

From the number of such "charismatic" persons who arose in Israel in this period and led them back to loyalty to Yahweh and forward to victory against their enemies, the whole period is known as the period of the "judges."

One of Gideon's sons, Abimelech by name, did not share his father's scruples about kingship. (He, however, was the son of a Canaanite woman and had been brought up with his mother's relatives at Shechem.) After his father's death he attempted to succeed to his power, exterminating most of the other members of Gideon's family in the process. For three years he reigned as king from Shechem, but his kingdom did not extend beyond Western Manasseh. His subjects soon grew tired of him, and he met his death in trying to put down their revolt.

[1] It has been suggested, however, that Gideon's deprecatory reply was a politely veiled acceptance of their offer.

CHAPTER II

THE PHILISTINES AND THE
HEBREW MONARCHY

(c. 1100—1010 B.C.)

THE SITUATION WHICH DID AT LAST LEAD TO THE ESTABLISHMENT OF a hereditary monarchy in Israel was brought about by invaders from another quarter. The downfall of the Mycenaean and Hittite Empires towards the end of the thirteenth century B.C. uprooted many of the populations of the Aegean lands and sent them faring forth over the eastern Mediterranean in search of new homes. One such group was called the Philistines, from the south-west of Asia Minor. Some of the Philistines settled in Crete; others attempted a landing on the Egyptian coast, and when they were repulsed, sailed east and landed on the Mediterranean coastland of Canaan. Here they were able to settle. They organized themselves in the five city-states of Ashdod, Ashkelon, Ekron, Gath and Gaza – former Canaanite cities – each of the five city-states being under the control of a ruler whom they called in their own language a *seren* (an Aegean word akin to the Greek *tyrannos*). The Philistines intermarried with the Canaanite women of the area and quickly adopted Canaanite language and religion. They were capable military organizers, and when once they had established themselves in their pentapolis, they began to extend their control over the rest of Canaan. They were not long in making contact with the Israelites, and militarily the Israelites were no match for them. Although the Israelites had entered Canaan some time after the beginning of the Iron Age, they were slow in taking over the facilities of the Iron Age themselves. Sisera[1] might have nine hundred chariots shod with iron, but the tribesmen who overthrew him had no thought of creating such a force for themselves. Apart from technical and organizational problems involved, there was the consideration that a chariot force required a troop of horses, and the horse, for reasons which we shall see,[2] was a foreign animal to Israel until the reign of Solomon.

The Philistines, however, had mastered the art of iron-working, and when they began to assert their suzerainty over the Israelites they saw

---

[1] At the battle of Kishon (p. 19).   [2] See page 32.

21

to it that they kept the monopoly of iron-working in their own hands. When the Israelites began to use iron implements of agriculture, the Philistines insisted that they must come to Philistine smiths to have them sharpened. They realized that if they allowed smiths to ply their craft among the Israelites, they might not only forge and sharpen agricultural implements but instruments of war as well, to be used in rebellion against their overlords. The Philistines thus extended their power steadily along all the lines of communication in the land, as far as the eastern end of the Plain of Jezreel. Although they made the Israelites tributary, their domination was not extraordinarily oppressive; they certainly did not menace the very existence of the people as the Midianite raiders had done in Gideon's day. Some of the Israelites were quite content to live peacefully under Philistine domination, as the story of Samson makes plain, and they resented the way in which Samson's attacks on the Philistines brought their wrath not only upon himself but on his fellow-countrymen as well.

But if the very existence of the Israelites was not menaced by their Philistine overlords, their national survival was menaced. The centre of the national life at this time was at Shiloh, an Ephraimite sanctuary, where the ark of the covenant was housed in a more permanent structure than the old tent-shrine of the wilderness days, and where the God of Israel was worshipped as "Yahweh of hosts". The priestly family in charge of the sanctuary of Shiloh traced its descent from Moses' brother Aaron (who had been chief priest of the tent-shrine in the wilderness). The last of the chief priests of Shiloh, Eli by name, discharged more than priestly duties; as priest of the amphictyonic sanctuary he acted as inter-tribal judge. In his days the tribes of Israel, intent on repelling further Philistine encroachment, raised the standard of revolt against their overlords, coming first to Shiloh no doubt in order to receive the priestly blessing on their enterprise. But they met with ill success, and decided that they must have the sacred ark itself, the palladium of Israel's God, to go before them into battle and assure success against the enemies of Yahweh. But even the presence of the ark was insufficient; they were beaten, and more decisively than before, at Aphek, some 12 miles east of Joppa. The two sons of Eli, who attended the ark as it led Israel into battle, were killed in action; worse still, the ark itself was captured by the enemy. The disastrous news was taken back to Shiloh and was the death of Eli himself; Shiloh itself with its sanctuary was destroyed by the Philistines – an event which the evidence of Danish archaeological research on the site dates about 1050 B.C.

The bond which united the tribes of Israel together was broken: the central shrine was no more; its priesthood was wiped out (apart from two infants, the grandsons of Eli); the very symbol of Yahweh's presence with His people was in alien hands. The Philistines had triumphed indeed; and it looked as if Israel's glory and national identity had departed for ever.

That it did not depart is due to the character and enterprise of one man, Samuel. Samuel has often received much less than his due from historians, but his name deserves to stand alongside those of Moses, Joshua and David in the annals of Israel. Samuel was a native of the region of Ramah, in the tribal territory of Ephraim; he had grown up from boyhood at Shiloh, where he was in attendance on the sanctuary under the direction of Eli. Even before the overthrow of Shiloh he had manifested the prophetic gift, and when the disaster took place, he proved equal to the task of rallying the shattered morale of his people. He showed them that their God was still in their midst even if the sacred ark was in the hands of the Philistines; and indeed, when the Philistines after a short time restored the ark to Israelite territory it remained in the obscurity of a private house in Kiriath-yearim, on the border between Judah and Benjamin, throughout Samuel's lifetime and for several years more. The judicial functions which Eli had carried out at Shiloh could no longer be performed there, but Samuel continued to carry them out, and went annually in circuit to the ancient sacred centres of Mizpah in the central highlands (which in some degree served as a new amphictyonic rallying-point), Gilgal and Bethel, as well as to his own homestead of Ramah, to pronounce judgment on the cases submitted to him. And although he did not belong to the priestly family, he undertook the priestly duties with widespread acceptance.

At Mizpah, Gilgal and Bethel there were ancient altars where sacrifice might be offered, and at Ramah too he erected an altar and sacrificed there. The central sanctuary was decentralized, but one man, under God, served as the focus of national life. He has well been described as "God's emergency man".

Under his direction Israel returned to its old covenant-loyalty to Yahweh, and with the return of their former faith came a resurgence of national spirit: they went out again against the Philistines and on the field where they had suffered such a crushing defeat a few years before they routed the Philistines to such good purpose that for many years the Philistines left the central highlands in peace.

But Samuel grew old, and then the question arose who should take his place. He had two sons who acted as deputy judges for him, but they did not show their father's strict impartiality and were suspected of venality. The people had no desire to be judged by them when Samuel could no longer discharge his judicial functions. The old desire to have a hereditary monarchy which had found expression in Gideon's day was voiced anew with greater persistence. But a hereditary monarchy introduced a principle which was bound to change the character of civil rule in Israel. Hitherto they had been ruled by charismatic judges raised up by God from this tribe or that in His sovereign good pleasure; the hereditary principle meant that their rulers in future would not necessarily have the special spiritual endowment which had marked Samuel and his predecessors, but would more probably resemble the kings of Israel's neighbours. But if they wanted a king, there was only one man who could give them a king, and that man was Samuel. Samuel expostulated with them, telling them that their request marked a lack of faith in Yahweh, their true King, who had never failed to raise them up a champion of His choice in time of need heretofore. Since they persisted, he acquiesced in their demand, and nominated as their king a man named Saul, from Gibeah in the tribal territory of Benjamin, who may have been chosen by Samuel some time earlier to act as military commander under his direction. But Saul came from an obscure family, and many despised him in spite of his impressive stature. Their attitude was changed, however, when a sudden cry for help came from across Jordan, from the men of Jabesh-gilead, closely related to Saul's own tribe of Benjamin, who were threatened by the Ammonite king with dishonourable servitude. When the appeal came to Saul at his home farm at Gibeah, he sent a summons to united action throughout the tribes and arrived to give effective succour to Jabesh-gilead in an astonishingly brief space of time. The energy which he showed on this occasion impressed the popular imagination: the people united to acclaim him as their king, the chosen of Yahweh, at Mizpah. Not only so, but the approval of Yahweh Himself seemed assured when Saul suddenly manifested the prophetic gift and thus entered the succession of Israel's charismatic rulers. Samuel had by no means abdicated his authority, which was essentially moral and religious in character; but if Saul were content to act as king – *i.e.* as judge and military leader – under the old man's guidance, the combination might work out most happily for Israel and the decision to institute the monarchy might appear to have been justified. This, however, was not to be.

The Ammonite threat had provided Saul with a timely occasion for demonstrating his kingly qualities. But it was the Philistine domination that chiefly lay behind the people's demand for a king, and it was against the Philistines that the first two kings of Israel must make real proof of their worth. The Philistines were not, like the Ammonites, kinsfolk of the Israelites, with much the same way of life; they were heirs of the ancient civilization of the Aegean. Their chief buildings and temples (like the one at Gaza which Samson brought down upon himself) were constructed on Aegean models; their leading warriors (like Goliath of Gath) were accoutred like Homeric heroes.

It was no light matter to challenge the might of overlords like these. Yet they did so, by the very fact of electing a king: the Philistines knew what that meant, and would know what action to take. But Jonathan, the daring and intrepid young crown-prince, took matters into his hands by killing the Philistine prefect at Geba, not far from his father's headquarters at Gibeah. This action resulted in punitive raids by a Philistine band which established itself at Michmash, at a point which enabled them to cut the line of communications between Ephraim and Benjamin and thus proceed more conveniently to the destruction of the rebel force. The followers of Saul, a volunteer peasant army, saw with dismay the vengeance that their revolt was like to bring upon them, and they began to melt away. The remnant would soon be left defenceless before the Philistines. But Jonathan, who had done so much to bring this critical situation about, resolved it by a daring commando stroke. Accompanied by his armour-bearer only, he climbed up the rock of Michmash by the steepest ascent, and when the Philistine garrison, thinking that a considerable band of Israelites had come to attack them, came out to deal with them, Jonathan and his batman picked them off one by one at a narrow point where only one man could pass at a time. The garrison panicked, for they imagined that a large force was upon them. Saul's scouts, looking north from Gibeah towards Michmash, saw the panic, and when Saul consulted the sacred oracle, and received a response from the priest that the time was propitious for attack, he led his army against the fleeing Philistines and inflicted great slaughter on them. The central territory was once more cleared of the invaders, and for a time Saul's control was firmly established over Central Israel. Other foes who had profited by the Philistine invasion to encroach on Israelite territory from other directions were pushed back, and Saul reached the highest pinnacle of his success and power.

But the tragedy which increasingly marred the later part of Saul's reign had already begun to unfold. At an early point in his campaign against the Philistines, when Saul gathered his army to the sanctuary at Gilgal to receive the divine blessing through Samuel for the inauguration of the holy war, Samuel was late in arriving, and to prevent the army from dispersing Saul performed the sacred rites himself. This encroachment upon the priestly prerogatives of Samuel was the beginning of a growing alienation between the two. The alienation was intensified when Samuel conveyed a divine communication to Saul commanding him to march into the Negev and wipe out Israel's ancestral enemies, the Amalekites, and Saul failed to "devote" the whole community to Yahweh. That Saul spared Agag the Amalekite king must not be ascribed to any humanitarian sentiment (he had no compunction in slaughtering the rest of the community whose bloodguiltiness was less than Agag's); it may have been due to private ideas of his own about the sort of treatment that befitted a holder of the kingly office. Samuel despatched Agag with his own hands, and assured Saul that he had proved unworthy of the kingship and had been rejected by Yahweh.

The tragedy of Saul is that he was a sincerely religious man, deeply concerned to do the will of Yahweh, and Samuel's announcement that Yahweh had rejected him as king preyed upon his mind as it would not have done if he had been an irreligious man. He became a victim to melancholia and persecution mania, and required to have his dejected spirits soothed by music. It was in this way that he first met the young man who, unknown to him, had been anointed by Samuel as his successor, for David, member of a family in Bethlehem, a town in the tribal territory of Judah, was a skilful harpist.

David was not only a skilful harpist but a gifted warrior as well, and his prowess against the Philistines when they resumed their encroachments on Saul's territory led to his being made commander of the royal army and receiving one of Saul's daughters in marriage. But his success made him a target for Saul's suspicions – and it may be that Saul suspected that Samuel had his eyes on him as prospective successor to Saul. It was all the more bitter for Saul that his eldest son Jonathan and David were bosom friends. But David's personal charm was such that Saul himself was won over by it, and in his more lucid moments he addressed David in terms of warm affection.

Time and again, however, Saul's suspicion returned and broke out in murderous threats and attacks upon David, until David was forced to take refuge in the wilderness of Judah. There he became the leader of a band of malcontents and fugitives from justice and the like whom he welded into a first-class force of fighting men, warmly attached to himself to the point where, if necessary, they were prepared to die for him. In fact, the name David[1] may have been given to him as a term of affection by his comrades; it has been thought that his personal name was Elhanan.[2] A great access of prestige to David's cause was the arrival of Abiathar, a young priest who fled from the sanctuary of Nob, near Jerusalem, at the time when the whole priestly family there was wiped out at Saul's command for having given aid and comfort to David as he fled from the royal court. Abiathar was a great-grandson of Eli, the last priest of the sanctuary at Shiloh, and he brought with him the inter-tribal "ephod," the oracular apparatus by which the will of Yahweh was ascertained.

[1] The most probable meaning of David is "beloved"; a widely-held opinion, based on the evidence of Old Babylonian inscriptions from Mari on the Middle Euphrates, that it meant "leader", is now regarded as doubtful.

[2] In II Sam. 21:19 the slayer of Goliath, the Philistine giant of Gath cf. I Sam. 17:4 ff.), is called Elhanan.

Several of the men who joined David in the wilderness retreat, in the cave of Adullam, were later to hold high position in his kingdom, like Joab, who became commander of the army, and Benaiah, who became captain of the royal bodyguard.

Saul saw in David's band of followers a rival force to his own army, and decided that there was no room in one kingdom for both military formations. He therefore took advantage of a spell of quiescence on the Philistine front to sweep the wilderness of Judah until David realized that there was no place there for himself and his followers. He therefore crossed the Philistine frontier and offered the services of his band as a mercenary force to Achish, ruler of the Philistine city of Gath. Achish, who remembered David's prowess when he led Saul's army against the Philistines, was delighted to have him on his side, and made David's band his personal bodyguard.

Saul, having cleared David out of Judah and thus brought most of the southern part of his kingdom under his control, planned to bring the northern tribes into the unity of Israel as well. They lay north of the Plain of Jezreel, which was controlled by the Philistines. In order to establish his sovereignty effectively over these tribes, therefore, it was necessary to fight a decisive action against the Philistines. As the Philistine contingents prepared for the battle, murmurs arose against the presence of David and his men in their ranks. The other Philistine rulers pointed out to Achish that, if David wished to be reconciled with his former master, he had now a marvellous opportunity for doing so – by changing sides in the course of the forthcoming battle, to the grave prejudice of the Philistine forces among which he and his men occupied a key position. Their suspicions may have been well founded, despite Achish's personal confidence in David. Achish was compelled to dismiss him, and he led his followers back to Ziklag, the town in the south of Judah which Achish had allotted to them, to await news from the north. When news came, a few days later, it was tragic news indeed. The Israelites had lost the fight at Mount Gilboa, Saul with Jonathan and two other sons had fallen in battle, and the Philistine grip on the whole land of Israel was firmer than before (c. 1010 B.C.)

CHAPTER III

THE REIGN OF DAVID

(*c.* 1010—970 B.C.)

A FEW OF SAUL'S FOLLOWERS WERE ABLE TO ESCAPE TO TRANSJORDAN, and there they proclaimed Saul's remaining son Eshbaal king in his father's place. Eshbaal remained east of the Jordan, making his court at Mahanaim; there was no place for an independent king of Israel west of the river. In Judah, however, a new king was proclaimed. David, after consulting the oracle of Yahweh, left Ziklag for Hebron, an ancient city in the territory of Judah, and his fellow-tribesmen sent a deputation to him there and acclaimed him king of Judah. What was a distant and ineffective Transjordanian ruler, a Benjamite by birth, in their eyes by comparison with their own valiant fellow-Judaean David?

The Philistines tolerated David's assumption of this new dignity. He was still their vassal, and in any case the fact that the Judaeans made him their king meant that the tribes of Israel were now divided in their allegiance. A policy of "divide and rule" seemed proper for the Philistines to pursue. Events seemed to play into their hands still further when war broke out between David's followers and the supporters of Eshbaal. The commander of Eshbaal's army was his uncle Abner. In one of the engagements between the two parties Abner killed a brother of Joab. This was his undoing a short time afterwards when he took offence at an untimely rebuke by Eshbaal, and led a party of his men over to David's side. David gave Abner a warm welcome, for Abner's defection from Eshbaal bade fair to be taken as an example by many other Israelites. Joab, however, seized an early opportunity of assassinating Abner in revenge for his brother's death at his hands. David, in dismay, made it as clear as he could that he dissociated himself entirely from Joab's treacherous act, following Abner's bier as chief mourner.

With the defection of Abner, Eshbaal's cause was irrevocably doomed. Two of his officers, realizing this, decided to exploit the situation in their own favour by murdering him and carrying his head to David at Hebron, expecting a reward. The reward they received was an ignominious death, as befitted their perfidy; but Eshbaal's death hastened the inevitable conclusion towards which events were tending in any case. The other tribes of Israel, now left leaderless, sent delegates to David, whom they remembered as their beloved commander during the reign of Saul, and anointed him king over all Israel. The anointing ceremony was accompanied by a covenant, in which king and people undertook mutual obligations. The king of Israel was no absolute monarch, for all the sacrosanctity of his anointed person; he was as much bound by his covenant to the people as they were by theirs to him.

The Philistines had now to reckon with a situation in Israel which had turned sharply to their disadvantage. The tribes were now reunited under a man who was no puppet ruler. David could no longer be counted upon as their dutiful tributary; he must be put down at once. They marched against him; David withdrew to his old base at Adullam, and from there he made a surprise attack upon them on their way to Hebron, and defeated them at Baal-perazim in the Valley of Rephaim, south of Jerusalem. A second defeat inflicted upon them in the same area effectually expelled them from Judaean territory. Their dominion over Israel was broken, never to be renewed.

The ancient citadel of Jerusalem remained a Canaanite enclave on the southern border of the tribal territory of Benjamin, between the two constituent parts of David's kingdom, Israel and Judah. It was originally a joint Hittite and Amorite foundation, and its inhabitants called themselves Jebusites. A king who aimed at uniting Israel and Judah into one realm could not afford to leave this foreign state between the two areas. David therefore, having driven the Philistines out of Judah and Central Canaan, determined to reduce Jerusalem. But this was no easy task; otherwise it would have been reduced long before. Both by nature and by art it was strongly fortified. The citadel stood on the hill Ophel, south of what was later to become the temple area. So confident were the defenders of their impregnable position that they taunted David and his men when they came to invest their citadel, saying that the blind and lame among the population would suffice to keep the besiegers out. But David knew what stuff his mighty men were made of. He announced that whoever succeeded in capturing the fortress would be made commander-in-chief of his forces. Joab, David's cousin, succeeded in leading a band of followers into the city by an unsuspected route, the water shaft[1] by which water was drawn up from the cave forty feet below into which the Gihon spring empties. The idea that this vertical shaft would ever be used as a means of ingress by a hostile force was never taken seriously by the Jebusites,

[1] Another interpretation of the Hebrew word *sinnōr*, which R.S.V. renders "water shaft" in II Sam. 5:8, is "hook", *i.e.* scaling-hook; so W. F. Albright, in *Old Testament Commentary*, ed. H. C. Alleman and E. E. Flack (1954), p. 149.

until they found the enemy in their midst. Their strong fortifications were useless to them now; Jerusalem was at last in Israelite hands, and the fortress became known as the City of David, for David made it his headquarters, and the capital of his kingdom.

The importance of David's capture of Jerusalem can hardly be exaggerated. The strategic advantages of the place now turned to David's favour, and we may be sure that care was taken that no future invader should find the same way into the city as Joab did. It served as a centre from which David could dominate the land and complete the subjugation of the Philistines. Politically it was admirably adapted to be his royal city, for it was neither Israelite nor Judaean, and neither Israel nor Judah could complain that the other was favoured in this respect. It remained a city-state in its own right, governed by the king of Israel and Judah, who now succeeded to its ancient dynasty of priest-kings. A sacred city of such ancient prestige was a worthy capital for the founder of a new dynasty under which all elements in the population of Canaan were to be united; it had venerable associations in Israelite as well as in Canaanite eyes, for did not Melchizedek, priest of 'El 'Elyon, come forth from there to greet Abraham when the patriarch returned from the rout of the invading kings from the east? Did he not bestow his priestly blessing on Abraham and receive tithes of the spoil from him? And did not David now sit on the throne of Melchizedek as king of Jerusalem as well as on the joint throne of Israel and Judah?

But David bethought himself of a way in which the sacred prestige of his new capital, already great, might be further enhanced, especially in Israelite eyes. Since the days of Samuel when the ark of the covenant was restored by its Philistine captors, it had remained in obscurity in Kiriath-yearim. If this ancient palladium of the tribes of Israel were publicly brought to Jerusalem and ceremoniously installed there, Israel and Judah would once more have one inter-tribal sanctuary, and Jerusalem would become the spiritual centre of the united nation as well as the political and military capital. This then David proceeded to do. His first attempt to bring the ark to Jerusalem was marred by the untoward death of an attendant who laid his hand on the ark to steady it; but three months later the operation was completed without any such disaster, and the ark was brought into the city of David, into a tent-shrine that David had prepared for it, amid scenes of enthusiastic rejoicing. Here in Jerusalem was a dwelling place for Yahweh of hosts, the God of Israel. In Abiathar David had a scion of the ancient Elide priesthood of Shiloh, and now priesthood and ark were reunited as they had been in the sanctuary at Shiloh.

The recognition of Jerusalem as a holy city by three world faiths is to be traced back to its capture by David in the seventh year of his reign. Nor must we overlook the extraordinary way in which the names of Zion and Jerusalem have entered into the religious terminology of Christianity, as symbols of the church both militant and triumphant, and of the heavenly abode of the people of God.

From Jerusalem David made himself master of all the land of Israel. Not only were the Philistines expelled from Israelite territory, but they in turn became David's vassals. From their ranks he manned his personal bodyguard of Cherethites and Pelethites; nor had he a more loyal band of soldiers than the six hundred men of Gath, under their commander Ittai, who were attached to him since the days when he himself served as a mercenary leader in the pay of the Gittite king Achish.

But it was not enough for him to bring the whole land of Israel under united control for the first time in history. The situation outside the frontiers of Israel gave him the opportunity of founding an empire for himself, and his military and diplomatic ability matched the opportunity. The conquest of Edom made David master of the territory as far south as the head of the Gulf of Aqaba; its rock capital Petra (Sela) fell into David's hands. Moab, east of the Dead Sea, was added to his empire; so was Ammon, whose king Hanun rashly incurred David's enmity by insulting the ambassadors whom David sent to congratulate him on his accession to the throne. The whole of Transjordan was now in David's hands, in addition to all the land between Jordan and the Mediterranean. This situation is reflected in the oracle quoted in Ps. 60: 6–9:

> God has spoken in his sanctuary:
> "With exultation I will divide up Shechem
> and portion out the Vale of Succoth.
> Gilead is mine; Manasseh is mine;
> Ephraim is my helmet;
> Judah is my sceptre.
> Moab is my washbasin;
> upon Edom I cast my shoe;
> over Philistia I shout in triumph."
> Who will bring me to the fortified city?
> Who will lead me to Edom?

To the north of his kingdom the signs were also propitious. There were no powerful rulers at this time in the valleys of the Nile or of the Euphrates and Tigris to control the highway that ran from the Egyptian border to Carchemish. Hadadezer, king of Zobah, a state to the north of Damascus, had lent his aid to the Ammonites against David. Therefore, when Rabbah, the Ammonite capital, had fallen to David's men, and David had set the crown of Ammon on his own head, David turned against Hadadezer, and defeated him. He defeated also the army of Damascus, which came to Hadadezer's help. Zobah and Damascus thus became tributary to David, and garrisons of David's troops were placed in Damascus and other Aramaean cities. Farther north lay the Hittite kingdom of Hamath on the Orontes, whose king Toi made haste to enter into friendly relations with David, and became in effect his tributary. David's sphere of influence now extended from the Egyptian frontier on the Wadi el-Arish (the "brook of Egypt") to the Euphrates; and these limits remained the ideal boundaries of Israel's dominion long after David's empire had disappeared.

David also entered into alliance with his neighbour to the north-west, Hiram, king of Tyre and overlord of Phoenicia. This alliance was economic rather than military, and was mutually beneficial, for the Phoenicians could import grain from the fertile parts of David's kingdom and other merchandise through the Gulf of Aqaba, while David had some share in the proceeds of the wider Phoenician maritime trade, and hired Phoenician architects to build in Jerusalem royal quarters worthy of the ruler of such an empire.

David's conquest of the Aramaean kingdoms beyond his northern border gave him the opportunity to acquire a modest chariot-force. Consisting as it did of a hundred chariots and horses, it was indeed modest by comparison with the scale on which it was developed by Solomon and later kings of Israel. But it marked a tendency which was deprecated by the prophetic genius of Israel. The introduction of the horse into the Western Asian states, from the eighteenth century B.C. onwards, brought about in them, as in Greece and Rome and mediaeval Europe, a division in the free population. The men who owned horses – the chivalry or the "knights" – were inevitably accorded a higher rank than their freeborn brethren who did not possess horses, and this menaced the free equality of Israel's covenant-constitution. This effect did not become manifest in the time of David, for he seems to have reserved his hundred horses for military purposes only. He did not have a horse for his own use; whereas earlier rulers in Israel had ridden on white asses, David compromised to the extent of riding on a mule.

David's court now began to present a marked contrast to the simplicity of the fortress at Gibeah which served as Saul's head-quarters throughout his reign. And we are indebted for a wonderfully vivid and honest picture of David's court life to the court chronicler whose account is preserved in II Sam. 9–20, and continued as the succession narrative of I Kings 1–2. David began to affect the style of other eastern kings, and the unhappiest aspect of his court-life was the domestic rivalry between the children of his numerous wives – a rivalry which was to continue to the closing moments of his life.

In the later part of David's reign two serious revolts broke out

PLATE I

Figure of a Canaanite
noble; bronze plaque of
c. 1400 B.C. found at
Hazor. Height approx.
3½ inches. (Dept. of
Archaeology, Hebrew
University, Jerusalem.)

Stone statue of a god,
Ammonite, *c.* 800 B.C.
found in Amman. Height
31½ inches.
(Courtesy Dept. of
Antiquities, Hashemite
Kingdom of Jordan.)

Egyptian relief showing
the king as Horus (a
falcon) smiting a Philistine
captive. From the temple
of Ramesses III at
Medinet Habu.
(Courtesy, K. A. Kitchen.)

Potsherd from Tell Qasile near Jaffa bearing the words 'Gold of Ophir for Beth Horon: 30 shekels' in Old Hebrew script. Eighth century B.C. Cf. pp. 36, 48.
(Dept. of Archaeology, Hebrew University, Jerusalem.)

Impression of the seal of Asani-el, 'God made me', Hebrew or possibly Phoenician work of the eighth or seventh century B.C. Below the lion is an Egyptian winged beetle. Twice natural size.
(Dept. of Western Asiatic Antiquities, British Museum.)

PLATE II

Clay figure of a horse bearing a disc on its brow, probably symbolic of the sun, found in a ritual deposit in Jerusalem (Ophel), c. 700 B.C. Cf. pp. 73, 77.
(Courtesy, K. M. Kenyon.)

Sketch of an arrowhead with three flanges and a barb, a type possibly spread by the Scythians. Variations in form occur. See p. 75, n. 3.

against his authority. Of these the first and more serious was organized within his own family, the leader being his favourite son Absalom (by this time probably also his oldest surviving son). Absalom paved the way for his revolt carefully, by setting himself deliberately to win the affection of the people, especially in Judah, and seduce them from their allegiance to his father. When he judged the time ripe, he had himself proclaimed king in Hebron, David's old capital and Absalom's own birthplace. The situation was so serious that David and those who remained loyal to him (including his Philistine bodyguard) had to escape to Transjordan, leaving Jerusalem to Absalom. Absalom knew that his position was not secure so long as his father was alive and at large, so he led a force across the Jordan against him. The rebel force was completely defeated, and Absalom himself met his death at the hands of Joab, despite David's charge to his men to do no harm to Absalom. Joab considered that he knew David's best interests better than David himself did – and in this instance he was certainly right. With the death of the usurper, the rebellion was dissolved, and first Israel and then Judah renewed their allegience to David and escorted him back in triumph to Jerusalem.

It may have been partly as a gesture of conciliation that David transferred the chief command of his army from Joab to Amasa, another of his cousins, who had commanded the rebel force; but probably he could not forgive Joab for killing Absalom. It was not long before Amasa had to take the field in David's service. The men of Israel were enraged because David allowed the Judaeans to take the lead in escorting him back to his kingdom, although these same Judaeans had been foremost in Absalom's cause. Their resentment was fanned into disaffection and fresh revolt by one Sheba, a member of the tribe of Benjamin to which Saul had belonged; and before David was well established again at Jerusalem, his army had to put down this second revolt. At an early stage in operations, Joab found an opportunity to assassinate Amasa, and took over the command from him. Joab then pursued Sheba through all the tribes of Israel until at last he besieged him in a city near the northern limit of the kingdom. The men of that city judged that their welfare would be best served by getting rid of their embarrassing guest, so they killed Sheba and threw his head over the wall to Joab. Thus the second revolt collapsed.

The last intrigue of David's reign was not directed against his authority but concerned the succession to the throne. David, now about seventy years of age, lay on his deathbed. His oldest surviving son, Adonijah, considered that he was the proper successor to his father, and several of his father's most loyal servants thought so too, among whom were Joab and the priest Abiathar. But Adonijah and his party knew that his succession would not be undisputed; they judged it wise therefore to have Adonijah proclaimed as king while his father was yet alive and thus present the nation with a *fait accompli*. The proclamation was accordingly carried out, with sacrifice and feasting, at a spot about a quarter of a mile south-east of Jerusalem called "Serpent's Stone" – possibly the spot where kings of Jerusalem had been installed in the Jebusite era.

But while the ceremony was going on, and shouts of "Long live King Adonijah!" were arising, news of what was happening came to Nathan the prophet, who informed Bathsheba, David's favourite wife. David had already promised her that her son Solomon would succeed him as king; and this succession would certainly be more pleasing to the people of Jerusalem, who would prefer to be ruled over by a native of their city (as Solomon was) rather than by a son born to David before he became king of Jerusalem. Adonijah and his supporters were probably well aware of this, for when the proclamation ceremony was arranged, no invitation was sent to Solomon, nor yet to those court officials – Zadok the priest and Nathan the prophet and Benaiah, captain of the royal bodyguard – who were known to favour Solomon's claims.

Bathsheba entered the king's presence and reported Adonijah's action. David acted quickly. He ordered that Solomon, mounted on David's special mule, should be escorted by the royal bodyguard down to the spring Gihon (the Virgin's Fountain) in the Kidron valley and proclaimed king there. So it was done, and when Zadok the priest poured the anointing oil on Solomon's head, the roar of acclamation was such that Adonijah and his guests heard it where they were feasting nearly half a mile away. Hard upon the noise itself came a messenger to tell what it signified, and the guests in dismay broke off their banqueting and went home with haste. Adonijah himself fled for sanctuary to the altar at the central shrine, and did not cease to cling to its horns until he received a personal assurance from Solomon that his life would be spared.

Solomon's succession was thus assured, and the old king breathed his last in the knowledge that his pleasure in this matter had been carried out.

CHAPTER IV

SOLOMON AND HIS SUCCESSORS

(c. 970—881 B.C.)

SOLOMON'S REIGN HAD NOT LONG BEGUN BEFORE HE GOT RID, BY ONE means or another, of those who had supported Adonijah's claim as well as the luckless Adonijah himself.

Solomon was no warrior, as David was, but he set himself to exploit the commercial possibilities of the empire which his father had conquered and bequeathed to him as a glorious inheritance. Much of the wealth of the empire he used to affect a much more grandiose style of court life than his father's. He amassed a very large harem, consisting in large part of daughters of neighbouring princes and sheikhs with whom he had political and commercial agreements. He engaged in a magnificent building programme at Jerusalem. The complex of buildings which constituted his new court included his royal palace; a palace for his queen, who was a daughter of one of the last kings of the weak twenty-first Egyptian Dynasty; the "hall of pillars" or assembly room, the throne-room of justice, and a treasury or armoury, called "the house of the forest of Lebanon," probably because it was panelled in cedar-wood. But more important and imposing than any of these was "the house which King Solomon built for Yahweh" north of the citadel of Jerusalem, on a site which David his father had bought from its Jebusite owner to use as a place of propitiatory sacrifice at a time when Jerusalem was devastated by a pestilence. Here was a natural rock-altar where, according to later Jewish tradition, Abraham had prepared to offer up Isaac his son.[1] And here was erected the great temple of Solomon, on a spot where sacrifices were to be offered to the God of Israel with but two interruptions[2] for a full millennium.

For carrying out this elaborate architectural programme, which took twenty years to complete, Solomon hired workmen from Hiram of Tyre, his father's friend, with whom he maintained a close alliance.

[1] It was only later that "the land of Moriah" of Gen. 22:2 (perhaps originally the land of Moreh or Shechem) was identified with Mount Moriah, the name given to the temple hill in II Chron. 3:1.
[2] That is, after the destruction by Nebuchadrezzar in 587 B.C., and during the profanation under Antiochus Epiphanes, from 167 to 164 B.C.

But the consequence was that Solomon fell heavily into debt and had to mortgage part of his territory to Hiram.

With the aid of Hiram and his Phoenician fleet, too, Solomon developed the commercial opportunities which arose from the fact that the road from the Mediterranean to the Red Sea and Indian Ocean ran through his kingdom. Solomon himself had a fleet of merchantmen based on Aqaba, which sailed with the Phoenician fleet to the Red Sea and Indian Ocean ports, bringing home from "Ophir"[1] almug wood and precious stones, and from other parts "gold, silver, ivory, apes, and peacocks" – or were the "peacocks" really baboons?[2]

At Aqaba, too, was a refinery, mainly for copper (great quantities of which are to be found in the vicinity) but used for iron as well. The refinery was built at a point where full use could be made of the violent "winds and sandstorms from the north, that blow along the centre of the Wadi Arabah as if forced through a wind tunnel." "A forced draft system for the furnaces was employed, and later abandoned and forgotten, to be re-discovered only in modern times." The "strong and continuous winds" from the north made it possible, by means of a system of flues and air-channels, to operate the smelting plants economically without employing an expensive bellows system.[3] Here, no doubt, the copper was refined which was used in such abundance for the vessels of the temple. When the metal had been smelted at Aqaba, the vessels were cast farther north, in the Jordan valley. "In the plain of the Jordan the king cast them, in the clay ground[4] between Succoth and Zarethan" (I Kings 7:46).

Nor was it only from seaborne trade that Solomon amassed his wealth. He acquired large revenues because his kingdom lay across the main route from Egypt to Asia Minor and Mesopotamia, and the trade routes across the Syrian and Arabian deserts. One valuable source of income was the horse and chariot trade with Asia Minor, in which he acted as middleman. "Solomon's import of horses was from Musri and Kue [probably Cappadocia and Cilicia], and the king's traders received them from Kue at a price. A chariot could be exported from Musri for six hundred shekels of silver, and a horse for a hundred and fifty; and so through the king's traders they were exported to all the kings of the Hittites and the kings of Syria."[5]

[1] Probably modern Somalia.
[2] The Hebrew word in I Kings 10:22 is *tukkiyyim*, which may be connected with Sinhalese *tokei*, "peacock", or (more probably) with Egyptian *kyw*, a kind of monkey.
[3] N. Glueck, *The Other Side of the Jordan* (1940), pp. 92–94.
[4] Or "earthen foundries" or "thickened earthen moulds"; *cf.* N. Glueck, *The River Jordan* (1946), pp. 145 f., 156. For a critique of Glueck's thesis and an alternative account see B. Rothenberg, "Ancient Copper Industries in the Western Arabah", *PEQ* 94 (1962), pp. 5 ff.
[5] I Kings 10:28 f. "Egypt" in R.S.V. and the older versions should be replaced by Musri, a district in S.E. Asia Minor.

Trade with Egypt was no doubt facilitated by Solomon's alliance with the Egyptian king, his father-in-law. When Solomon received the Egyptian princess in marriage, he received a handsome dowry with her, for her father captured the city of Gezer from the Canaanites who occupied it and handed it over to Solomon, who rebuilt and fortified it. Other cities which Solomon fortified (apart from Jerusalem itself) were the strategic stronghold of Megiddo, Hazor in the far north, Beth-horon in the central area, and Baalath and Tamar in the territory of Judah.

Solomon not only acquired a large revenue from the horses and chariots which passed through his hands; he built up a large force of chariots and horses for himself. The narrative of I Kings refers to the cities which Solomon built for his chariots and horsemen.[1] We may be sure that Solomon's horses were better housed than many of Solomon's subjects were.

But the ordinary income of his empire and the revenue which came to him from the commerce that passed through his realm were not sufficient to maintain the expensive establishment which Solomon set up and the building programme which occupied so much of his forty years' reign. He found it necessary to impose increasingly heavy taxes on his subjects, and to exact forced labour from them. At first this forced labour was supplied by his non-Israelite subjects but later it was extended to Israelites as well. "He sent them to Lebanon," we are told, "ten thousand a month in relays; they would be a month in Lebanon and two months at home" (I Kings 5:14). This corvée system was a serious departure from the ideals of Israel's early free polity, and was regarded as a breach of Yahweh's covenant which bound king and people alike. Nothing did so much to alienate the tribes of Israel from the dynasty of David. Moreover, the kingdom of Israel was divided into twelve administrative districts, largely, but not entirely, following the old tribal boundaries. Each of these districts was administered by a royal commissioner, and was responsible to send food supplies for the court for one month in the year.[2]

Israel and Judah enjoyed peace throughout the reign of Solomon, but the prosperity and joy which accompanied that peace to begin with turned to disillusionment towards the end of his reign. He placed on his realm burdens too heavy to bear, and it fell to pieces at his death. Nevertheless, the memory of his earlier years, before the burden of forced labour and taxation became so heavy, was cherished by the people for long; and in later days, when Israel and Judah fell

---

[1] I Kings 9:19; 10:26. The remains of stables at Megiddo, formerly thought to be Solomon's, have been shown by Y. Yadin to belong more probably to Ahab's reign ("New Light on Solomon's Megiddo", BA 23 [1960], pp. 62 ff.).

[2] I Kings 4:7-19.

into harder times, the glories of a golden age to come were based to a considerable extent on the recollection of the time when peace and prosperity were established under a king of Israel who ruled the territory between the wadi at Egypt's frontier and the great river Euphrates, while the coming King was pictured as combining in his person the military genius of David and the arts of peace associated with Solomon.

Among the arts of peace which flourished under Solomon may be reckoned literature of various kinds. The architectural achievements of his reign were Phoenician rather than Israelite, but the national epic and the court-chronicle flourished, together with the "wisdom" for which Solomon became renowned in all succeeding ages. For he "uttered three thousand proverbs", we read; "and his songs were a thousand and five;" while his acquaintance with natural lore won him fame among all his neighbours and more distant peoples as well.[1] Yet the features of his reign that mattered most for Israel at the time were features that marked a departure from the ancient ideals of the nation.

Towards the end of Solomon's reign a change of régime took place in Egypt. The weak twenty-first dynasty (to which Solomon's father-in-law belonged) came to an end, and a new and ambitious king, Sheshonq by name – or Shishak, as the Biblical narrative calls him (c. 945–914 B.C.) – assumed the double crown as first ruler of the twenty-second dynasty.

The main direction in which ambitious kings of Egypt had looked in centuries gone by was towards Asia. The Mediterranean coastal road ran north to Megiddo, where it turned east through the pass into the Plain of Jezreel and crossed the Jordan, to turn north again and run through Syria as far as Carchemish, where the Euphrates might be forded. But when Shishak came to the throne this road, from his own frontier as far as the Euphrates, was controlled by Solomon. It was therefore to his interest to weaken Solomon's power. This he did in particular by encouraging any movement for independence that showed itself among Solomon's subject-peoples. And there was no lack of such movements. Early in Solomon's reign a former officer of Hadadezer king of Zobah, Rezon by name, led an independence movement which made its headquarters at Damascus, and he became the founder of a royal dynasty which ruled in Damascus for two hundred years. Again, Hadad, crown prince of Edom, who had been carried to Egypt as a child when David conquered Edom, grew up at the Egyptian court and in due course returned to Edom with Egyptian backing to raise the standard of revolt in his native land.

[1] I Kings 4:32 ff.

These were non-Israelites, but more ominous still was the encouragement which Shishak gave to Jeroboam the son of Nebat. Jeroboam was one of Solomon's officials, whose organizing capacity shown at the repair of the fortifications of Jerusalem won for him the charge of the corvée provided by the tribes of Ephraim and Manasseh. But the prophetic party, which was opposed to the innovating trends of Solomon's policy, marked out this Jeroboam as one to whom the national loyalty could be diverted; and the suggestion was sown in Jeroboam's mind by the acted prophecy of one of their number, Ahijah of Shiloh. When Solomon got wind of the matter, Jeroboam escaped to Egypt, and remained under Shishak's protection until Solomon died.

Solomon's death (c. 930 B.C.) coincided with the collapse of David's empire, and was followed by the disruption of the united kingdom of Israel and Judah itself. The long separation of Judah from the northern tribes made them think of Judah as almost alien territory. When a Judaean dynasty acquired supreme power, the situation called for special qualities of diplomacy and consideration if the loyalty of the northern tribes was to be retained. Unfortunately, the northern tribes found cause to suspect that Judah was being increasingly favoured at their expense. When, therefore, the tribes came together after Solomon's death to elect his successor, great care and tact were called for if the unity of the realm was to be maintained.

The tribal delegates met at Shechem, one of the most venerable of the holy places in Central Canaan. The dynasty of David had not completely dissipated the fund of goodwill which it once enjoyed; its prestige was still very great; and the people were prepared to accept Solomon's son Rehoboam as king if he would return to the terms of the ancient covenant which his father's oppressive measures had violated. But Rehoboam, with almost incredible folly, refused to give them the satisfaction which they requested or to promise an alleviation of the burden which Solomon had placed upon them. The reaction was immediate and violent; the northern tribes threw off their allegiance to a dynasty which would not recognize that it had obligations to its subjects. Nor had they far to look for an alternative choice to Rehoboam. Jeroboam had lately come back from Egypt and in fact took the lead among the tribal delegates who stated their terms to Rehoboam. There at Shechem they proclaimed Jeroboam king; and there he made his capital.

Rehoboam, seeing the hostility of the delegates, hurried home in his chariot to Jerusalem. He had good cause to seek the safety of Jerusalem, for when he tried to assert his authority over the rebel tribes by sending the officer in charge of the corvée to the delegates, they showed what they thought of him and his royal master by stoning him to death.

As a result of his folly, Rehoboam was left with a tiny kingdom, consisting of the tribe of Judah and the small tribe of Benjamin on its northern boundary, within whose territory Jerusalem was situated. He was, however, not resourceless; he still had great wealth and a powerful army at his command, and he prepared to invade the northern territory and put down the revolt by force. But a spokesman of the prophetic party forbade him to do so, and such was the respect that the prophets could command that Rehoboam stayed his hand. The division between the two parts of the nation had come to stay.

The immediate cause of the division was economic: the people were tired of the burdensome taxation and forced labour which they had to endure under Solomon, and they saw no prospect of an alleviation of their burden under his son. The jealousy of the northern tribes against Judah played its part, as also did Egyptian intrigue. But the action of the prophetic party must not be forgotten. Samuel the prophet had played his part in preparing the way for David's rise to power, and in succeeding generations members of the prophetic guilds which he appears to have founded continued to remind the kings of both north and south that the principles of "democratic Yahwism" could not be lightly disregarded.

The kingdom, then, was divided politically, but religiously it was united in terms of the inter-tribal covenant. The ark, symbol of this unity, was enshrined in the temple at Jerusalem, which thus remained the central sanctuary of the amphictyony. Had Jerusalem and its temple had nothing more than this religious significance, all might have been well. But Jerusalem was also Rehoboam's capital and the temple was his royal chapel as well as being the central shrine for all Israel. Jeroboam was afraid that if the northern Israelites continued to visit Jerusalem for religious purposes something of their old feelings of allegiance to the house of David might revive. He therefore raised two ancient sanctuaries in his realm to the status of national shrines. One was the sanctuary of Dan, in the extreme north, served by a hereditary priesthood which traced its lineage back to Moses. The other was the sanctuary of Bethel, near the southern frontier of his kingdom, whose sacred associations were still more venerable, going back to Abraham and Jacob, both of whom had offered sacrifice there. What offended even more against the principles of Israel's worship under the covenant than the erection of rival sanctuaries to that at Jerusalem was that in both these sanctuaries golden images of bull-calves were installed, to serve as the visible pedestal for the invisible throne of Yahweh. This infringed the aniconic principle laid down for Israel's worship in the days of Moses, and it represented a dangerous assimilation to Canaanite religious practice (although among the Canaanites a *visible* representation of the divinity was supported by the animal).

It may be asked whether there was any difference in principle between the use of bull-calf images to support Yahweh's invisible presence and the use of cherubs for the same purpose in the holy of holies at Jerusalem. The answer probably is that the cherubs were symbolical beings (representing originally the storm-winds) and their images were therefore not "any likeness of anything that is in heaven above, or that is in the earth beneath, or that is in the water under the earth",[1] whereas the bull-calf images were all too closely associated with Canaanite fertility ritual. It appears from the ritual texts of Ugarit that El, the supreme god of the Canaanite pantheon, was on occasion actually hypostatized as a bull (shor), and known as Shor-El.[2]

At any rate, Jeroboam's elevation of the shrines of Dan and Bethel to be rivals to Jerusalem, and his installation of the golden bull-calf images in these shrines, are together stigmatized throughout the narrative of the book of Kings as "The sin of Jeroboam the son of Nebat, which he made Israel to sin".

In the fifth year after the disruption of the kingdom (c. 925 B.C.), Shishak mounted an invasion of Palestine from Egypt. We have two accounts of the invasion: the Judaean account preserved in I Kings 14-25 ff. and in II Chron. 12:1 ff., and an Egyptian account preserved on a pylon of the temple of Amun at Karnak. The Judaean account concentrates on Shishak's appropriating the ceremonial shields of gold in Jerusalem carried by the royal bodyguard when the king entered the temple, and on their replacement by shields of bronze. The Egyptian account gives us further information: in addition to a relief picturing Shishak's victory there is a list of conquered cities of Asia, of which about 120 names are legible and a number of these are identifiable as Israelite cities. It is plain that his invasion was not confined to Judah, for the list includes cities which he took in the northern kingdom as far north as Megiddo and the Plain of Jezreel and eastward across the Jordan. Probably Jeroboam, whom Shishak regarded as his vassal, did not pay him the respect which he claimed but conducted himself as an independent king; and so he as well as Rehoboam suffered at Shishak's hands.

The southern kingdom in particular was gravely weakened, both in money and in manpower, as a result of Shishak's invasion, and the kings of Judah could no longer think seriously of reconquering the revolted tribes to the north. This did not lead them to make peace, however; it led them to seek allies, and they found them in the kings of Damascus, the successors of that Rezon who founded a dynasty there in the reign of Solomon. Abijah, Rehoboam's son, enlisted the

---

[1] Ex. 20:4; Deut. 5:8.
[2] It is relevant to recall here the Greek myth of Europa and the bull, which has Phoenician affinities.

aid of Tabrimmon, king of Damascus, against Israel, and the alliance was renewed between their sons, Asa and Benhadad I respectively. The kings of Israel had thus to keep watch on their southern and north-eastern frontiers simultaneously. If they tried to take offensive action against Judah, they had to expect an invasion from the north. Thus, about 890 B.C., Baasha fortified the frontier town of Ramah as an outpost against Judah and also, it appears, to prevent any of his own subjects going over to Judah; the pull of Jerusalem and the Davidide dynasty was still strong! Asa, king of Judah at the time, sent a message to Benhadad, who responded by invading Israel and overrunning a good part of the territory north of the Plain of Jezreel. Baasha had to hasten north to deal with this greater threat, and during his absence the king of Judah organized compulsory work parties from Judah who demolished the fortifications of Ramah and carried away all the material to build two fortresses in his own Benjamite territory against the northern realm.

The name of Asa is also associated with a religious reformation in Judah; he made a clean sweep of Canaanite cultic objects and institutions which were included in the apparatus of Yahweh-worship at various local shrines ("high places") throughout the land. Stern measures were adopted even in his own household; the queen-mother Maacah was deposed from her dignity (which was more than a nominal one) because she maintained a shrine of her own with an image or sacred pole representing the Canaanite goddess Asherah.

Weak though the southern kingdom was, it remained loyal to the house of David, which remained in power so long as the kingdom itself did, a period of 340 years after the death of Solomon. There was much less dynastic stability in the northern kingdom. There only two dynasties – those founded by Omri about 881 B.C. and by Jehu forty years later – lasted for more than two generations. Jeroboam's son was assassinated by Baasha, one of his army officers, in the year after he succeeded to the kingdom; when Baasha had reigned twenty-four years, a similar fate befell *his* son and successor. A few years of civil war followed, between various rivals for the succession; the survivor, Omri, was one of the greatest kings of the northern kingdom.

CHAPTER V

THE HOUSE OF OMRI

(881—841 B.C.)

THE CIVIL WAR IN THE NORTHERN KINGDOM WHICH FOLLOWED THE assassination of Baasha's son in 884 B.C. came to an end with the victory of Omri, commander-in-chief of the armed forces. Omri reigned only eight years after his triumph, but during his brief reign he gave his kingdom a direction, by internal consolidation and foreign conquest and alliance, which it continued to follow during the forty years that his dynasty lasted.

One important internal measure was the choice of a new site for the capital of his kingdom. Jeroboam had fixed his capital at Shechem, probably because of the ancient prestige of the place (the place where Abraham built his first altar after arriving in the land of Canaan). Later the capital was moved to Tirzah, about seven miles north-east of Shechem.

But Omri found a more suitable position and built the city of Samaria, seven miles north-west of Shechem. Samaria had the central advantages of Shechem and Tirzah, but it also occupied a strong strategic position and its natural strength was increased by fortification. The wisdom of Omri's choice was shown on more occasions than one during the remaining century and a half of the northern kingdom's existence, when Samaria withstood several sieges conducted by well-equipped armies.

Omri extended his Transjordanian control by imposing tribute upon the land of Moab, which had regained its independence since the time when David conquered it. He renewed Solomon's policy of alliance with Phoenicia, and this alliance was confirmed by the marriage of his son Ahab to Jezebel, daughter of the Phoenician priest-king Ethbaal (878–866 B.C.). But whatever commercial advantages were secured by this alliance, its religious consequences were such that the prophetic party looked upon Omri as a greater offender against Yahweh than any of his predecessors, surpassed only by his son Ahab himself.

It was a common practice that a foreign princess who married the ruler of a neighbouring state should have facilities for practising her native religion in her new home. So Solomon's many foreign wives had shrines provided for their native cults on the western slope of the Mount of Olives – an action which is reprobated in the narrative of I Kings 11. Whether such a practice was common diplomatic form or not elsewhere, the prophetic party would have preferred no foreign alliances rather than alliances which involved the installation of ethnic cults in the presence of the God of Israel.

But the religious practices of Solomon's wives made little impact on the life of his subjects. Far different was it with the religious practices of Ahab's wife. Phoenicia was a powerful state, and correspondingly great respect had to be paid to Phoenicia's gods, and especially to Melqart,[1] the chief god of Tyre, whose devotee Jezebel was.

It is unlikely that there was a plan to make the worship of Melqart the dominant or sole form of worship in Israel. Ahab, while he patronized the new cult, appears to have been a Yahweh-worshipper, to judge by the names borne by those of his children whose names we know – Jehoram[2] ("Yahweh is high"), Ahaziah ("Yahweh has taken hold"), Athaliah ("Yahweh is exalted"). But Jezebel was plainly not content with maintaining a private shrine where she herself might practise her own religion; she appears to have organized the worship of Melqart on a fairly large scale and maintained a large staff of cultic officials, who enjoyed positions of influence at court. The worship of Melqart was essentially Canaanite in character, and its introduction into Israel led to a great revival of the old Canaanite worship of Baal and Asherah. Melqart himself was, from one point of view, the Tyrian counterpart of Baal, and in fact is called Baal throughout the Biblical narrative. There was a large measure of syncretism between the Tyro-Canaanite cult and Israel's religion, and a popular landslide away from the purer forms of Yahweh-worship. The prophets of Yahweh protested against this apostasy, but their protests were treated as treasonable, because the apostasy enjoyed court patronage, and at Jezebel's instigation many of these prophets were put to death.

The leader of these protesting prophets was Elijah, a man of exceptionally powerful personality, who announced a three years' famine throughout the land as a divine judgment for the apostasy and became the special target for Jezebel's enmity. He had to take refuge from her wrath, first in Transjordan and later in Phoenicia; but came forth from his retreat at the end of three years to lead the people back to Yahweh-worship.

The impressive occasion when the "fire of God" came down on Elijah's sacrifice on Mount Carmel and convinced the people that

---

[1] Phoenician *melk-qart*, "king of the city".

[2] Abbreviated as Joram, by which form he is referred to below (pp.48 ff.), to distinguish him from his namesake Jehoram, king of Judah (pp.46, 49, 51).

Yahweh and not Baal was the true God is described in I Kings 18. The summit of Carmel, which juts out into the Mediterranean, was an ancient holy place, and Elijah built no new altar there, but repaired an old Yahweh-altar which had fallen into ruin. But even as he did so, he arranged his sacrifice to synchronize with the daily afternoon oblation that was offered in the temple at Jerusalem. It would be precarious to argue that because no protest on Elijah's part is recorded against the cults of Dan and Bethel, therefore he approved of them. These were corrupt forms of Yahweh-worship, but the far greater menace of Baal-worship engaged Elijah's active opposition.

The people who gathered on Carmel, no longer content to limp between two opinions, acclaimed Yahweh as the real God, and at Elijah's instigation slaughtered the cult-officials of Baal in the Kishon ravine at the foot of the hill. These events were followed quickly by a cessation of the long drought and a downpour of rain, which further confirmed the people in their return to covenant-loyalty. But Elijah, though vindicated so signally, panicked when Jezebel threatened to serve him as he served the prophets of Baal, and fled south to Arabia, where he held communion with God and received fresh courage thereby at the sacred hill of Horeb, the place of Moses' theophany four hundred years earlier. Thus strengthened, he returned to his homeland to put into effect a programme which envisaged the extermination of the dynasty of Omri as the only way to purify the land completely of the Baal cult.

The prophetic opposition to the policy of the house of Omri was not concerned simply with the external forms of the national religion, but with its social content as well. The covenant with Yahweh safeguarded the rights and privileges of the meanest and obscurest of the sons of Israel. But the influence of foreign alliances led to a weakening of the covenant in this as in other respects. It had turned out so under Solomon, and this was largely responsible for the breach in the unity of the kingdom. How it worked in Ahab's reign is well illustrated by the story of Naboth the Jezreelite.

Ahab had a country house at Jezreel in the Plain of Jezreel. Hard by his estate lay the small vineyard of Naboth, a freeborn Israelite of the place. Ahab thought that Naboth's vineyard would make a convenient addition to his own grounds, and offered to buy it from Naboth at a good price or to give him a better vineyard in exchange. Ahab was perfectly free to make such an offer, and Naboth was equally free to accept it or reject it. Naboth rejected it. The vineyard was one which had come down from his ancestors; he did not choose to let it go, even for the sake of getting a better vineyard somewhere else. When Naboth said "No", Ahab accepted his "No": he could do nothing else. He was displeased, and went home and sulked; but he knew that

Naboth was completely within his rights by the ancient law of Israel, and the idea of violating that law did not occur to him. But Jezebel his wife had been brought up to quite a different idea of kingship. "Is this the way you play at being king in Israel?" she scornfully asked. Then by the suborning of false witnesses, who accused Naboth of blasphemy and sedition before the elders of Jezreel, she procured Naboth's judicial murder by stoning. His property was now confiscated to the crown; and when the foul deed was done, Jezebel announced to her husband that he might now without more ado take possession of the coveted vineyard. And as the wretched king went to inspect his ill-gotten gain, who should meet him in Naboth's vineyard but Elijah the Tishbite, lately returned from Horeb? From Elijah's lips the conscience-stricken monarch then heard a fearful sentence pronounced on himself and his family – a sentence which involved their utter and shameful extermination. And the prophets maintained their opposition to the house of Ahab until the extermination was accomplished.

The war against Damascus that had been waged sporadically for several decades continued with one important interval throughout the reign of Ahab. But Ahab was diplomat enough to avoid waging a war on two fronts. Instead of having to defend himself against Syria and Judah simultaneously he brought the feud with the dynasty of David to an end, making an alliance with King Jehoshaphat of Judah (c. 870—845 B.C.), Asa's son, and cementing the alliance matrimonially by giving his daughter Athaliah as wife to Jehoshaphat's son Jehoram. (It is not said in so many words that Athaliah's mother was Jezebel, but Athaliah's subsequent behaviour suggests that she was.) The restoration of peace on Jehoshaphat's northern frontier enabled him to reconquer Edom, to the south. When the kingdom of Judah was strong, Edom was regularly reduced to subjection; any weakening on Judah's part was the constant signal for the reassertion of Edomite independence. The Judaean conquest of Edom and alliance with Ahab, and Ahab's alliance with Phoenicia, meant that the trade-routes between the Mediterranean and the Red Sea via the Gulf of Aqaba were open again.

When Benhadad of Damascus invaded Ahab's kingdom with a large army, Ahab succeeded in inflicting two successive defeats on him, one outside the walls of Samaria, and the other the following spring at Aphek in the Plain of Jezreel. After the second battle Benhadad had to sue for his life, and Ahab granted him peace on condition that he restored the Israelite cities which his father, Tabrimmon, had taken and permitted the establishment of Israelite bazaars with extra-territorial rights in Damascus. The peace thus concluded lasted for three years.

During these three years an event took place which would in any case have compelled the small states of Syria to forget their private quarrels and unite to meet a common peril. The fortunes of Assyria, which had been at a low ebb for two centuries because of raids by Aramaean nomads, were restored about 900 B.C. under a succession of vigorous kings, who carried Assyrian arms westwards from the Tigris to the Mediterranean Sea. In 853 B.C. one of these, Shalmaneser III (859—823 B.C.), was met by a coalition of Syrian and Cilician states at Qarqar on the Orontes. To Shalmaneser's record of the battle we owe our information of the identity of these confederate kings and the military contingents supplied by each. Among the twelve kings who fought him he mentions Benhadad of Damascus – or, as he calls him, Adad-idri (the equivalent of the Biblical name Hadadezer) – and Ahab of Israel. While Benhadad supplied the largest contingent of soldiers (20,000 men), Ahab supplied the largest chariot-force (2,000 chariots). (Ahab is credited with supplying 10,000 soldiers – a very respectable figure considering the contingents of some of his stronger allies.) The heritage of Solomon in horses and chariots had not been squandered: the stables at Megiddo were still maintained at a high level of efficiency.[1]

Shalmaneser claims a sweeping victory; the corpses of his foes, he says, covered the plain of the Orontes and dammed the stream itself. But the fact that he did not pursue his alleged advantage but returned home and did not trouble these parts for twelve years suggests that his confederate opponents gave a good account of themselves.

When the Assyrian threat receded, the anti-Assyrian alliance quickly broke up, and it was not long before Ahab and Benhadad resumed mutual hostilities. The Israelite frontier city of Ramoth-gilead in Transjordan had remained in Benhadad's hands in spite of the terms of the truce three years earlier. Ahab decided to make a bid to recapture it, and King Jehoshaphat led a military force from Judah to cooperate with him. The narrative of I Kings 22 draws a memorable picture of the two kings sitting robed upon their thrones at the gate of Samaria, while complaisant prophets foretold complete success for the enterprise – until the honest Micaiah ben Imlah described the vision in which he had seen the people of Israel scattered on the mountains like shepherdless sheep. Ahab, feeling in his bones that the truth lay with the one independent prophet rather than with the four hundred who had given a more comfortable response, disguised himself when battle was joined at Ramoth-gilead, and entered the fray as a common chariot-soldier. But when "a certain man drew his bow at a venture" and his arrow pierced Ahab between the joints of his armour, he recognized that no disguise could protect him from

[1] See p. 37, n. 1.

his predicted destiny. Yet his last hours were worthy of a royal warrior: he had himself propped up in his chariot till evening fell, lest his followers should panic if they knew their king was mortally wounded. At sunset he died from loss of blood and the battle was broken off.

His son Ahaziah succeeded him. The only recorded event of his short reign is his cooperation with Jehoshaphat to send a merchant fleet from Aqaba to import a cargo of gold from Ophir: the ships never set sail, for they were wrecked in a storm while they were still in harbour at Aqaba.

Ahaziah died in consequence of a fall in the year after he came to the throne, and was succeeded by his brother Joram. Joram is credited in the Hebrew record with doing something to discourage Baal-worship in Samaria: in particular he removed a sacred pillar or *massebah* which his father had erected in honour of Melqart.

Ahab's death had been the signal for a revolt of the Moabites, who had been made tributary by his father Omri. The tribute was paid in sheep and wool, which constituted Moab's chief wealth; year by year King Mesha of Moab had to pay to his Israelite overlord 100,000 lambs and the wool of 100,000 rams. The statement in II Kings 1:1;3:5, that when Ahab died Moab rebelled against Israel is considerably elaborated in Mesha's own account of the revolt, recorded on the victory stele which he set up at Dibon near his frontier with Israel – the so-called Moabite Stone, discovered in 1868. In his inscription Mesha ascribes the period of Moabite subjection to the fact that Chemosh, the god of Moab, was angry with his people; similarly the praise for the successful revolt and the victories which Mesha won when he tried to extend his territory at the expense of Israel in Transjordan is ascribed to Chemosh. The rebellion was, in fact, a holy war waged by Moab, and the frontier towns taken from Israel were "devoted" to Chemosh as Jericho had once been devoted to Yahweh. Here is part of the inscription:—

> I am Mesha the son of Chemosh – [kan], king of Moab, the Dibonite. My father reigned over Moab for thirty years and I became king after my father. I made this high place for Chemosh at Qorhah, [a high place of] salvation, because he saved me from all my assailants and caused me to see my desire upon my enemies. Omri, king of Israel, oppressed Moab many days, for Chemosh was angry with his land. His son succeeded him and he too said, "I will oppress Moab". In my days he spoke th[us], but I saw my desire upon him and his house, and Israel utterly perished for ever. Now Omri had taken possession of the land of Medeba and [Israel] dwelt in it during his days and half the days of his son, forty years; but Chemosh restored it in my days. I built Baal-meon and made the reservoir in it, and I built Qiryathen. Now the men of Gad had dwelt in the land of Ataroth for long, and the king of Israel had built Ataroth for himself.

But I fought against the city and took it, and I killed all the people in the city, a spectacle for Chemosh and Moab. And I took captive from there the altar-hearth of David and dragged it before Chemosh in Qeriyoth. And I settled therein the men of Sharon and the men of Mahrath. Then Chemosh said to me, "Go, take Nebo against Israel". I went by night and fought against it from daybreak till noon, and I took it and killed them all – seven thousand men, boys, women, [girls] and female slaves, for I had devoted it to Ashtar-Chemosh.[1] I took the vessels of Yahweh from there and dragged them before Chemosh. Now the king of Israel had built Jahaz and he dwelt there while he fought against me; but Chemosh drove him out before me. I took two hundred men of Moab, all of them chiefs, and led them up against Jahaz, and I took it to annex it to Dibon. I built Qorhah, the wall of the woodlands and the wall of the mound; I built its gates, I built its towers and I built the royal palace; and I made the two reservoirs for water inside the city. There was no cistern inside the city of Qorhah, so I said to all the people, "Each of you make a cistern in his house." I had ditches dug for Qorhah by Israelite prisoners. I built Aroer and made the road by the Arnon; I built Beth-bamoth, for it had been demolished; I built Bezer, for it lay in ruins, [with] fifty me[n] of Dibon; for all Dibon owes allegiance to me. I reigned over hundreds of cities which I annexed to the country. I built Medeba, Beth-diblathen and Beth-baal-meon, and I led up there the sheep-breeders of the country . . .[2]

In II Kings 3 we have the story of an attempt made by Joram, with the aid of his ally King Jehoshaphat of Judah and Jehoshaphat's vassal the king of Edom, to bring Moab back under his control. The battle went against Moab until Mesha in desperation offered his firstborn son as a sacrifice to Chemosh on the city wall. The spectacle of this desperate act of supplication nerved the hard-pressed Moabites for one final rally, and they turned the tide of battle and repelled the Israelites and their allies.

The narrative of the battle is also interesting for the part that the prophet Elisha plays in it, directing the strategy of the confederate forces. Elisha was the attendant of Elijah, who succeeded his master as chief prophet in the land of Israel, recognized as such by the prophetic guilds. He was to prove a trusty adviser to the kings of Israel for several decades, especially after the fall of the house of Omri. In fact, he was largely responsible for instigating the revolt which led to its fall.

Soon after the campaign against Moab, Jehoshaphat died and was succeeded on the Judaean throne by his son Jehoram, son-in-law to Ahab. This Jehoram was a weak king, and during his reign Edom rebelled against Judah and established its independence once more.

The hostilities which were renewed between Israel and Damascus

---

[1] The female consort of Chemosh.
[2] See translation and notes by E. Ullendorff in DOTT, pp. 195 ff.

in the year of Ahab's death continued for a long time, with fluctu-
ations this way and that. At one point during the reign of Joram the
Damascene army penetrated into the heart of the land of Israel, and
besieged Samaria so closely that they were on the point of reducing it
by famine when a rumour of the approach of an army of Cilicians and
Hittites from the north to aid the Israelites made them raise the siege
suddenly – to the immense and bewildered relief of the people of
Samaria, who had been reduced to cannibalism by the extremities of
the famine.

In this continued fighting Ramoth-gilead remained a disputed point.
Here Damascene and Israelite troops continued to face each other
throughout the reigns of Ahab's sons. And it was here in 841 B.C. that
the conspiracy came to a head which caused the downfall and extermination of the family of Ahab.

The commander of the Israelite army at Ramoth-gilead was Jehu
the son of Jehoshaphat the son of Nimshi. Several years before, when
the prophet Elijah received a communication from God at Horeb in a
"still small voice" which was more powerful for destruction than
wind, earthquake or fire, he was commanded to go back and not only
anoint Elisha as his successor in the prophetic office but also to anoint
this Jehu as king of Israel and one Hazael as king of Damascus. Elijah
did in fact take Elisha as his disciple and successor, but the two other
acts of anointing he did not carry out in person but bequeathed to
Elisha as duties for him to perform. Hazael, an officer of Benhadad I,
had already succeeded his master. We are told how Benhadad fell ill
and sent Hazael to Elisha (whose fame as a prophet was well known in
Syria) to ask if he would get better. Elisha replied that the illness was
not a mortal one, but added, eyeing Hazael meaningly, that Benhadad
would die none the less. Hazael pretended not to understand, but
Elisha told him plainly that he would be king of Syria, and wept as he
thought of the depredations that Hazael would perpetrate within the
frontiers of Israel. Hazael went out from Elisha's presence, and when
he arrived back at the palace he smothered his sick master by pressing
a wet cloth on his face, and took the throne for himself.[1]

There remained only the anointing of Jehu to complete the three-
fold commission. Elisha sent a member of a prophetic guild to Ramoth-
gilead with a small flask of oil, and told him to request a private interview with Jehu. This the prophet did, and when Jehu and he were
alone, he poured the oil over Jehu's head, hailed him in Yahweh's
name as king of Israel and exterminator of the family of Ahab – and
fled. Jehu's fellow-officers chaffed him over the visit of this unkempt
madman, but when Jehu told them what had happened, the idea
appealed to them instantly. They blew the trumpet, and proclaimed

[1] II Kings 8:7–15.

Jehu king, placing their military cloaks under his feet as he stood on the steps of the barracks.

The only justification for such a conspiracy must be its success.

> Treason doth never prosper. What's the reason?
> For if it prosper, none dare call it treason.

But treason indeed it was on Jehu's part. Not only did he rebel against the king to whom he had sworn allegiance, but by leaving his post of duty at Ramoth-gilead he weakened the frontier defences of Israel in a manner that he and his successors had good cause to rue for many a day.

At present, however, Jehu must make good his newly acquired title. Joram had recently been wounded in battle against the Damascenes, and was recuperating from his wounds at his summer palace at Jezreel. His nephew Ahaziah, king of Judah (who had succeeded his father Jehoram the year before), was paying him a friendly visit. Suddenly the approach of a party of charioteers was reported to the two kings. They both set out to meet the party: this must be important news from the battle-front, for the leader of the party was said to be Jehu himself. But when they reached the charioteers, they learned the truth. Joram received a forbidding answer to his query "Is all well?" "It's treason, Ahaziah!" he called out to his nephew, and they both turned to flee. Too late: Joram was pierced to the heart by an arrow, and died on the spot (the spot, the narrator notes, was the former vineyard of Naboth); and Ahaziah was also shot at and fatally wounded. Jehu, like the reckless revolutionary he was, took no thought of possible diplomatic repercussions from the murder of the king of another realm: "Shoot him too", he shouted (perhaps because he was a grandson of Ahab). Ahaziah died of his arrow-wound at Megiddo, and his body was carried home to Jerusalem for burial.

Meanwhile Jehu pressed on with the work of wiping out the royal family. Jezebel, the queen-mother, was in residence at Jezreel, and met her death with queenly dignity: nothing in her life became her so much as the leaving of it. The other members of Ahab's household at Jezreel were massacred, but most of his family lived at Samaria, the capital. On receipt of a letter from Jehu, the elders of Samaria realized that they had a new master who must be placated; how better could he be placated than with the heads of the sons of Ahab? So the male descendants of Ahab were slaughtered, seventy in all, and their heads were despatched to Jehu at Jezreel. Some forty relatives of Ahaziah of Judah, on their way to greet the royal family of Israel, were also slaughtered: they had not heard of the rebellion. Thus the dynasty of Omri was wiped out. It was a popular dynasty: hence (from Jehu's point of view) the necessity of leaving no member of the family who might become a focus for the people's loyalty to it. But the extermination of the family of Ahab chimed in with the policy of the prophetic guilds; it was retribution for the hostile action which Jezebel had once taken against them.

Something else figured on the prophetic programme: the wiping out of Baal-worship. This foreign cult had declined during Joram's reign, but Melqart still had a shrine in his honour in Samaria. Jehu therefore made his way to Samaria in the rôle of a religious reformer, and this rôle was strengthened by his securing the cooperation of Jonadab the Rechabite, leader of a strictly puritanical group, who bore much the same relation to other Yahwists as the Wahhabi bear to other Muslims. The Rechabites had not exchanged the desert way of life for the agricultural economy of Canaan as the other Israelites did at the time of the settlement; they continued to live in tents, they sowed no seed, planted no vineyards and drank no wine; in fact, they abstained from everything that had the remotest connexion with the Canaanite fertility-cults, and were accordingly foremost in their detestation of Baal-worship.

On arriving at Samaria, Jehu, with low cunning, proclaimed a solemn assembly in honour of Baal, giving out that he would patronize Baal-worship even more than Ahab had done, and celebrate a splendid sacrifice in his honour. When a large concourse of worshippers had come together on the appointed day – many of them no doubt simply desirous of pleasing the new ruler – they were treacherously massacred. The Baal shrine and all its installations were destroyed; every relic of the Tyrian cult was suppressed.

Thus Jehu carried out the prophetic programme. But the manner in which he did it – the wholesale massacres, and the treachery of the suppression of Baal-worship – was unpardonable, and a century later another prophet, Hosea, announced in Yahweh's name that retribution would fall upon the house of Jehu for the bloodshed at Jezreel.

CHAPTER VI

THE SYRIAN WARS AND THE RISE
OF THE PROPHETS

(841—745 B.C.)

WHEN KING AHAZIAH OF JUDAH DIED AT MEGIDDO OF THE WOUND inflicted by one of Jehu's archers, his mother Athaliah, the daughter of Ahab, decided that the moment was opportune to seize power for herself in Jerusalem. She was able to secure the support of the royal bodyguard, and had all the royal family massacred. Only Ahaziah's six-month-old son Joash escaped her notice; he and his nurse were smuggled out of her way and the infant prince was brought up in the temple precincts.

The worship of Melqart appears to have flourished in Jerusalem during Athaliah's reign of six years: this suggests that she was a daughter of Jezebel. But in the seventh year there was a popular rising, led by the priest Jehoiada, who succeeded in getting the royal bodyguard to transfer their allegiance from Athaliah to the young prince Joash. They guarded the temple while the boy Joash was brought forth and proclaimed king of Judah. Athaliah did not get wind of what was afoot until it was too late; when she came into the temple with a cry of "Treason!" on her lips, she was immediately hustled out and put to death as soon as she was outside the sacred precincts. The installation of Joash as king was marked by a tripartite covenant-ceremony between Yahweh, the king and the people.

The dynasty of Jehu lasted for nearly a hundred years. At the beginning of Jehu's reign, Shalmaneser III of Assyria paid a return visit to the west, and Jehu is recorded as one of the western rulers who paid him tribute. He is called "Jehu son of Omri" in the Assyrian account – ironically enough, when one recalls that he had so lately exterminated the dynasty of Omri, but the title simply marks him out as king of "the land of Omri". Jehu probably welcomed the Assyrian protection against his Damascene neighbours to the north-east, and thought it cheaply bought at the price of the tribute paid. But Shalmaneser returned to Assyria, and after 839 no Assyrian army appeared in these western lands for nearly forty years. No protection came from that direction against the Syrians. Jehu's precipitate departure from

Ramoth-gilead to seize the throne for himself weakened the Israelite defences there, and the bloodshed that accompanied his revolt weakened the state internally. The menace of Syrian encroachment kept on growing during the reign of Jehu (841—814 B.C.) and reached its climax under his son Jehoahaz (814—798 B.C.). Hazael of Damascus and his son and successor Benhadad II pressed home every advantage, until it looked as if Israel's independence as a nation would be lost altogether. So low was Israel brought that Jehoahaz could muster no more than 10,000 infantry, with fifty horsemen and *ten* chariots – an eloquent index of Israel's decline since the day when Ahab was able to send two thousand chariots to the confederate army that faced Shalmaneser at Qarqar.

The Syrians invaded Israel from the north and east. They occupied all Transjordan and infiltrated down the western coastal plain as far south as Gath. This occupation of Gath was a threat to Jerusalem, and Joash had to buy them off with the treasures of his temple. The priesthood and people appear to have been alienated from Joash in consequence, and he was assassinated about 800 B.C. Other enemies of Israel profited by their distress. The Ammonites, for example, encroached from the south-east upon Israel's territory east of Jordan, massacring the population to acquire more living space for themselves. But when the fortunes of Israel were at their lowest ebb, "Yahweh gave Israel a deliverer."[1] This deliverer can be identified as the Assyrian king Adadnirari III, who in 803 B.C. led an expedition against Syria, in the course of which he raided Damascus and made it tributary. Syrian pressure on Israel relaxed. Jehoash, who succeeded Jehoahaz as king of Israel (*c.* 798—782 B.C.), was able to beat the Syrians off and to recover the Israelite cities which they had taken in his father's reign.

All through the long-drawn-out tribulation of these years Israel had one man whose morale and confidence in Yahweh never wavered. The prophet Elisha was a tower of strength to his people, and when at last he lay on his death-bed, King Jehoash came down to see him and wept over him. "My father, my father," he cried, "Israel's chariots and horsemen!" – echoing the words spoken by Elisha himself when his master Elijah was taken from him. Elisha's last words presaged Israelite victory over the Syrians, and Jehoash inflicted three defeats on them.

Jehoash also took Jerusalem, after receiving a foolish challenge from Amaziah, the successor of Joash as king of Judah. Amaziah had conquered Edom, and thought himself strong enough to face Israel in battle. But he was beaten and made tributary, and a good part of Jerusalem's fortifications were dismantled. Amaziah was discredited

[1] II Kings 13:5.

and had to flee from Jerusalem, where the people made his son Uzziah[1] king in his place (c. 791—740 B.C.). A few years later Amaziah was assassinated at Lachish, where he was able to hold out for some time after leaving Jerusalem.

About the same time as Uzziah was proclaimed king in Jerusalem, Jehoash of Israel died and was succeeded by his son Jeroboam II (c. 782—745 B.C.). Uzziah and Jeroboam II both enjoyed long and prosperous reigns. At the death of Adadnirari III in 782 B.C. the Assyrian tide receded for forty years, but Damascus was now too weak to undertake renewed aggression against Israel and Judah.

Uzziah recovered and fortified Elath on the Gulf of Aqaba and reasserted Judaean supremacy over the Philistine cities of the Mediterranean coastland. The agricultural economy of Judah received special attention. The prosperity of the kingdom may be judged from the variety of "consumer goods" enjoyed by the urban population. The character of his reign is mirrored in the early oracles of the prophet Isaiah, a native of Jerusalem who was called to his prophetic ministry "in the year that King Uzziah died".[2] The catalogue of female finery in Isa. 3:18 ff. suggests a high level of material prosperity and sophistication of polite society. But the underlying condition of the body politic was not so healthy as the outward adornment might suggest. The wealth was concentrated in the hands of the few, who had extended their property at the expense of their poorer brethren:

> Yahweh has taken his place to contend,
>   he stands to judge his people.
> Yahweh enters into judgment
>   with the elders and princes of his people:
> "It is you who have devoured the vineyard,
>   the spoil of the poor is in your houses.
> What do you mean by crushing my people,
>   by grinding the face of the poor?" says the Lord Yahweh
>   of hosts.[3]
>
> Woe to those who join house to house,
>   who add field to field,
> until there is no more room,
>   and you are made to dwell alone
>   in the midst of the land![4]

Nor could the poor secure justice when they sued for it; their wealthy dispossessors were in a position to bribe venal judges:

[1] Also called Azariah.   [2] Isa. 6:1.
[3] Isa. 3:13-15.   [4] Isa. 5:8.

> Your princes are rebels
>   and companions of thieves.
> Every one loves a bribe
>   and runs after gifts.
> They do not defend the fatherless,
>   and the widow's cause does not come to them.[1]
>
> Woe to those who decree iniquitous decrees,
>   and the writers who keep writing oppression,
> to turn aside the needy from justice
>   and to rob the poor of my people of their right,
> that widows may be their spoil,
>   and that they may make the fatherless their prey![2]

Isaiah was a city dweller. The oppression of the poorer peasantry is even more vigorously described by his contemporary prophet, the countryman Micah, who lived in the south-western part of the kingdom of Judah:

> Hear, you heads of Jacob
>   and rulers of the house of Israel!
> Is it not for you to know justice? –
>   you who hate the good and love the evil,
> who tear the skin from off my people,
>   and their flesh from off their bones;
> who eat the flesh of my people,
>   and flay their skin from off them,
> and break their bones in pieces,
>   and chop them up like meat in a kettle,
>   like flesh in a caldron.[3]

The small peasant-proprietor tended to be more and more at the mercy of his wealthier neighbours. One bad harvest was a disaster; two or three in succession might make life impossible. He could only mortgage his small-holding to his wealthy neighbour, who would seize an opportunity to foreclose, and add the small-holding to his own estate, while the peasant and his family were compelled to work as his serfs.

If this took place in Judah, it took place also, and on a larger and more alarming scale, in the northern realm, where the peasantry had been hardest hit by the Syrian invasions.

Jeroboam II continued his father's work of winning back Israelite territory from Syria. He completed the reconquest of Transjordan as far south as the Dead Sea, while to the north he extended his power as far as the Hamathite frontier-post of Labo (Lebweh). Yet his reign, for all its political importance, is sketched but briefly in II Kings. He is reprobated for his maintenance of the schismatic bull-calf cults in the

---

[1] Isa. 1:23.   [2] Isa. 10:1 f.   [3] Mic. 3:1–3.

shrines at Dan and Bethel; but for the rest, his victories are presented as a merciful relief from the Damascene tribulation given to Israel by Yahweh, who "saw that the affliction of Israel was very bitter, for there was none left, bond or free, and there was none to help Israel. But Yahweh had not proposed to blot out the name of Israel from under heaven, so he saved them by the hand of Jeroboam."[1]

Some of the details, however, can be filled in from the prophetic oracles of Amos and Hosea. They make some reference to details of his military career, as the reconquest of the Transjordanian cities of Lo-debar and Karnaim.[2] But they are most concerned with the religious and social condition of the nation. There was a superficial prosperity, but it had been gained by depressing the status of the small independent peasants, who had hitherto constituted the backbone of the nation. The respect for the ancient covenant-laws which had deterred even Ahab from taking Naboth's vineyard by force had disappeared. The rich landowners had discovered means of appropriating vineyards like Naboth's without breaking the law:

> Thus says Yahweh:
> "For three transgressions of Israel,
>   and for four, I will not revoke the punishment;
> because they sell the righteous for silver,
>   and the needy for a pair of shoes –
> they that trample the head of the poor into the dust of the earth,
>   and turn aside the way of the afflicted; . . .
> they lay themselves down beside every altar
>   upon garments taken in pledge;
> and in the house of their God they drink
>   the wine of those who have been fined."[3]

They and their wives lived in ease and luxury on the wealth which they had extorted from the poor, with no thought for the evils which such a course of life must bring in its train:

> Woe to those who lie upon beds of ivory,
>   and stretch themselves upon their couches,
> and eat lambs from the flock,
>   and calves from the midst of the stall;
> who sing idle songs to the sound of the harp,
>   and like David invent for themselves instruments of music;
> who drink wine in bowls,
>   and anoint themselves with the finest oils,
>   but are not grieved over the ruin of Joseph!
> Therefore they shall now be the first of those to go into exile,
>   and the revelry of those who stretch themselves shall pass
>   away.[4]

---

[1] II Kings 14:26 f.   [2] Amos 6:13, R.S.V.
[3] Amos 2:6–8.   [4] Amos 6:4–7.

Yet these same people were punctilious in their religious observances. Never did such abundant sacrifices smoke to Yahweh from the altars at Dan and Bethel and other sanctuaries in Israel; and the note of praise rose regularly and loudly from tongue and harp. Was not this the worship in which Yahweh delighted? So they thought, but the voice of Yahweh through His prophet told a different story. Their unrighteousness and disregard of covenant-obligations tainted their devotions and made them abominable in His sight:

> I hate, I despise your feasts,
>   and I take no delight in your solemn assemblies.
> Even though you offer me your burnt offerings and
>   cereal offerings,
>   I will not accept them,
> and the peace offerings of your fatted beasts
>   I will not look upon.
> Take away from me the noise of your songs;
>   to the melody of your harps I will not listen.
> But let justice flow down like waters,
>   and righteousness like an everflowing stream.[1]

They talked glibly about the Day of Yahweh – the day when Yahweh would deal in judgment with His enemies. But did they not realize that Yahweh's judgment was to be executed in righteousness, and that iniquity would be punished in whomsoever it was found? And if it were found in Israel, it would be punished more severely in them than in others, for other nations had not enjoyed the knowledge of Yahweh and His will as Israel had done. Yahweh had no favourites; if He brought up Israel from the land of Egypt, He also brought their neighbours, the Syrians and the Philistines, from their former habitations to settle them in their present territories. And if He had driven out the former inhabitants of Canaan before Israel because of their sin, He would on the same principle dispossess Israel too.

The external form of worship was valueless without those inward and practical virtues which were lacking in Israel. Amos would have agreed completely with the words of Micah in Judah:

> What does Yahweh require of you
> but to do justice, and to love kindness,
>   and to walk humbly with your God?[2]

But that was not all: the external forms of popular worship themselves were corrupted by imitation of the old fertility cults of Canaan with its blunting of their ethical perception. Ritual prostitution was practised at the solemn festivals:

---

[1] Amos 5:21–24.   [2] Micah 6:8.

> A man and his father go in to the same maiden,
> so that my holy name is profaned.[1]

Further details of these practices are given by Hosea, whose own wife was seduced by them. But it was Hosea's forgiving love for his errant wife that brought home to him the persistence of Yahweh's love for His unfaithful people. He would bring them back to their old covenant-loyalty, but first they must be broken of their addiction to Canaanite idolatry by being uprooted and carried away from their land, back to the wilderness to renew their allegiance to their God, who had first made Himself known to them and won their love there.

In a situation of this kind, as T. H. Robinson has pointed out,[2] one of two things is bound to happen, and either way involves ruin. Either the point will come where the downtrodden peasantry will revolt, and overthrow the civilization erected on their oppression; or if they have lost sufficient spirit even to do this, then the nation has rotted from within and will fall, an easy prize, into the hand of the first aggressive adventurer who comes that way.

> Ill fares the land, to hastening ills a prey,
> Where wealth accumulates, and men decay.

The "hastening ills" followed swiftly upon the death of Jeroboam II about 745 B.C. His son Zechariah reigned only six months, and was then assassinated at Ibleam, in the plain of Jezreel, by Shallum ben Jabesh, apparently one of his military officers. The dynasty of Jehu thus came to an end in the fourth generation. It ended as it had begun, in rebellion and assassination. Not long before, Hosea had been commanded to give his first-born son the symbolic name of Jezreel, "for yet a little while", said Yahweh, "and I will punish the house of Jehu for the blood of Jezreel, and I will put an end to the kingdom of the house of Israel. And on that day, I will break the bow of Israel in the valley of Jezreel."[3] Amos too had foretold that Yahweh would "rise against the house of Jeroboam with the sword";[4] it was in fact this prophecy that constituted the final provocation to the chief priest of Bethel, and made him send Amos back to his own home in Judah.

But Shallum did not enjoy the kingdom long; in a month's time he fell in turn before another military leader, Menahem ben Gadi, who assumed the royal dignity, subdued the cities which held out against him, and by a display of frightfulness made sure that there would be no rebellion against *his* rule.

---

[1] Amos 2:7.
[2] W. O. E. Oesterley and T. H. Robinson, *A History of Israel* (1932), i, pp. 366 f.
[3] Hos. 1:4 f.   [4] Amos 7:9.

CHAPTER VII

DECLINE AND FALL OF THE
NORTHERN KINGDOM

(745—721 B.C.)

THE QUARTER OF A CENTURY THAT FOLLOWED THE FALL OF THE house of Jehu witnessed the collapse of the northern kingdom. Amos and Hosea had foretold what would happen: the plumb-line of God was set against the wall of the state of Israel, and revealed it to be hopelessly out of plumb and ready to fall.

> The high places of Isaac shall be made desolate,
>   and the sanctuaries of Israel shall be laid waste.[1]

The people had lost its former cohesion: social corruption was followed by political anarchy, and the swift succession of kings mirrored the instability of the nation:

> I have given you kings in my anger,
>   and I have taken them away in my wrath.[2]

One strong push was sufficient to bring down the edifice in ruin, and the push was administered by the Assyrians.

About the same time as the house of Jehu fell in Israel, a new ruler seized supreme power in Assyria. This was a man named Pulu, who, when he became king of Assyria, assumed the throne-name Tiglath-pileser, which had been held by two earlier kings of Assyria. One of these, Tiglath-pileser I (1114—1076 B.C.), had been a great conqueror in his day, and it may have been from a desire to emulate his achievements that Pulu assumed the same name.

For the first few years of his reign Tiglath-pileser III engaged in campaigns against his northern neighbours in Armenia, in the land called Urartu (the biblical Ararat). Then, having secured his northern position, he turned west and invaded the numerous states of Syria, as his predecessor Shalmaneser III had done a century before. The rulers hastened to make their submission and pay tribute to the invader. From Cilicia to Arabia Tiglath-pileser III lists them: they embraced Hittite, Aramaean, Phoenician and Hebrew rulers, including

---

[1] Amos 7:9.   [2] Hos. 13:11.

Rezin of Damascus, Menahem of Samaria, Hiram of Tyre, and (after stubborn resistance) Azariah of Judah. This expedition is usually dated in 738 B.C., but probably took place some five years earlier.[1]

The Israelite account is found in the Biblical narrative: "Pul[2] the king of Assyria came against the land; and Menahem gave Pul 1,000 talents of silver, that he might help him to confirm his hold of the royal power. Menahem exacted the money from Israel, that is, from all the wealthy men, fifty shekels of silver from every man, to give to the king of Assyria. So the king of Assyria turned back, and did not stay there in the land".[3] Menahem, feeling the need of external aid after his seizure of the Israelite throne, was glad of Assyrian support, even at the price of tribute. But the manner in which he raised the sum was bound to make him all the more unpopular: he imposed a capital levy of fifty shekels (one mina) apiece on the men of substance in the kingdom, 60,000 in all.

Unlike previous Assyrian kings who had campaigned in the west for a few years at a time, Tiglath-pileser III intended to establish his empire on a more permanent footing. Where local monarchs were able to control their states in the Assyrian interest and pay tribute as appointed, he left them in possession. Other areas were organized as Assyrian provinces, under a governor whose responsibility it was to maintain peace in his territory and collect and deliver the tribute regularly. The sanction underlying this extension and maintenance of imperial power was the Assyrian army, a superbly organized body of fighting men. The states of the west had never seen anything like the efficiency and speed of this army:

> None is weary, none stumbles,
>   none slumbers or sleeps,
> not a waistcloth is loose,
>   nor a sandal-throng broken;
> their arrows are sharp,
>   all their bows bent,
> their horses' hoofs seem like flint,
>   and their wheels like the whirlwind.[4]

The Assyrian army consisted of the regular soldiers, together with the militia who were mobilized in time of war. The regular soldiers wore a uniform of tunic, crossbelt, plumed helmet, kilt, and high boots. The militia were distinguished by the conical shape of their helmets. A company of infantry consisted of twenty-five files; each

---

[1] Cf. E. R. Thiele, *The Mysterious Numbers of the Hebrew Kings* (1951), pp. 75 ff.
[2] Note that here the biblical writer calls the Assyrian king by his personal name; elsewhere he calls him by his throne-name.
[3] II Kings 15:19 f.   [4] Isa. 5:27 f.

file comprised two men – an archer, and a spearman with a shield; these two stuck close together. There were also units of chariotry, slingers and sappers. The sappers were of considerable importance, for the Assyrians specialized in siege warfare.

Tiglath-pileser took this instrument of aggression over from his predecessors and built it up to carry out his imperial policy. Assyrian military operations were attended by ruthless brutality; but whereas some earlier kings had indulged in indiscriminate frightfulness, Tiglath-pileser and his successors made frightfulness part of their settled policy. Those states which submitted at once and remained loyal received *relatively* mild treatment, though they were heavily taxed. Those which resisted were crushed with great severity, but the worst fate was reserved for those who, having sworn allegiance, broke their oath and rebelled. These were treated as impious wretches who had committed perjury not merely against the Great King but against the Assyrian God Ashur, and the most exemplary penalties were therefore exacted from them – rulers and ruled alike.

Menahem remained the faithful vassal of Tiglath-pileser for the duration of his reign, as also did his son and successor Pekahiah. But there were forces in the west which were not willing to remain under Assyrian domination, and these found supporters in the land of Israel. One Transjordanian captain, Pekah by name, determined to bring Israel into an anti-Assyrian alliance headed by Rezin of Damascus. He therefore staged a revolt against Pekahiah, assassinated him, and seized the crown for himself.

The time seemed propitious for throwing off the Assyrian yoke, as Tiglath-pileser was once more engaged in fighting against the people of Urartu. They had not realized that this Assyrian king was not the kind of man who was content to make sporadic raids in the western territories, collect as much tribute from them as possible, and then go home and forget about them. But their alliance would be stronger if they could bring the kingdom of Judah into it and thus extend the anti-Assyrian front as far south as the Gulf of Aqaba. So they made overtures to the Judaean king, Ahaz, grandson of Uzziah. When he refused to join them, they decided to use force. They invaded Judah with the intention of deposing Ahaz and placing on the throne in Jerusalem one Tabeel, a Syrian pawn of their own, who could be trusted to carry out their will. Edom profited by Judah's preoccupation with this menace from the north to regain its independence and occupy the Judaean port of Elath (734 B.C.).

The invasion of Judah by the united army from Damascus and Samaria threw the court at Jerusalem into a panic. There was one man there – the prophet Isaiah – who saw the hopelessness of the Syro-Ephraimite policy, and urged his king and people to keep calm and trust in Yahweh, but he was not heeded. Ahaz had (as he thought) a better plan. He would send to Tiglath-pileser and call him in to help.

This, as Isaiah insisted, was an unnecessary and foolish move. It was unnecessary, because Tiglath-pileser was bound in any case to march west as soon as he could and deal with this anti-Assyrian rising. Ahaz's invitation would bring him no sooner, but (and herein lay its folly) it would draw the attention of Tiglath-pileser to the kingdom of Judah and involve the entry of Judah into the Assyrian sphere of control. Otherwise he might not have paid much attention to the small state in the hill country, lying away from the main lines of communication. But Isaiah's motives were not primarily geopolitical; they were religious. He knew that the Assyrian connexion would have disastrous results for the moral and spiritual condition of his fellow-countrymen. The proper course for Judah to pursue was not foreign entanglement, but steadfast trust in God. Let Ahaz and his people but place their faith in God, and they would surely be upheld and preserved. But if they called in the Assyrians, the Assyrians would in the long run bring destruction and not aid.

Isaiah's advice, although communicated in the name of Israel's God, was unheeded. Ahaz had made up his mind, and he carried out his plan. Tiglath-pileser came ere long, and dealt faithfully with the rebellion. Damascus was taken, the monarchy was abolished, and the kingdom, which had come in with a Rezin, went out with a Rezin, and was transformed into the Assyrian province of Damascus. The Israelites saw their fate approaching, realized the disastrous pass to which Pekah had brought them, and decided to act before Tiglath-pileser came. They assassinated Pekah and elected a new king, Hoshea, who immediately offered his submission to Tiglath-pileser (732 B.C.). This timely action meant the preservation of part of the kingdom of Israel, but all the territory north of the Plain of Jezreel and the Israelite lands in Transjordan were detached from the kingdom and reduced to the status of Assyrian provinces – Megiddo, Karnaim, and Gilead. The upper strata of the population of these areas, both of Syria and of Israel, were deported to other parts of the Assyrian Empire and replaced by colonists from elsewhere. This policy of deportation was inaugurated by Tiglath-pileser, and followed by his successors in the Assyrian and Babylonian Empires, as a means of discouraging revolt. Those who, if left in their homelands, would be the natural leaders of rebellion would have less opportunity and less inclination to start anything of the kind if they were transplanted to distant parts and settled among aliens. As a short-term policy, this plan seemed promising: people would not be so ready to fight for a land not their own, and thus the will to resistance would be broken. But in the long run it meant that the whole imperial territory was full of discontented communities of displaced people, and when at last a conqueror appeared who had sufficient political wisdom to allow these exiles to return home, he was assured of an immediate and inexpensive fund of goodwill.

The deportation of Israelites from the northern and Transjordanian territories was so thorough that these territories quite lost their Israelite character. The Transjordanian provinces have remained predominantly Gentile ever since; the territory north of the plain of Jezreel remained predominantly Gentile until it was conquered and judaized by a Hasmonaean king at the end of the second century B.C.[1] The change in the population of that area is indicated by the name now given to it – "the circuit (Heb. *galil*) of the nations," as it is called in a passage of Isaiah which depicts this depopulation but looks forward to a day of glorious hope for the same land, in words which the First Evangelist finds fulfilled in the Galilaean ministry of Jesus:[2]

> They will pass through the land, greatly distressed and hungry; and when they are hungry, they will be enraged and will curse their king and their God, and turn their faces upward; and they will look to the earth, but behold, distress and darkness, the gloom of anguish; and they will be thrust into thick darkness.
>
> But there will be no gloom for her that was in anguish. In the former time he brought into contempt the land of Zebulun and the land of Naphtali, but in the latter time he will make glorious the way of the sea, the land beyond the Jordan, Galilee of the nations.[3]

Only the central portion of the land, around Samaria, was left as the truncated kingdom of Israel, ruled by Hoshea as Tiglath-pileser's vassal. "The country of the house of Omri", says Tiglath-pileser, " . . . all its people [and their possessions], I carried away into Assyria. Pekah their king they had overthrown; Hoshea as king over them I placed. Ten talents of gold and . . . talents of silver I received as tribute from them."[4]

Among the other kings from whom Tiglath-pileser received tribute at the same time he mentions "Jehoahaz" of Judah. This Jehoahaz is the biblical Ahaz. One may wonder whether the shorter form of his name in the Bible is due to the fact that the biblical scribes considered that a king guilty of such apostasy against Yahweh did not deserve to retain in his name the element Yahweh (of which Jeho- or Yeho- is a reduced form, the whole meaning "Yahweh has taken hold"). For when the rebellion was put down, the Great King held a durbar at Damascus, and his tributaries, Ahaz included, were summoned to meet him there.

---

[1] See page 172.   [2] Matt. 4:15 f.
[3] Isa. 8:21 f., 9:1.   [4] *Cf. DOTT*, p. 55.

PLATE III

Stone stele sculptured
with the storm god walk-
ing on a bull, perhaps
comparable with Jero-
boam's bulls at Bethel
and Dan, see p. 40.
Assyrian style, from
Arslan Tash, Syria, *c.*
740 B.C. Height approx.
54 inches. (Musée du
Louvre, Paris.)

Ivory plaque from Megiddo showing a Canaanite ruler seated on a throne supported by winged animals ('cherubim'?) and drinking from a cup proffered by his queen. A lyre-player stands behind her. To the right is shown a victory procession. *C.* 1200 B.C. Length 10¼″.   (Dept. of Antiquities and Museums, Israel.)

PLATE IV

Stone relief depicting a war chariot of Assyrian style, from Carchemish, ninth century B.C.   (British Museum; original in Hittite Museum, Ankara.)

And now it became apparent what Ahaz's thoughtless enlisting of Assyrian aid involved. It meant that the kingdom of Judah became tributary to Assyria, and if that had had political implications only, it would not have been so bad; but there were religious implications as well. For he who paid homage to the king of Assyria must at the same time pay homage to Assyria's gods, in particular to the chief god Ashur. As Damascus had been given the status of an Assyrian province, the cult of Ashur was established there, and the vassal-kings were expected to instal the cult in their own domains. It mattered little that the kings of Moab and Ammon should set up the cult of Ashur alongside those of Chemosh and Milcom, but that Ahaz should set up an altar of Ashur in the temple of the God of Israel at Jerusalem involved a denial of the first principle of the covenant: "You shall have no other gods before me (*i.e.*, in my presence)". Yet, having taken the first step by calling in Tiglath-pileser's aid, Ahaz could not refuse to take the second. The record of apostasy thus inaugurated was to have devastating consequences for the realm of Judah, and brought about a corruption of the national character which two reformations of religion could not undo, and which could only be purged at last in the furnace of the Babylonian exile. In the light of this sequel, we can see how prophetically right Isaiah was in opposing Ahaz's policy. "Ahaz by his unbelief had not only *disestablished* himself; he had mortgaged the hope of Israel."[1]

The closing years of Tiglath-pileser's reign were marked by his conquest of Babylon, with all the prestige which control of that city of sacred antiquity carried with it. He had himself solemnly installed as king of Babylon by taking the hand of Marduk, the chief deity of Babylon, in the temple of Esagila on the Babylonian New Year festival in the spring of 729 B.C.

When Tiglath-pileser died at the beginning of 726 B.C., he was succeeded by his son Shalmaneser V. The change of king was attended by unrest in Syria, and this unrest was fomented by Egypt. Tefnakht, a ruler in the Western Delta (*c.* 727—716 B.C.), attempted to establish a unified kingdom in Lower Egypt, for the country had been split up among a number of local princes. He felt the proximity of the Assyrian power on the Asian frontier of Egypt to be inconvenient to his plans. Among the Syrian vassals of Assyria who were inclined to listen to the seductive voice of Egypt was Hoshea, whom Tiglath-pileser had confirmed as king in Samaria. Hoshea withheld his annual tribute from Assyria and at the same time probably tried to purify the national worship of Assyrian influences, if this is what is meant by the qualified commendation given him in II Kings 17:2b, that the evil which he did in the eyes of Yahweh (by maintaining the Bethel cult)

[1] G. A. Smith, *The Book of Isaiah*, i (1927), p. 114.

was "not as the kings of Israel who were before him". But he found, as too many rulers in Western Asia were to find in the following century and a half, that Egypt could not be relied upon to give any effective aid to those who tried to pull her chestnuts out of the fire by rebelling against the Mesopotamian power.

> Ephraim is like a dove,
>   silly and without sense,
>   calling to Egypt, going to Assyria.[1]

Hoshea was summoned to the Great King's presence and thrown into prison (724 B.C.). An Assyrian army besieged his city of Samaria, and so strong were the defences of the city that even experts in siege warfare like the Assyrians took three years to storm it. About the end of the siege there was a change of dynasty in Assyria, and Sargon II, the new king who displaced Shalmaneser, claims the capture of Samaria as his own work:

> At the beginning of my reign, in my first year, . . . I besieged and cap-tured Samaria. I carried captive from the midst of it 27,290 people. Fifty chariots I took there to be an addition to my royal force . . . I returned and caused more people than formerly to dwell there; I settled in the midst of it people from lands which my hands had captured. I appointed my officers over them as governors; I imposed tribute and taxes on them after the Assyrian manner.[2]

The last part of the former kingdom of Israel was now reduced to the status of an Assyrian province under the name of Samaria. An Assyrian governor was appointed to administer the area, and the tribute which had been exacted from it under King Hoshea continued to be exacted at an increased rate. The upper classes were deported to eastern parts of the Assyrian Empire, and replaced by settlers from other parts of the Empire – from Hamath in 720 B.C., from North Arabia in 715, and from Babylonia in 709 B.C. (Further colonists were sent there by later kings of Assyria – Esarhaddon and Ashurbanipal.) These settlers on their first arrival were worshippers of various foreign deities, but in the land of Israel they soon learned "the law of the God of the land"[3] and intermarried with the Israelite population whom they found there and became indistinguishable from them. Since Samaria, originally the name of the capital city, was now the name of the whole province as well, all the inhabitants of the province came to be called Samaritans.

The deportation policy of the Assyrian kings had important lingu-istic consequences. Aramaic, the language spoken by the majority of the states between the Euphrates and the Mediterranean, became the

---

[1] Hosea 7:11.   [2] Cf. DOTT, p. 59.   [3] II Kings 17:26 f.

general medium of communication in Western Asia, and retained that status for several centuries.

If Assyrian conquest meant the domination of the Assyrian gods, it also meant the weakening and ultimate disappearance of the gods of the conquered. To the Assyrians the God worshipped in Israel and Judah was another petty divinity like the gods of Hamath and Arpad and the gods of all the other states overrun by the Assyrian forces. But, whereas the gods of these states depended for their vitality and their very existence upon the continuing national identity of their worshippers, the God of Israel was the Living God, whose survival was not bound up with the fortunes of His people. Not only the gods of Hamath and Arpad, but the gods of Assyria as well, have disappeared: the God of Israel lives.

CHAPTER VIII

HEZEKIAH AND THE ASSYRIAN PERIL
(721—686 B.C.)

ALTHOUGH SARGON'S ACCESSION TO THE IMPERIAL THRONE OF Assyria synchronized with the capture of Samaria and the deportation of its inhabitants, it was the signal for revolts in many parts of the empire. In Babylon a Chaldaean prince from the land at the head of the Persian Gulf, Merodach-baladan by name, led a successful revolt against the Assyrian overlordship, and had himself solemnly installed as king of Babylon on the Babylonian New Year's Day, 1st Nisan, 721 B.C. He strengthened his position by allying himself with the King of Elam, which lay along the eastern shore of the Gulf. When Sargon attacked the allies, he was defeated, and Merodach-baladan ruled in Babylonia for twelve years.

In Syria and Palestine, too, a number of states which had been tributary to Assyria revolted, under the leadership of Hamath. Sargon's measures against these were more successful. Hamath was treated with special severity; its population was deported (many of them to Samaria) and replaced by settlers from Assyria, Armenia and Media. Farther south some of the Philistines – Gaza in particular – had revolted at the instigation of Egypt; when the Egyptians marched to their aid, they were defeated and thrown back at the frontier town of Raphia (720 B.C.). The other Philistine cities, together with Judah, Edom and Moab, continued quietly, and wisely, to pay tribute.

For several years after 720 Sargon was preoccupied on the northern frontier of his empire – in Armenia and Eastern Asia Minor. His northern and western neighbours in those parts (including the peoples called in the Bible Meshech, Tubal and Togarmah) were gravely weakened about this time by raiders called the Cimmerians (the biblical Gomer) from the steppe-lands of South Russia and Crimea, and Sargon profited by their inroads to secure his northern frontier from the river Halys in Asia Minor to the Elburz mountain range in North-West Persia. But his preoccupations there were for a considerable time not disturbed by further revolts in Syria and Palestine – partly because of the stern lesson he had taught the vassal-states in 720, partly because of a revolutionary situation in Egypt. The Nubian king Piankhi invaded Egypt shortly after the Egyptian defeat at

68

Raphia in 720, and pressed ever more inexorably on the territory ruled by Tefnakht until in 716 Tefnakht, who had once been foremost in fomenting disaffection among Sargon's Syrian and Palestinian vassals, begged for aid from the Assyrian king, and sent him a present. But it was no use: the Nubians encroached more and more on Egyptian territory, until the time came when Sargon could describe Egypt as belonging to the land of Nubia. For several decades (715—663 B.C.) Egypt was dominated by a Nubian dynasty (the XXVth). Once established in control of all Egypt, this new dynasty followed ancient precedent in inciting the border-states to revolt against their Mesopotamian overlords.

In 711 the people of Ashdod accepted a Greek adventurer as their ruler and revolted against Assyria. An Assyrian army came to besiege Ashdod and stormed the city. Hezekiah, son of Ahaz, who by this time had succeeded his father as king of Judah, was inclined to listen to Egyptian blandishments and join in the revolt. He and his people were solemnly warned against paying any heed to Egypt by the prophet Isaiah, who added force to his admonition by an acted prophecy, walking disrobed and unshod like a prisoner of war in token not only that Ashdod would fall to the Assyrian but also that the Egyptians themselves would be conquered and led captive in like manner.[1] According to Sargon's own account, Judah was actually implicated in this revolt. The Greek ruler of Ashdod, he says, tried to persuade the rulers of Judah, Edom and Moab to join his revolt, and also invoked the aid of "Pharaoh king of Egypt, a prince who could not save them." In their accurate assessment of the value of Egyptian aid, the Assyrians talk quite like Hebrew prophets! And in fact when the Greek fled for refuge to Egypt, the Egyptian king judged it wisest to deliver him up to Sargon. Ashdod was now made the headquarters of an Assyrian governor, who had the greater part of Philistia as his province. The king of Ekron, however, who had remained loyal to Assyria, was confirmed in his position as Sargon's vassal. It has sometimes been suggested that the description in Isa. 10:27-32 of an Assyrian force advancing on Jerusalem from the north belongs to this setting:

> He has gone up from Rimmon,
>   he has come to Aiath;
> he has passed through Migron,
>   at Michmash he stores his baggage;
> they have crossed over the pass,
>   at Geba they lodge for the night;
> Ramah trembles,
>   Gibeah of Saul has fled.

[1] Isa. 20:1 ff.; cf. DOTT, pp. 60 ff.

Cry aloud, O daughter of Gallim!
Hearken, O Laishah!
Answer her, O Anathoth!
Madmenah is in flight,
    the inhabitants of Gebim flee for safety.
This very day he will halt at Nob,
    he will shake his fist
    at the mount of the daughter of Zion,
    the hill of Jerusalem.

Whether Hezekiah took any overt part in the revolt of 711 or not, he took a leading part in an anti-Assyrian revolt some years later. Sargon died in 705, and was succeeded by his son Sennacherib. As usual, the accession of a new Assyrian king was the signal for widespread revolt, and the new king had to spend the first years of his reign putting down the revolts systematically in province after province of his empire. Merodach-baladan, whom Sargon had expelled from Babylon in 709 B.C. returned and reclaimed the sovereignty. He took an active part in stirring up disaffection elsewhere, and the biblical record tells how he sent an embassy to Hezekiah, ostensibly to congratulate him on his recovery from a serious illness, but actually (we may suppose) to assess the contribution that Hezekiah could be counted upon to make to the anti-Assyrian cause. Egypt was also busy with her usual incitements to revolt. Isaiah warned the king against listening to either Merodach-baladan or the Egyptian king Shabaka, advocating a policy of patience:

In returning and rest you shall be saved;
    in quietness and in trust shall be your strength.[1]

But the pro-Egyptian party at court was too influential, and the prophet's warnings passed unheeded – until the ensuing disaster proved his policy right. Elulaeus king of Tyre, Sidqa king of Ashkelon, whose realm stretched as far north as Joppa, the kings of Moab and Ammon, and Hezekiah withheld tribute from Assyria. The king of Ekron refused to join them, remaining faithful to his overlord, but the people of Ekron rose against him, deposed him, handed him over in chains to Hezekiah for safe keeping at Jerusalem, and joined the revolt.

An anti-Assyrian policy meant the purification of the national worship from Assyrian cultic elements. Hezekiah had probably embarked on a policy of this nature even earlier in his reign, and had also endeavoured to purify Judah from old Canaanite ritual practices.

[1] Isa. 30:15.

To do this more effectively, he proceeded to close down the local sanctuaries in the kingdom of Judah and concentrate the national worship at Jerusalem. Even at Jerusalem he purified the temple worship of other than Assyrian elements: he destroyed the bronze serpent Nehushtan, a sacred object of ancient prestige. He went further: now that the northern monarchy was no more he invited the Israelites from the provinces of Samaria and Megiddo to join their southern brethren in worship at Jerusalem, but these overtures met with a poor response.

Hezekiah took steps to reinforce the defences of Jerusalem; in particular, he improved the city's water-supply by having a new channel cut to carry the water from the Virgin's Fountain[1] to the upper pool of Siloam in the south-east quarter of the city. These precautions were wise; it would have been better to have followed Isaiah's advice and not revolted, but having revolted he did well to count on the certainty of an Assyrian siege. And before long the Assyrian army came.

Methodically, Sennacherib put down the revolts in the various parts of his empire. In 703 B.C. he expelled Merodach-baladan from Babylon, and installed an Assyrian prince as vassal-king there. Then he turned west, and marched to Phoenicia. The Phoenician cities which had revolted under the aegis of Tyre made their submission to the Assyrian; the mainland city of Tyre was reduced and the island city besieged for five years. From there Sennacherib marched south down the coastal road, receiving the submission of Acco, Joppa and Ashkelon on the way, and advanced on Ekron. An Egyptian force, marching north in response to the urgent appeal of the men of Ekron, was defeated at El-tekeh, in the Judaean foothills. Ekron submitted to the conqueror, those who had mutinied against their king were executed, and the king himself was handed over by Hezekiah and restored to his throne.

It was now the turn of Judah to suffer for her part in the revolt. All the fortified places in the kingdom, forty-six in number, were taken and over 200,000 of their inhabitants were driven from them as refugees. Jerusalem itself was closely besieged. The whole realm was reduced to a wilderness, and the capital was left amid the desolation "like a lodge in a garden of cucumbers",[2] says Isaiah – like a toolshed in an abandoned allotment. Hezekiah realized too late the folly of heeding his pro-Egyptian counsellors; he sent an embassy to Sennacherib offering his abject submission and undertaking to accept any terms which the Assyrians chose to impose. Sennacherib imposed a crushing tribute on him, and reduced his territory by bestowing parts of it on the king of Ekron and other faithful vassals of the Philistine

---

[1] I.e., the spring of Gihon.　　　　　　　　[2] Isa. 1:8.

seaboard (701 B.C.). To such straits was Judah reduced that, in the words of Isaiah:

> If Yahweh of hosts
>   had not left us a few survivors,
> We should have been like Sodom,
>   and become like Gomorrah.[1]

But the economic distress of the land was attended by a period of spiritual renewal, under the guidance of Isaiah, whose warnings the event had so tragically confirmed. And Isaiah's presence and encouragement were to prove a veritable tower of defence to Jerusalem when Sennacherib later decided to make a clean sweep of the Judaean monarchy and make the realm an Assyrian province. In the earlier stage of events Hezekiah was in the wrong, having broken his oath at the behest of his pro-Egyptian advisers; but now Sennacherib was guilty of unprovoked aggression against Jerusalem:

> Woe to you, destroyer,
>   who yourself have not been destroyed;
> you treacherous one,
>   with whom none has dealt treacherously!
> when you have ceased to destroy,
>   you will be destroyed;
> and when you have made an end of dealing treacherously,
>   you will be dealt with treacherously.[2]

Let Hezekiah and his people but put their trust in God, and He will be their defence against the Assyrians. Thanks to the faith of Isaiah, the morale of people and king did not break. An Assyrian force sent against Jerusalem to give effect to Sennacherib's new policy was diverted to the coastal road on the receipt of a report that an Egyptian force was marching against them, and near the Egyptian frontier the Assyrian army was ravaged by what appears to have been an attack of bubonic plague. Operations against Judah were broken off, and Hezekiah ended his days in peace.

It was in these days of reduced circumstances for Judah and Jerusalem that Isaiah had his vision of an era of perfect righteousness, peace and prosperity not only for all Israel but for the other nations of earth too, under a prince of the house of David – a vision which was to be of far-reaching importance in shaping the outlines of Israel's messianic expectation. But, as events quickly proved, the fulfilment of that vision was not for the near future.

[1] Isa. 1:9.   [2] Isa. 33:1 f.

CHAPTER IX

APOSTASY AND REFORMATION

(686—621 B.C.)

HEZEKIAH WAS SUCCEEDED BY HIS YOUNG SON MANASSEH, WHO FOR most of his long reign was the obedient vassal of Assyria. He accepted all the religious as well as the political implications of such a policy, and his reign marked a complete break with the reforming policy of his father and a reversion to the policy of Ahaz. Ahaz's reign had been short, and there was therefore not enough time for his religious policy to manifest its worst effects, although his whole policy brought disaster enough on his people. But Manasseh's long reign – he reigned for at least forty-five years after his father's death[1] – allowed the retrograde tendencies of religious syncretism to become ingrained in the life of the people, and their moral effect was such that no subsequent reformation, like that sponsored by his grandson Josiah, could undo the evil; nothing would serve but the purgatory of national collapse and exile. The worship of the sun and other planetary divinities ("the host of heaven"), became an integral element in the national cult in the Jerusalem temple itself. The local sanctuaries, which had been closed by Hezekiah, started up again, and the old Canaanite ritual flourished there – the worship of Baal and Asherah, and the attendant practices of necromancy, ritual prostitution and even, on occasion, human sacrifice – for Manasseh himself, like Ahaz before him, is said to have offered up his son as a sacrifice, presumably on some occasion of grave national peril.

All this was naturally opposed and denounced by the prophetic party, who recognized in the royal policy a landslide from pure Yahwism, but their opposition was drowned in blood. Such stern measures were no doubt judged to be in the national interest, lest an anti-Assyrian movement should bring down the wrath of Assyria on Judah once again. These foreign entanglements against which Isaiah had warned Ahaz and Hezekiah brought insoluble dilemmas in their train.

[1] The 55 years assigned to Manasseh in II Kings 21:1 may include up to 10 years during which he was coregent with his father; so Thiele, *The Mysterious Numbers of the Hebrew Kings*, pp. 155 ff. A different account is given by H. H. Rowley, "Hezekiah's Reform and Rebellion", *BJRL* 44 (1961–62), pp. 395 ff.

Sennacherib died in 681 B.C., assassinated by two of his sons, and was succeeded by his youngest son Esarhaddon. The most outstanding feature of Esarhaddon's reign (681—669 B.C.) was the Assyrian conquest of Egypt. This conquest reached its climax in 663, under Esarhaddon's son and successor Ashurbanipal (669—c. 630), when Thebes, the chief city of Upper Egypt, was sacked and destroyed by the Assyrians. The Nubian control of Egypt which had lasted for half a century was thus brought to an end. The fall of Thebes is described by the Hebrew prophet Nahum, when he addresses the Assyrian capital Nineveh and predicts a similar fate for her:

> Are you better than Thebes[1]
>   that sat by the Nile,
> With water around her,
>   her rampart a sea,
>   and water her wall?
> Ethiopia was her strength,
>   Egypt too, and that without limit;
>   Put and the Libyans were her helpers.
>
> Yet she was carried away,
>   she went into captivity;
> her little ones were dashed in pieces
>   at the head of every street;
> for her honoured men lots were cast,
>   and all her great men were bound in chains.[2]

Yet the Assyrian conquest of Egypt, complete as it was for the time being, did not last long. Ashurbanipal governed the country through a noble Egyptian house that had shown its loyalty to him. But twelve years later this house, under Psamtek I, was able to assert Egyptian independence of Assyria and rule the country as the twenty-sixth Dynasty. Ashurbanipal was unable to prevent Psamtek from doing this, because he was faced at the same time with revolts among his northern vassals and with a war against Elam on the east. Under Ashurbanipal the Assyrian Empire extended over its widest limits: from Sardis in the north-west and Thebes in the south-west to Susa in the east his power was felt. But the empire began to fall to pieces even in Ashurbanipal's lifetime.

Manasseh is mentioned in the records of both Esarhaddon and Ashurbanipal. Esarhaddon lists him among twenty-two kings of the western lands who were obliged to supply labour and building material for the construction of his new palace at Nineveh. Ashurbanipal includes him in a similar list of twenty-two kings who brought him gifts and escorted him on his progress against Egypt early in his

---

[1] Heb. No-'Amon; "No (Egyptian Nut), the city of the god Amon".
[2] Nahum 3:8-10.

reign. The Hebrew Chronicler preserves the account of an occasion when Manasseh was taken as a captive to Babylon by officers of the Assyrian king.[1] It is not certain to what period of his reign this event should be assigned, but it was doubtless bound up with the relations between Assyria and Egypt. There was a Sidonian revolt against Esarhaddon in 677, with which the Egyptian king Tirhakah had something to do; four years later Tirhakah formed an anti-Assyrian alliance with Tyre. Manasseh may have been implicated in one or the other of these; at any rate, the king of Assyria thought it wise to make sure of his loyalty. N. H. Baynes suggested that Manasseh was concerned in Psamtek's revolt in 654, but that when Psamtek stabilized his position Ashurbanipal realized the wisdom of having a reliable buffer-state between his empire and Egypt, and restored Manasseh.[2] About 665 B.C. we have an instance of the restoration of a prince (Necho, through whom Esarhaddon and Ashurbanipal governed Egypt) who had been suspected of disloyalty and brought in chains to the Assyrian court. That Manasseh is said to have been carried to Babylon and not to Nineveh need not surprise us: Esarhaddon was king of Babylon for the whole of his reign, and treated it as a second capital.

Esarhaddon and Ashurbanipal are both mentioned in the book of Ezra as sending further settlers to the province of Samaria; under Ashurbanipal ("the great and noble Osnappar" of Ezra 4:10) settlers were sent from as far east as Babylonia and Elam, when he reduced Babylon after a revolt in 648 B.C. and captured Susa, the Elamite capital, in 645 B.C.

The inner weaknesses in the Assyrian Empire were aggravated by the invasion of its northern territories by raiders called the Scythians from the Russian steppe-lands. They are first mentioned in Assyrian records in Esarhaddon's reign, but it was towards the end of Ashurbanipal's reign that they became a serious menace to the empire. Egypt and Lydia had secured their independence several years before; Media later did the same, and Elam, so recently conquered by Assyria, was seized by the Persians, an Aryan nation farther east. In 626 a Chaldaean prince, Nabopolassar, established himself as independent king of Babylon and founded a powerful dynasty there.

A graphic picture of the Scythian invasion is given by the Greek historian Herodotus,[3] although it is uncertain how accurate his account is. According to him, the Scythians dominated Western Asia for twenty-eight years, in the course of which they marched down the

---

[1] II Chron. 33:11-13.

[2] *Israel amongst the Nations* (1927), p. 92.

[3] *History*, i. 103 ff. Possible relics of the Scythian occupation or influence, in the form of bronze fibulae and triple-bladed arrowheads, have been found at Lachish (O. Tufnell in *PEQ* 91 [1959], p. 101, after *Lachish* III [1953], p. 57).

Mediterranean coastal road as far as the Egyptian frontier (where they were repulsed by Psamtek), and on their return plundered the temple of Astarte at Ashkelon.

The threat of such an incursion of northern barbarians may provide the background for the language of the young prophet Jeremiah when he describes the situation in which he was called to the prophetic ministry in 626 B.C. In that year the word of Yahweh came to him:

> Out of the north evil shall break forth upon all the inhabitants of the land. For, lo, I am calling all the tribes of the kingdoms of the north, says Yahweh; and they shall come and every one shall set his throne at the entrance of the gates of Jerusalem, against all its walls round about, and against all the cities of Judah. And I will utter my judgments against them, for all their wickedness in forsaking me; they have burned incense to other gods, and worshipped the works of their own hands.[1]

For the present, however, Judah and Jerusalem had a respite; and the judgment from the north, when it came, came by the hands of another nation. But the outlook was gloomy and menacing enough:

> Blow the trumpet through the land;
>   cry aloud and say,
> "Assemble, and let us go
>   into the fortified cities!"
> Raise a standard toward Zion,
>   flee for safety, stay not,
> for I bring evil from the north,
>   and a great destruction.
> A lion has gone up from his thicket,
>   a destroyer of nations has set out;
>   he has gone forth from his place
> to make your land a waste;
>   your cities will be ruins
>   without inhabitants . . . .
>
> I looked on the earth, and lo, it was waste and void;
>   and to the heavens, and they had no light.
> I looked on the mountains, and lo, they were quaking,
>   and all the hills moved to and fro.
> I looked, and lo, there was no man,
>   and all the birds of the air had fled.
> I looked, and lo, the fruitful land was a desert,
>   and all its cities were laid in ruins
>   before Yahweh, before his fierce anger . . . .

---

[1] Jer. 1:14–16. We must not say, however, that Jeremiah's first stimulus to prophecy was provided by the Scythian invasion itself. The effective occasion of his call may have been Josiah's first steps in reformation, begun in the preceding year (II Chron. 34:3). Cf. H. L. Ellison, *Men spake from God*[2] (1958), p.79.

At the noise of horseman and archer
every city takes to flight;
they enter thickets; they climb among rocks;
all the cities are forsaken,
and no man dwells in them.[1]

Manasseh had died in 641 and was succeeded by his son Amon, who continued his father's policy. But new influences were emerging at court, and in the assassination of Amon in 639 and his replacement by his eight-year-old son Josiah we may see the beginning of a new anti-Assyrian policy. By the time Josiah was old enough to assume control of his kingdom in person, the Assyrian grip on Palestine had slackened to such an extent (thanks mainly to the Scythian invasion) that Josiah could initiate and carry through without fear of Assyrian reprisals a policy of religious reformation such as his great-grandfather Hezekiah had been prevented from completing successfully.

The outstanding event of Josiah's reformation, and the one which gave the chief impetus to its most notable features, was the discovery of "the book of the law" in the temple while it was being repaired in the eighteenth year of the king's reign (c. 621 B.C.). Even before this date he had begun to purify his kingdom of the idolatrous installations which marred it. In Jerusalem particularly he cleansed the temple of all the apparatus of sun-worship and the other planetary cults which had been established there during the long period of Assyrian domination when his grandfather Manasseh was king.

The "book of the law" was handed by the chief priest Hilkiah, who found it, to Shaphan the royal secretary, who read it in the king's hearing. From the activity which followed immediately, when the king undertook to put the prescriptions of the scroll into operation, there is little doubt that it was (as Jerome discerned)[2] a copy of the book of Deuteronomy, or at least of the law-code which forms the kernel of that book (chapters 12–26).

The reading of this book threw the king into alarm and consternation. If these commands were the commands of Yahweh, then the nation had been guilty of flagrant disobedience to them, and had rendered itself liable to the judgments which the book pronounced against those who failed to keep the divine law. The recent abolition of the apparatus of Assyrian worship now appeared to be quite inadequate; there was much in the religious life of the nation which must be radically reformed if the precepts of this book were to be given effect. But no one within living memory had known anything of an attempt to give effect to them; perhaps it was now too late. An urgent message

[1] Jer. 4:5–7, 23–26, 29. This is not the only place in Old Testament prophecy where an incursion of northern barbarians is used as a symbol of divine visitation (cf. Ezek. 38–39; Joel 2:20).
[2] *Commentary on Ezekiel*, 1:1.

was sent to Huldah, a prophetess, to consult her on the matter and receive a response from Yahweh. The response was unpromising: the idolatrous worship denounced in the book had gone so far that it must inevitably bring divine judgment in its wake. But that judgment would not fall upon Josiah, because when the book was read to him, he had truly repented of the sins committed by his people and his predecessors in ignoring the commands of God.

Josiah therefore set himself to institute a thorough-going reformation. A solemn assembly was held in the temple, at which the newly-discovered book was read publicly, and the king led the chief representatives of the nation in binding themselves by a firm covenant to carry out all the things commanded by God in the book. Their act was in effect a reaffirmation of the earlier covenant inaugurated in the wilderness in the days of Moses, when the people of Israel heard the law for the first time and undertook to obey it. But was this reaffirmation of the covenant sufficient to undo the evil wrought by generations of idolatry? The conduct of the nation in the decades that followed proved that it was not.

The king lost no time in translating the words of his covenant into deeds. The temple had already begun to be purged of the Assyrian cult; but there were many other installations whose affinities were Canaanite rather than Assyrian: these too must be removed.

The shrine in the Valley of the Sons of Hinnom, south of the city, where a fertility cult had been carried on for long, involving on occasion human sacrifice, was demolished, and the valley which had been polluted by its presence was ceremonially defiled in order that the cult might never be re-established there. Where formerly fires had burned on the *topheth* or altar-hearth of Molech, now fires of another kind were to burn, for the place became the common refuse dump and incinerator of Jerusalem. From the constant fires which burned there to consume the rubbish the name Valley of Hinnom (Heb. *Gê-Hinnom*) came later to be used as the name of the place (*Gehenna*, in its Greek form) where the wicked are to be punished in the world to come, just as the Garden of Eden (Paradise) supplied the name for the future abode of the blessed.

Similar radical measures of reformation were carried out in the other cities of Judaea; idolatrous cults and priesthoods were suppressed everywhere. Nor was Josiah content to confine his reforming campaign within his own frontiers. The relaxing of Assyrian control in the west meant that he could enter the province of Samaria with impunity. This he did, and in particular he destroyed the schismatic sanctuary at Bethel, just over the border, which the first Jeroboam had made the southern of his two national shrines. Other local sanctuaries in the province of Samaria were similarly treated.

But the abolition of the relics of Canaanite worship and the destruction of idolatrous sanctuaries were not enough. Josiah went farther: the purity of Judah's worship could be best safeguarded if the sacrificial worship of the kingdom were concentrated exclusively in the Jerusalem temple, under the eye of the king and his ministers. The local sanctuaries of Yahweh throughout the kingdom were therefore closed down. Hezekiah, some eighty years before, had attempted a similar policy, but he was unable to carry it through effectively because of the Assyrian invasion. The Assyrians could now be safely disregarded and Josiah carried through his radical reformation unhindered by foreign intervention. The closure of the local sanctuaries of Yahweh would involve considerable hardship for the priests who served these shrines, but provision may have been made for attaching them to the priesthood of the Jerusalem temple. Both the centralization of the national cult and the attachment of the outlying priesthoods to the central shrine were prescribed in the Deuteronomic law.[1] But while the Jerusalem priests no doubt welcomed the centralization of worship at their own shrine, the idea of sharing the service and its emoluments with an accession of priests from the suppressed sanctuaries would not be so agreeable, and in the event the priests of the local sanctuaries evidently remained where they were.

When the initial stages of the reformation had been completed, a special celebration was held at the passover season of 621 B.C. The passover was held in accordance with the distinctive Deuteronomic regulations[2] as a festival at the central shrine; the passover lambs for the whole kingdom were slaughtered in Jerusalem and not (as heretofore) at several centres throughout Judah. The unprecedented character of this passover is emphasized by the statement in II Kings 23:22 that "no such passover had been kept since the days of the judges who judged Israel,[3] or during all the days of the kings of Israel or of the kings of Judah."

One important product of Josiah's reformation which did abide was the final recension of a body of historical writing covering the period from the beginnings of the settlement in Canaan down to Josiah's reign, which appears in our ordinary versions of the Old Testament as the books of Joshua, Judges, Samuel and Kings. The presentation of the history in these books is so informed with the ideals of the Deuteronomic legislation that they are commonly referred to, comprehensively, as the Deuteronomic historical writing. This history, however, was by no means composed at this time out of whole cloth;

[1] Cf. Deut. 12:5–14; 18:6–8.
[2] Deut. 16:1–8.
[3] The Chronicler states that "no passover like it had been kept in Israel since the days of Samuel the prophet" (II Chron. 35:18); the explicit mention of Samuel may be more significant than appears on the surface.

most of the material incorporated in it had probably existed in written form for long, a good part of it indeed being contemporary – or nearly so – with the periods covered by the various parts. In the Hebrew Bible these books are reckoned as the Former Prophets, and this gives us a clue to their recension. They are not intended to be a secular chronicle, but a record of Yahweh's dealings with His people Israel, presented from the prophetic view-point, and compiled probably for the most part by members of the prophetic guilds. But the reign of Josiah, after the discovery of the Deuteronomic law in the temple, is the most natural setting for the publication of this invaluable record.[1]

In carrying out his reforming work Josiah could count on the support of some at least of the prophetic party. Two young prophets in particular appear to have lent him their enthusiastic aid. One of these was (it appears) a cousin of his own, Zephaniah by name. Zephaniah's prophetic ministry should probably be dated a little earlier than Josiah's reformation; at any rate, several of the reforms instituted by Josiah are predicted in the book of Zephaniah, such as the abolition of the planetary cult and the relics of Baal-worship, the deposition of the kemarim, or priests of the idolatrous shrines, and the like.

More significant than Zephaniah is Jeremiah, whose prophetic ministry also began, as we have seen, about the time of the Scythian menace, five years before the reformation. Jeremiah himself belonged to the priestly family of Anathoth (in the tribal territory of Benjamin), probably descended from Abiathar, who was exiled there at the beginning of Solomon's reign. In whatever way his family may have been affected by Josiah's policy, Jeremiah must have approved of the reform so far as it went. He was only too well aware of the idolatrous tendencies of those local sanctuaries which Josiah suppressed even if they were formally sanctuaries of Yahweh and not of the Canaanite fertility gods. In the oracles which belong to the earliest period of his ministry, he denounces several of the abuses which were put down by Josiah – the multiplicity of false gods worshipped with incense throughout the cities of Judah, the installation of Asherah-poles and cult-pillars, idolatrous altars, and the monstrous cult of Molech in the Valley of the Sons of Hinnom.

When Jeremiah saw these abuses being abolished by the king, how could he fail to approve of what was done? And yet with all his approval went the conviction that all this work of reformation was insufficient to cure the disease from which the nation suffered. It did not go far enough; it did not touch the national conscience. He

---

[1] Originally the Deuteronomic history may have ended with the account of Josiah's passover, at II Kings 23:23; the following narrative of the last days of the kingdom of Judah will then be an appendix or series of appendices to the main narrative, completed about 562 B.C. (the date of the last event to be recorded).

recognized the sincerity and honesty of Josiah himself, but there were many others who acquiesced in the reform simply because the king had set the example; inwardly they resented his interference with forms of worship handed down by their ancestors. The covenant in which Josiah so solemnly led his people after the discovery of the law-book was but a repetition of the covenant of Moses' day, and suffered from the same defects; it could not change the people's nature, and would be kept with no greater success than the original covenant at Sinai had enjoyed. A covenant of a different kind – a new religious relationship – was called for, and in due course Jeremiah foresaw the nature and strength of this better covenant:

> Behold, the days are coming, says Yahweh, when I will make a new covenant with the house of Israel and the house of Judah, not like the covenant which I made with their fathers when I took them by the hand to bring them out of the land of Egypt, my covenant which they broke, though I was their husband, says Yahweh. But this is the covenant which I will make with the house of Israel after those days, says Yahweh: I will put my law within them, and I will write it upon their hearts; and I will be their God, and they shall be my people. And no longer shall each man teach his neighbour and each his brother, saying, "Know Yahweh", for they shall all know me, from the least of them to the greatest, says Yahweh; for I will forgive their iniquity, and I will remember their sin no more.[1]

Six hundred years and more had passed since the old covenant was inaugurated in Moses' day; six hundred years and more were again to pass before the new covenant which Jeremiah foretold was in-augurated (as the New Testament teaches) by Jesus of Nazareth. But on the eve of the national catastrophe, which none foresaw with such terrible clarity as Jeremiah did, this gleam of light appears to illuminate the future with divine hope.

For the immediate future, however, the outlook was quite un-promising, in spite of Josiah's zealous example. The demoralization of previous reigns had gone too deep to be undone by any such reform as he undertook. So long as he lived he maintained the religious purity which he had so drastically established; but the landslide which followed his death showed how truly Jeremiah had diagnosed his people's sore complaint.

[1] Jer. 31:31–34. On the authenticity of the oracle see J. Skinner, *Prophecy and Religion* (1922), pp. 325 ff. G. A. Smith, (*Jeremiah* [1929], pp. 292 f.) dates it during Gedaliah's governorship (see p. 93).

CHAPTER X

LAST DAYS OF THE KINGDOM OF JUDAH

(621—587 B.C.)

THE WEAKENING OF ASSYRIAN POWER IN THE WEST HAD ENABLED Josiah to assert his independence, carry through his reformation and extend his power over the former province of Samaria, at least as far north as the Plain of Jezreel. But it was bound up with world movements in which the hardly-won freedom of Judah was soon to be eclipsed.

In 616 Nabopolassar, founder of the new Chaldaean dynasty at Babylon, invaded the Assyrian territory, but the Assyrians received support from an unexpected quarter. For another former subject of their empire, Psamtek of Egypt, was not minded to see a strong successor to Assyrian power established on his Asian frontier. A weakened Assyria suited him well, and enabled him to extend his influence over the Syrian provinces, which had formed part of the Egyptian Empire in imperial days of old. For the next eleven years, therefore, the Egyptians appear in Western Asia as allies of the Assyrian Empire, endeavouring to shore up its tottering fabric against the blows directed against it by its assailants.

Nabopolassar had to give way in face of Psamtek's approach, but later in the year he routed an Assyrian force east of the Tigris. Next year he made an attack on Ashur, the former capital and most sacred city of Assyria, but failed to storm it. This was achieved, however, in 614, by the Median king, Cyaxares. Media, like Assyria, had suffered considerably from the Scythian incursion, but had made a speedy and vigorous recovery. The fall of Ashur was followed by a Medo-Babylonian alliance, which was cemented by the marriage of the Median princess Amytis to the Babylonian crown-prince Nebuchad-rezzar. In the summer of 612 B.C. the allies attacked Nineveh, which fell in August of that year after a siege of two and a half months. The destruction of the imperial city was hailed with delight by all the peoples of Western Asia who had had to endure so much barbarous oppression at her hands. The victory chant of Nahum must have found a widespread echo:

Woe to the bloody city,
　　all full of lies and booty –
　　no end to the plunder!
The crack of whip, and rumble of wheel,
　　galloping horse and bounding chariot!
Horsemen charging,
　　flashing sword and glittering spear,
hosts of slain,
　　heaps of corpses,
dead bodies without end –
　　they stumble over the bodies! . . . .

Your shepherds are asleep,
　　O king of Assyria;
　　your nobles slumber.
Your people are scattered on the mountains
　　with none to gather them.
There is no assuaging your hurt,
　　your wound is grievous.
All who hear the news of you
　　clap their hands over you.
For upon whom has not come
　　your unceasing evil?[1]

The Assyrian state outlived the collapse of the capital by a few years, thanks to the continued support of the Egyptians, now more concerned than ever to have what remained of Assyria as a buffer between the Egyptian sphere of influence and the rising powers east of the Euphrates. For two years Ashur-uballit II, the last Assyrian king, maintained himself at Harran, but Harran too fell in 610. In the summer of 609 Ashur-uballit endeavoured unsuccessfully to recapture it, with the aid of Psamtek's successor, Necho II. As Necho marched north to help Ashur-uballit, his advance was blocked at the Pass of Megiddo by King Josiah. Josiah must have made good use of the few years since 626 in developing a new Judaean army. The weakening and dis-appearance of Assyrian power, as he saw it, were essential for the maintenance of his own kingdom's independence, and Egypt's continued attempts to retard or reverse the process of Assyrian collapse must be withstood. At Megiddo, then, the patriot king endeavoured to bar the Egyptian advance. His motives were good, but his political wisdom must be questioned. He refused to listen to Necho's expostu-lation, gave him battle and was fatally wounded by the Egyptian archers. He was carried home to Jerusalem, and all Judah lamented his untimely death. How great cause they had to lament him they prob-ably did not fully realize at the moment; but the death of Josiah marked the end of Judah's independence. The prophet Jeremiah joined

[1] Nahum 3:1-3, 18 f.

in the general mourning over so good a king, but it is noteworthy that Jeremiah's eulogy of Josiah praises his personal qualities but makes no mention of his reformation. Addressing an unworthy son of Josiah, he asks:

> Did not your father eat and drink
>   and do justice and righteousness?
> Then it was well with him.
> He judged the cause of the poor and needy;
>   then it was well.
> Is not this to know me?
>   says Yahweh.[1]

There is a strange similarity between the death of Josiah and that of Ahab, a very different type of king. Not only was each fatally wounded by hostile archery and carried home in his chariot to his capital, but they both disguised themselves on the battle-field, and perhaps for the same sort of reason, for there are some grounds for thinking that Josiah's expedition to bar Necho's way at Megiddo was opposed by the faithful prophetic party.

A successor to Josiah was immediately elected, and the people had probably good cause to pass over his eldest son Eliakim and bestow the crown upon his second son Shallum, who took the throne-name of Jehoahaz. But his reign was brief. Necho failed to recapture Harran for Ashur-uballit; but he tried to establish the frontier of his own sphere of influence at Carchemish. When the campaigning season came to an end, he marched south from the Euphrates, and summoned the new king of Judah to his presence at Riblah, a Hamathite city on the main road. There he threw him into chains, to be taken captive to Egypt. He exacted homage from his elder brother Eliakim, whom he thereupon nominated as king in Jerusalem under the name Jehoiakim. Josiah's ill-timed venture thus resulted almost immediately in his country's becoming an Egyptian vassal-state.

Jeremiah, who had so recently mourned over the fate of Josiah, now judged that he was happy in his death compared with his luckless successor who was to wear out the remainder of his days in Egyptian captivity.

> Weep not for him who is dead,
>   nor bemoan him;
> But weep bitterly for him who goes away,
>   for he shall return no more
>   to see his native land.[2]

Jehoiakim lost no time in showing his subjects what an oppressive and impious tyrant Necho had appointed to be their king. Although

[1] Jer. 22:15 f.   [2] Jer. 22:10.

the land was crushed by the heavy tribute which Necho imposed upon it, Jehoiakim busied himself in having a new luxurious palace built with forced labour.

> Woe to him who builds his house by unrighteousness
>   and his upper rooms by injustice;
> who makes his neighbour serve him for nothing,
>   and does not give him his wages;
> who says, "I will build myself a great house
>   with spacious upper rooms,"
> and cuts out windows for it,
>   panelling it with cedar,
>   and painting it with vermilion.
> Do you think you are a king
>   because you compete in cedar? . . .
>
> But you have eyes and heart
>   only for your dishonest gain,
> for shedding innocent blood,
>   and for practising oppression and violence.[1]

And now it was seen how superficial the religious reformation under Josiah had been, when Josiah himself was no longer alive and on the throne. All the old idolatrous tendencies came flooding back into the nation's life. Not only were the prophets who protested against this retrograde movement disregarded; their lives were endangered.

Early in Jehoiakim's reign the prophet Jeremiah raised his voice in the temple court in Jerusalem and made one of his most daring pronouncements.[2] Because of the sin of the people, he declared, that sacred edifice which was intended to be a blessing to all the nations would become on the lips of all the nations a by-word for cursing. Just as the earlier shrine at Shiloh had been destroyed long before because of Israel's rebellion against Yahweh in days gone by (and its derelict site remained as a warning to all who cared to pay heed), so the temple at Jerusalem would go down in ruin unless there was a speedy repentance. It was of no avail for them to protest that this was Yahweh's own house and that He could never allow it to suffer such a fate. How could they imagine that Yahweh would extend to them the protection of His house when, as soon as Josiah was dead, they reverted to their former ways, burning incense to Baal, making cakes for the "queen of heaven" and pouring libations to other gods? If they sought security, let them deal justly with one another, give up oppressing the helpless, and have done with idolatrous worship. But if they persisted in theft, adultery and perjury, what was the use of coming to Yahweh's temple and fancying that it guaranteed their safety? "Has

---

[1] Jer. 22: 13–17.   [2] Jer. 7:1–20, condensed in Jer. 26:1–6.

this house, which is called by my name, become a den of robbers in
your eyes? Behold, I myself have seen it, says Yahweh."[1]

These words really shocked the people. This was the limit of
blasphemy, to speak such words against the holy house of Israel's God.
Many clamoured for the blasphemer's death, in particular the priests
and the cultic prophets; but when Jeremiah was put on his trial for
blasphemy, he was acquitted because the secular judges recognized
that he had not spoken of his own volition but "by the word of
Yahweh". They cited as a precedent the prediction of the destruction
of Jerusalem and its temple by the prophet Micah in Hezekiah's day.
Micah was not put to death, they pointed out; on the contrary, king
and people paid heed to his words and repented, and so the threatened
disaster was averted.

There were obviously some people in the land who maintained the
standards of justice set by Josiah. Jeremiah was acquitted. In this he was
fortunate. We are told of another prophet, Uriah by name, who
prophesied in the same terms as Jeremiah. King Jehoiakim decreed his
death, and when Uriah fled for refuge to Egypt, Jehoiakim had him
extradited and beheaded, and his body was thrown into a common
grave. That Jeremiah did not suffer the same fate was due to the
protection given him by a high officer at court, Ahikam ben Shaphan
(perhaps the son of that Shaphan who was secretary of state under
Josiah).[2]

Necho's domination of Western Asia did not last long. In the early
summer of 605 B.C. a Babylonian army, led by the crown-prince
Nebuchadrezzar, launched a surprise attack on Carchemish and routed
the Egyptian army which was based there. The fleeing remnants were
pursued to the very border of Egypt, and might have been pursued
farther, but that just then Nebuchadrezzar received news that his
father Nabopolassar had died (August 16), and he hastened back to
Babylon with a few attendants, by the shortest route across the
desert, to secure the succession for himself. The remainder of his
forces returned home by the longer route, via Carchemish, taking
with them captives from the Egyptian army and hostages from the
states of Western Asia which had hitherto been vassals of Egypt, including some from the nobility of Judah.[3] At one blow all those states
passed from the Egyptian into the Babylonian sphere of influence.

When Nebuchadrezzar returned to the west in the year after his
victory at Carchemish, he received Jehoiakim's formal submission.
At the time this made little difference to Jehoiakim; he simply paid
tribute now to Nebuchadrezzar instead of Necho. It certainly made

---

[1] Jer. 7:11.
[2] Jer. 26:7-24.
[3] This is probably the setting of Dan. 1:1-6.

no difference to his despotic behaviour, or to his dislike of the prophets of Yahweh.

In the year of Carchemish Jeremiah had warned the people of Judah and Jerusalem that because of their persistent impenitence seventy years of servitude under the Babylonians would be their lot. Next year witnessed the dramatic occasion when his secretary Baruch, having written down at Jeremiah's dictation all the oracles which the prophet had delivered during his twenty-three years' ministry, read them aloud to the people assembled at a solemn fast in the temple. The king heard of this, and the scroll was borrowed from Baruch and read to the king as he sat in his winter house in front of a charcoal brazier. As the reader "read three or four columns, the king would cut them off with a penknife and throw them into the fire in the brazier, until the entire scroll was consumed in the fire that was in the brazier".[1] Some of his courtiers who had more respect for the Word of God than their master tried to persuade him not to burn the scroll, but he paid no heed. In his folly he "thought the penknife was mightier than the pen";[2] he behaved as if the destruction of the scroll could nullify the divine oracles that had been written on it. Orders were given for the arrest of Jeremiah and Baruch, but they had been got safely away into hiding and could not be found. Jeremiah used the leisure of concealment to dictate his oracles to Baruch again, and further oracles with the same purport were added to those that had been written down on the first scroll. The warnings of Jeremiah, like those of the other prophets of Yahweh, were intended to lead the people to repentance, that the impending evils might be averted; but there was little hope of repentance and deliverance when the prophetic message received such contemptuous handling.

Jehoiakim appears to have made some attempt to extend his realm at the expense of his weaker neighbours in the years that followed Carchemish. At last they banded together and attacked him and brought him captive before Nebuchadrezzar (who visited the area year by year to collect the tribute from his new vassals). Something of this sort is presupposed in the prophet Ezekiel's poetic description of Jehoiakim's career:[3]

> He prowled among the lions;
>   he became a young lion,
> and he learned to catch prey;
>   he devoured men.
> And he ravaged their strongholds,
>   and laid waste their cities,

---

[1] Jer. 36:23.
[2] J. Paterson, *The Goodly Fellowship of the Prophets* (1948), p. 152.
[3] Ezek. 19:6–9; for this reconstruction see N. H. Baynes, *Israel amongst the Nations* (1927), pp. 99 f.

and the land was appalled and all who were in it
    at the sound of his roaring.
Then the nations set against him
    snares on every side;
they spread their net over him;
    he was taken in their pit.
With hooks they put him in a cage,
    and brought him to the king of Babylon;
    they brought him into custody,
that his voice should no more be heard
    upon the mountains of Israel.

But if this interpretation of Ezekiel is right, Jehoiakim must have been reinstated by Nebuchadrezzar, who may have regarded his attacks on his neighbours as directed against partisans of Egypt.

In 601 B.C. Nebuchadrezzar led an army to the Egyptian frontier to give battle to Necho, but this time he suffered severe losses, from which he took eighteen months to recover. Many of his new vassals immediately withheld tribute from him, including Jehoiakim. But when Nebuchadrezzar had repaired the losses in his manpower and equipment, he marched west again, and put down the rebels one by one. He dealt first with Arab tribes east and south of Judah, and meanwhile incited Jehoiakim's neighbours to attack him. Then a Babylonian army laid siege to Jerusalem; Nebuchadrezzar arrived in person while the siege was in progress. Not long before the siege began Jehoiakim met his death (December 7, 598 B.C.); he was succeeded by his son Jehoiachin (otherwise called Jeconiah). The city was taken on March 16, 597 B.C., and Jehoiachin, with many members of the royal family and the leading statesmen and courtiers, was taken captive to Babylon, as also were many other members of the higher ranks of Judaean society – three thousand in all. Among those captives was the prophet Ezekiel. The temple treasures were carried off from Jerusalem to grace the temple of Marduk in Babylon; gold objects which were too large for convenient transport were cut up.

Nebuchadrezzar had now reasserted his sovereignty over all the territory between the Euphrates and the Egyptian frontier. It is perhaps to this point of time that we must assign a despairing letter sent by the king of one of the Philistine city-states to his former overlord Necho,[1] imploring him to send help to a loyal vassal before the king of Babylon came and set up a governor of his own. But no help could be sent: "the king of Egypt did not come again out of his land, for the king of Babylon had taken all that belonged to the king

---

[1] This Aramaic document was found at Sakkara in Egypt in 1942. One widely held view is that its author, Adon, was king of Ashkelon, which was captured and destroyed by Nebuchadrezzar at the end of 604 B.C. (cf. D. J. Wiseman, *Chronicles of Chaldaean Kings* [1956], p. 28; *DOTT*, pp. 79 f.).

of Egypt from the brook of Egypt to the river Euphrates."[1] Assyria had disappeared beyond recall: the Babylonian Empire now covered all the southern area of the former Assyrian Empire, while the Median Empire took over its northern provinces, and continued to expand westward through Asia Minor until in 585 B.C. the river Halys was fixed as the common frontier between the Median dominions and the Lydian Empire farther west. The kings of Babylon and Cilicia acted as intermediaries on this occasion between the Median and Lydian kings.

Nebuchadrezzar appointed Jehoiachin's uncle Mattaniah to rule over a diminished population of Judah in his place, with the throne-name of Zedekiah, and exacted a solemn oath of fealty from him. Actually Zedekiah was a regent rather than king in the full sense of the term, for it appears from Babylonian records that Jehoiachin, even in captivity, continued to be regarded as the legitimate king of Judah. He continued to be so regarded also by his fellow-exiles, as is evident from the book of Ezekiel, where dates are reckoned by Jehoiachin's regnal years.

It was an unwise act on Nebuchadrezzar's part to deport so many of the leading statesmen of Judah with Jehoiachin. This meant that those who were left as advisers of the new ruler were men of less sagacity and maturity. Many of them, unable to profit by experience, pinned their hopes of restored national independence to Egyptian intervention. Zedekiah, having sworn an oath of loyalty to the Babylonian king, wished to keep it, but he was too weak to resist his foolish advisers. There was, indeed, one man in Jerusalem whose clarity of vision was undimmed; and if Jeremiah's advice had been heeded even at this late date the worst disasters might have been averted. Jeremiah warned the king and his advisers that their one hope of salvation lay in maintaining obedient allegiance to Nebuchadrezzar. But this insistence of his served only to win him the reputation of a defeatist and traitor.

At last the seduction of Egypt proved too strong, and Zedekiah was persuaded to rebel against Nebuchadrezzar.[2] He hoped that Egyptian aid would protect him and his people against the inevitable Babylonian reprisals. But at the end of 589 B.C. a Babylonian army arrived, the kingdom of Judah was overrun, Lachish[3] and other fortified cities were quickly stormed, and Jerusalem was besieged.

---

[1] II Kings 24:7.

[2] It was shortly before this that a body of Jewish mercenaries was hired by Psamtek II (594—588 B.C.) to help to garrison the southern frontier of Egypt, and settled with their families, at Syene and Elephantine (see p. 112).

[3] The *Lachish Letters*, discovered in 1935 and 1938, illustrate the jingoism and defeatism of public opinion in Judah at this time; cf. the translations by W. F. Albright in *ANET*, pp. 321 f., and D. W. Thomas in *DOTT*, pp. 212 ff.

Even during the siege Jeremiah maintained his point of view that only in submission to the Babylonians did any hope lie for the king and people of Jerusalem. For this he was fiercely attacked by the pro-Egyptian party, and accused of treason. At one time, indeed, it seemed that the pro-Egyptian policy was going to be vindicated, for Hophra (the Apries of the Greek historians) who became king of Egypt in 588, sent a force to the relief of Jerusalem. The siege was raised for a short time.[1]

But the people of Jerusalem showed no sign of repentance. On the contrary, they seized the opportunity provided by the raising of the siege to do a particularly mean action. When the siege began, the well-to-do citizens manumitted their slaves – probably not so much as an act of kindness as to relieve themselves of the necessity of finding food for them in the straitened conditions of the siege. But when the Babylonian army departed from Jerusalem, they revoked the act of manumission and recalled their slaves. Jeremiah was deeply moved by this piece of treacherous oppression, and declared that it had sealed the citizens' doom: the Babylonian army would return and reduce the city with the aid of famine and plague, until they stormed and destroyed it together with its inhabitants.[2]

Jeremiah himself availed himself of the opportunity provided by the raising of the siege to go out to his native town of Anathoth to redeem a plot of his ancestral land. But he was arrested as he was leaving the city by the north gate, charged with defection to the enemy, and thrown into prison, where he remained until the fall of the city.

For, as he foretold, the Babylonians were not long in dealing with the Egyptian force that had come to the relief of Jerusalem, and when it had been repulsed, they resumed the siege. Jeremiah continued to insist that the city's only hope of survival lay in submission to the Babylonians. This insistence enraged the king's advisers, who attempted to take Jeremiah's life; and while the king himself was personally inclined to listen to the prophet, he acknowledged that he was unable to go against his ministers. The siege continued, and the city began to endure the horrors of famine. The plight to which the people were reduced is movingly told by one who shared it himself, the author of the book of Lamentations:

> My eyes are spent with weeping;
>   my soul is in tumult;
> my heart is poured out in grief
>   because of the destruction of the daughter of my people,
> because infants and babes faint
>   in the streets of the city.

---

[1] Jer. 37:5 ff.   [2] Jer. 34:8 ff.

They cry to their mothers,
"Where is bread and wine?"
as they faint like wounded men
in the streets of the city,
as their life is poured out
on their mothers' bosom. . . .

The tongue of the nursling cleaves
to the roof of its mouth for thirst;
the children beg for food,
but no one gives to them.

Those who feasted on dainties
perished in the streets;
those who were brought up in purple
lie on ash heaps. . . .

Now their visage is blacker than soot,
they are not recognized in the streets;
their skin has shrivelled upon their bones,
it has become dry as wood.

Happier were the victims of the sword
than the victims of hunger,
who pined away, stricken
by want of the fruits of the field.[1]

Even the ultimate horror of cannibalism was not absent from the city's last days.

At last, at the end of July, 587 B.C., the Babylonian armies forced an entrance through a breach which they made in the city wall. The king and his principal officers attempted to escape to the south-east, but were pursued and caught, and led before Nebuchadrezzar, who had taken up his headquarters in the Syrian city of Riblah. Here stern vengeance was exacted from those who had forsworn their allegiance to him. The sons of Zedekiah were put to death before their father's eyes, he himself was then blinded, and taken to Babylon, where he spent the remainder of his life in prison.

Zedekiah was a weak character – as one writer puts it, he "had a wishbone where a backbone should have been"[2] – and could not resist his foolish pro-Egyptian counsellors. But in the eyes of the prophets his crowning sin was his perjury: after swearing fealty to Nebuchadrezzar in the name of Yahweh, he rebelled against him, and brought disgrace upon the crown of David.

[1] Lam. 2:11 f.; 4:4 f., 8 f.
[2] J. Paterson, *The Goodly Fellowship of the Prophets*, p. 152.

And you, O unhallowed wicked one, prince of Israel, whose day has come, the time of your final punishment, thus says the Lord Yahweh: Remove the turban, and take off the crown; things shall not remain as they are; exalt that which is low, and abase that which is high. A ruin, ruin, ruin, I will make it; there shall not be even a trace of it until he comes whose right it is; and to him I will give it.[1]

So spoke the prophet Ezekiel; but in the very hour of doom his word of judgment contained a gleam of hope – the hope that one day a worthier king than Zedekiah would receive the crown of David.

A month after the storming of Jerusalem, Nebuzaradan, captain of Nebuchadrezzar's bodyguard, arrived in Jerusalem to execute the royal vengeance against the city. The temple, the palace-buildings, and all the great houses of Jerusalem were set on fire, and the wall round the city was demolished. The metal work of the temple and the costly vessels of divine service were removed to Babylon. A number of the principal citizens, including the chief priests as well as military and civil leaders, were executed. Many members of the upper and middle classes were deported to Babylonia, to swell the numbers of those who had been deported earlier.[2]

More bitter than the vengeance of the Babylonians was the action of the Edomites, Judah's old enemies. They did not try to conceal their joy over the straits to which Judah and Jerusalem were reduced, and openly exulted over the fall of the city. The words of Ps. 137:7 express Judah's bitter resentment:

> Remember, Yahweh, against the Edomites
> the day of Jerusalem,
> how they said, "Raze it, raze it!
> Down to its foundations!"

Edom's unbrotherly conduct was severely reprehended by the prophets, and the memory of it remained for long to poison the relation between the two peoples. Nor were the Edomites content to rejoice in Judah's misfortune; they overran and occupied the southern part of the territory of Judah, and in post-exilic times Edom (or Idumaea, to give it its Graeco-Roman name) is no longer the area between the Dead Sea and Aqaba, but the Negev of Judaea. Possibly the Chaldaeans allocated the Negev to Edom.

[1] Ezek. 21:25-27.
[2] In addition to those deported in 597 B.C. others were perhaps deported from the cities of Judah at the beginning of the siege of Jerusalem in 588.

CHAPTER XI

THE EXILE

(587—550 B.C.)

WHEN VENGEANCE HAD BEEN TAKEN FOR THE REVOLT, JUDAH WAS given provincial status, but Nebuchadrezzar showed his statesmanship by appointing as governor over the sadly reduced territory of Judaea a Jew, Gedaliah, who had been a palace official of Zedekiah and was known to have opposed the pro-Egyptian policy. Gedaliah set up his administration at Mizpah, and in his entourage was the prophet Jeremiah, who had been given his liberty by the Babylonians, and allowed to go where he wished, to Babylonia, to Mizpah, or anywhere else.

Even so, the devastated land was not permitted to enjoy peace. In the eyes of the irreconcilable resistance-party, Gedaliah and his supporters were traitors to the national cause. One of these groups, headed by a member of the royal family named Ishmael, who had received harbourage from the king of Ammon,[1] came to Mizpah and treacherously assassinated Gedaliah and his supporters. But they could not remain in Judah and face Nebuchadrezzar's vengeance after this, so they went to Egypt, compelling the people of Mizpah to accompany them, to join many of their fellow-countrymen who had settled there already. One of these who were forced to go to Egypt with them was the aged prophet Jeremiah. He warned them that they would not escape Nebuchadrezzar by fleeing into Egypt, for Nebuchadrezzar would pitch his military tent in the forecourt of the royal palace of Tahpanhes (Daphnae), the frontier city of Egypt in which the fleeing Jews settled for the time being. But he was no more regarded now than he had been throughout his forty years' prophetic ministry in Jerusalem. Far from acknowledging that Jeremiah had been right all along, and that their disasters had befallen them because of their rebellion against God, they insisted that things had never gone right since Josiah's reformation, and put their troubles down to that. They decided that the best thing they could do was to resume the pagan

---

[1] Ammon had rebelled against Nebuchadrezzar about the same time as Judah, but Nebuchadrezzar decided to reduce Judah first, and Ammon still remained a pocket of anti-Babylonian intrigue (see Ezek. 21:18–23).

practices which Josiah had abolished. So, in response to Jeremiah's last appeal to all the Jews in Egypt to turn to the God of their fathers and serve Him only, they said:

> As for the word which you have spoken to us in the same of Yahweh, we will not listen to you. But we will do everything that we have vowed, burn incense to the queen of heaven and pour out libations to her, as we did, both we and our fathers, our kings and our princes, in the cities of Judah and in the streets of Jerusalem; for then we had plenty of food, and prospered, and saw no evil. But since we left off burning incense to the queen of heaven and pouring out libations to her, we have lacked everything and have been consumed by the sword and by famine.[1]

And that is the last authentic record in the career of Jeremiah.

A further deportation from Judaea which is assigned to the year 582 B.C. may have been a sequel to the assassination of Gedaliah or may be connected with some further revolt.[2] Probably about this time the whole of Judaea except the Negev (now occupied by the Edomites) was added to the province of Samaria; all corporate life in Judaea ceased.

There were other states in western Asia which resisted Nebuchadrezzar's supremacy. Prominent among these was Tyre, which preferred an alliance with Egypt to one with Babylonia, and sustained a thirteen years' siege from 585 to 573 B.C. At last Tyre was reduced, but the Babylonians found but an empty shell, for the men and wealth had been evacuated – probably to Egypt.[3] The siege of Tyre was followed by operations against Egypt itself. Hophra was defeated, deposed and replaced by Amasis, an Egyptian general. But in 568 B.C. Amasis revolted against Nebuchadrezzar, who then invaded and occupied part of the Egyptian frontier lands.

Nebuchadrezzar's empire did not long survive the great king himself. The years that followed his death were marked by usurpation and civil strife, with threatening moves on the imperial frontiers.

His son Evil-merodach (Amel-Marduk), who succeeded him in 562 B.C., figures in the Biblical record as the king who liberated Jehoiachin from custody and gave him a place of dignity at his court. Jehoiachin appears to have been recognized as the legitimate king of Judah throughout his captivity – all the more so (we may suppose) after the revolt and deposition of Zedekiah.

But two years after his succession Evil-merodach was assassinated in a palace revolt, and his brother-in-law Nergal-sharezer (Neriglissar in the Greek historians) succeeded him. The principal event of his reign is the campaign which he led in 557—556 B.C. into Cilicia, which had become tributary to Babylon under Nebuchadrezzar. Not long

[1] Jer. 44:16–18.   [2] Jer. 52:30.
[3] See Sidney Smith, "The Ship Tyre," PEQ 85 (1953), pp. 97 ff.

afterwards Neriglissar died and was succeeded by his infant son
Labashi-Marduk. But the time seemed to demand a strong hand at
the helm, and a further conspiracy was formed in which Labashi-
Marduk was assassinated. The conspirators elevated to the kingship
one of their own number, Nabonidus by name. The fact that they
chose Nabonidus to be king at such a time suggests that he was a man
of outstanding ability, and not the weakling or mere antiquarian
that he is frequently represented as having been. For the growing
power of the Median Empire, north of the Babylonian, made a strong
and wise ruler necessary in Babylonia.

The Medes had begun to encroach on the Babylonian territories in
North Syria, so much so that Babylonian control of the usual trade
route from the Egyptian frontier to Mesopotamia *via* Carchemish was
in danger. Nabonidus took various measures to counter this threat.
One was direct: he campaigned against the Medes in Syria in an
endeavour to drive them out of Babylonian territory. Secondly, to
strengthen his position against them, he allied himself with the small
but growing Indo-European kingdom of Anshan, a former province
of Elam, which had extended its territories westwards as a result
of the fall of the kingdom of Elam in 645 B.C., but was now over-
shadowed by the dominant power of Media. This kingdom, known
farther west as the kingdom of Persia, was ruled at this time by a
young monarch of exceptional military and political ability, Cyrus II,
who had succeeded to the throne of his fathers in 559, and was allied
by marriage to the royal house of Media.

Thirdly, Nabonidus made it his business to impose Babylonian
control more firmly over the southern part of his empire, between
the Persian Gulf and the Egyptian frontier, and to develop alternative
trade-routes in that area, in view of the Median threat to those in the
north. To do this more effectively, he seized the oasis of Tema in
North Arabia, the centre of several important trade-routes, and laid
it out almost as a second capital city for his empire. He made Tema
his headquarters for the development of these southern trade-routes,
and as this involved him in long absences from Babylon, he appointed
his eldest son Belshazzar as viceroy in his absence. Nabonidus's absence
from Babylon caused considerable discontent there, especially as
for several years on end he did not trouble to attend the New Year
ceremony and play the part which was proper to a Babylonian king;
this was one of his functions which a viceroy, even if that viceroy
was also crown-prince, could not discharge for him.

His neglect of this ceremony was due not only to his preoccupation
with affairs in North Arabia, but also to his deliberate neglect of
Marduk, the chief god of Babylon, in favour of the moon-god Sin.
It appears that he aimed at reducing the polytheistic chaos of the

imperial religion to some sort of order, and establishing Sin as the chief god of the imperial pantheon.

It has been suggested that Nabonidus's religious policy brought him into conflict with the Jews throughout his empire.[1] There are indeed, a few lines of evidence pointing to the conclusion that the fortunes of the Jewish exiles, who had hitherto settled down fairly comfortably in their new homes, underwent a considerable reversal during his reign, so that the change of régime which brought it to an end was hailed with equal joy both by those who availed themselves of the opportunity to go home and by those who elected to stay where they were.[2]

The first event which foreshadowed the advent of this change of régime came in 550 B.C., when the Median and Persian armies met in decisive battle, and victory went, not to the more numerous and powerful Median army, but to the better led army of Persia, thanks to the strategic genius of the Persian king Cyrus. The power of Media was overthrown at one blow. Cyrus immediately displayed the qualities of a statesman as well as those of a military commander. Instead of treating the Medes as a beaten foe and a subject nation, he had himself installed as king of Media and governed Media and Persia as a dual monarchy, each part of which enjoyed equal rights.[3] The basis of Babylonia's alliance with Persia – the common fear of Media – disappeared overnight. Nabonidus now had along his whole eastern flank one powerful neighbour, whose realm extended from the Persian Gulf to the river Halys in Central Asia Minor.

[1] See T. H. Robinson, *Prophecy and the Prophets in the Old Testament* (London, 1923), pp. 161 f.; *A Companion to the Bible*, ed. T. W. Manson (Edinburgh, 1939), p. 256.
[2] See J. M. Wilkie, "Nabonidus and the Later Jewish Exiles", *JTS*, N.S., 2 (1951), pp. 36–44.
[3] Hence the frequent references in the Old Testament literature of the post-exilic period to the *Medes and Persians* as the component nations of this dual monarchy; hence too, the Greek historians' habit of using *Medes* as synonymous and interchangeable with *Persians*.

PLATE V

Assyrian relief from the palace of Tiglath-pileser III at Nimrud, depicting the spoliation of Ashtaroth in Galilee; sheep are being driven off and the citizens with their belongings in bags taken to exile. Below Tiglath-pileser rides in a triumph. Mid-eighth century B.C. *Cf.* pp. 60 ff. (Dept. of W. Asiatic Antiquities, Brit. Mus.)

One panel of the Black Obelisk of Shalmaneser III of Assyria showing Jehu of
Israel or his emissary paying homage. *Cf.* p. 53.
(Dept. of Western Asiatic Antiquities, British Museum.)

PLATE VI

Drawing of an Assyrian relief from the palace of Tiglath-pileser III at Nimrud showing images of gods being carried away from a captured town.
(A. H. Layard, *Monuments of Nineveh* I, pl. 65; photograph, British Museum.)

CHAPTER XII

WHEN THE LORD TURNED AGAIN THE
CAPTIVITY OF ZION

(550—465 B.C.)

ACCORDING TO THE LATE DOM GREGORY DIX, "THE TAPESTRY OF history has no point at which you can cut it and leave the design intelligible. Yet the sudden rise to Empire *c.* 550 B.C. of Cyrus, the prince of a petty Persian tribe, is almost such a point. Herodotus saw in this event the turning point of all *Greek* history. That is only a part of the truth. Deutero-Isaiah, who saw in Cyrus God's Shepherd of the nations, the man whose right hand God Himself had held, 'to open the doors before him and the gates shall not be shut,' suggests a wider vision. The life's work of this one man moulded the destiny of three great civilizations and set the main lines upon which universal history would run for more than fifteen hundred years, with consequences that are still potent today."[1]

Cyrus's annexation of Media in 550 B.C. completely upset the balance of power in Western Asia. The alliance between himself and Nabonidus evaporated when Media was no longer their common enemy; Nabonidus allied himself instead with Lydia and Egypt. Instead of ruling over a small territory on the eastern shore of the Persian Gulf, Cyrus was now king of a realm that extended westwards across northern Mesopotamia well into Asia Minor. Croesus of Lydia now had the Persian Cyrus as his neighbour on the east instead of the Median rulers. Would Cyrus observe the truce which his Median predecessors had concluded with Lydia in 585 B.C., or would his imperial ambitions, fed by his recent conquest, carry him into Croesus's territory? Herodotus tells us how Croesus, in his perplexity, sought advice from the renowned oracle of Apollo at Delphi. The oracle returned an ominous response, warning Croesus to take measures for his safety when a mule ruled over the Medes. But how could a mule rule over the Medes – unless, indeed, the reference was to Cyrus, who was the son of a Persian father and a Median mother? The more Croesus pondered the matter, the more certain he was that Cyrus's

---

[1] G. Dix, *Jew and Greek* (1953), pp. 14 f. The "three great civilizations" which he mentions are those of Greece, Syria, and Persia.

97

rise to power boded no good for Lydia. There was only one thing to be done – not to wait for Cyrus to attack him but to take the initiative against Cyrus and get his blow in first. Such an important decision, however, must await the oracle's advice. Should Croesus, or should he not, lead his armies across the Halys into Cyrus's territory? "By crossing the Halys", said the oracle, "Croesus will destroy a great empire." Enough: the oracle had shown the green light (as Croesus in his haste imagined), and so he crossed the Halys. But the great empire which perished as a result of this step was not the Medo-Persian but the Lydian; Cyrus repulsed the invaders, pursued them back across the Halys into their own land of Lydia, pressed westwards until he stormed and sacked Croesus's royal city of Sardis and took Croesus himself captive (546 B.C.). All Lydia fell into Cyrus's hands. His empire now extended west to the Aegean Sea; the Greek cities of the Aegean coast of Asia Minor, which had hitherto been tributary to Croesus, had now to transfer their allegiance and their tribute to Cyrus.

We can imagine the alarm which the apparently irresistible progress of Cyrus produced in the ruling classes of Babylon. But in the hearts of the subject-races of the Babylonian Empire, and especially in the hearts of the displaced persons from Palestine and elsewhere, the news of his conquests brought strange surmises and wild hopes to birth.

This situation forms the background to Chapters 40 to 55 of the book of Isaiah. At the beginning of this body of oracles Cyrus's rise to power and conquering progress are depicted; his conquest of Babylon is foretold. But Cyrus is shown to be one raised up by the God of Israel to fulfil, all unconsciously, His purpose. Yahweh has anointed Cyrus to be His agent; by his overthrow of Israel's oppressors he will enable the exiles of Judah and Jerusalem to return home and rebuild their commonwealth. But this is not the end of the divine purpose; it is for something far greater than this that so much wealth has been expended in the rapid growth of Persian dominion and the restoration of Israel's exiles; it is in order that through Israel the knowledge of the true God may be carried to all the nations. For Israel's God is the only real God; all the other so-called gods are mere nonentities. The gods of the nations overrun by Cyrus were unable to give their worshippers wise counsel and powerless to deliver them. Greek historians told how Croesus consulted the most renowned oracles of their land, only to receive responses which were "ambiguous, and with double sense deluding." But Israel's God could foretell the future by His wisdom, and by his power He had raised up Cyrus and directed his victorious career, with a view to the accomplishment of His own will in His people's deliverance from bondage and restoration to their own land, that they might be the messengers of His truth to the ends of the earth.

But Israel's mission, these chapters further declare, is to be brought to its consummation by one called the Servant of Yahweh, who is closely associated with the Israelite nation and yet is distinguished from it. Like Cyrus, he is raised up to accomplish the purpose of God, but while Cyrus promoted that purpose unconsciously, the Servant promotes it intelligently and gladly. Nor are his methods those of Cyrus; instead of making a noise in the world and imposing his will on others by force he works quietly and obscurely, maintaining his obedience to God in the face of unjust judgment, suffering, contempt and death.[1] But by such endurance he carries his obedience to God to its appointed consummation and achieves the divine purpose to bring the knowledge of God and forgiveness of sins to the nations of the earth:

> It is too light a thing that you should be my servant
>   to raise up the tribes of Jacob
>   and to restore the preserved of Israel;
> I will give you as a light to the nations,
>   that my salvation may reach to the end of the earth.[2]

As the prophet foretold, so it came to pass: Cyrus added Babylon to his conquests on October 12, 539 B.C., and entered the city on October 29. This was followed quickly by two decrees authorizing the Jewish exiles to return and to rebuild their temple in Jerusalem.

As Cyrus marched through Babylonia, city after city opened its gates to him. While the crown-prince Belshazzar lost his life in the course of the Persian entry into Babylon, that city was taken over with as little fighting as the others. Such at any rate is the account given by Cyrus himself, and preserved in two inscriptions: the "Verse Chronicle of Nabonidus" and the "Cyrus Cylinder".[3] Cyrus won over the official classes to his side by representing himself as the champion of the gods of the various cities to whom Nabonidus had done despite; he restored to the other cities of Babylonia the images which Nabonidus had brought to Babylon, and in Babylon itself he gave himself out as the vindicator of the rights of Marduk, which had been so shamefully neglected by Nabonidus in favour of the moon-god, claiming that Marduk had for this very reason given him victory. Nabonidus had forfeited the goodwill of his people in Babylon by omitting the New Year ceremony in which he ought to have taken the hand of Marduk and thus been solemnly re-installed in his royal office for a further year. Cyrus in 537 B.C. took the hand of Marduk and thus legitimated his status as rightful king of Babylon. This act betokened no special devotion to Marduk on Cyrus's part, but he was sensible enough to realize the rich dividends of submission and even of gratitude which

---

[1] Isa. 42:1–4; 49:1–6; 50:4–9; 52:13–53:12.
[2] Isa. 49:6.
[3] Cf. DOTT, pp. 81 ff., 92 ff.

would accrue from such an inexpensive policy of outward respect to the deities of his subject nations.

In this respect, as in many more, Cyrus's conception of empire was widely different from Assyria's. The Assyrians imposed the worship of their chief gods on their subjects, and boasted in the subjugation of their subjects' gods. Cyrus, whose personal religious views are not easy to determine, had no intention of offending his subjects' religious susceptibilities by such a policy; on the contary, he would conciliate these susceptibilities by playing the part of a worshipper of their various gods. "The Great King", as one scholar has remarked, "had no objection to bowing in the house of Rimmon if there was anything to be picked up on the floor." There is evidence from other parts of the Persian Empire that this policy was not followed in Babylonia only.

Against this background we can appreciate the political motives of Cyrus's action with regard to the Jews. The Assyrian and Babylonian policy of deportation filled their empires with groups of discontented "displaced persons"; it was easy for Cyrus to win the gratitude of these exiles by rescinding his predecessors' edicts of deportation. As a wise administrator, he knew that an empire was more satisfactorily managed with contented subjects than with discontented ones.

Probably two decrees were issued by Cyrus with regard to the Jews, one authorizing the rebuilding of the temple at Jerusalem and the other authorizing the return to Judaea of a body of exiles. The original Aramaic text of the former decree is preserved in Ezra 6:3-5 (Aramaic was the common and official administrative language throughout the Persian Empire):

> Concerning the house of God at Jerusalem, let the house be rebuilt, the place where sacrifices are offered and burnt offerings are brought; its height shall be sixty cubits and its breadth sixty cubits, with three courses of great stones and one course of timber; let the cost be paid from the royal treasury. And also let the gold and silver vessels of the house of God, which Nebuchadrezzar took out of the temple that is in Jerusalem and brought to Babylon, be restored and brought back to the temple which is in Jerusalem, each to its place; you shall put them in the house of God.

The conveying of the temple vessels back to Jerusalem and the supervising of the work of rebuilding the structure were entrusted to Sheshbazzar,[1] who is given the title "prince of Judah" (Ezra 1:8) and appears to have been a younger son of King Jehoiachin.

The edict authorizing the return of a body of Jewish exiles to their homeland is not preserved in its Aramaic form; the sense of it is given in the Hebrew text of II Chron. 36:23 and Ezra 1:2-4. The exiles who

---

[1] Possibly identical with Shenazzar of 1 Chron. 3:18, both forms being abbreviated from Babylonian Sinabusur, "May Sin (the moon-god) protect the father", which is best preserved in the LXX form Sanabassaros (I Esdras 2:12, 15).

returned at this time were led by another scion of the house of David –
Zerubbabel, son or grandson of Jehoiachin's eldest son Shealtiel.
The altar of burnt-offering was set up and the sacrificial ritual was
re-inaugurated; the foundation of a new temple was laid.[1] Having
fulfilled his commission thus, Sheshbazzar seems to have gone back
to Persia. The small community which remained behind found so
many obstacles and discouragements in the way that they did not press
on with the work of rebuilding the temple. During the exile some
attempt had been made to maintain a centre of worship at the old
sanctuary at Bethel, and there were those who thought that instead
of rebuilding the Jerusalem temple it would be best to maintain the
sanctuary at Bethel. It could have been argued that this would have the
advantage of uniting the northern Israelites with their southern kinsfolk in Judaea, whereas the northerners would not look so kindly on
the restoration of the Jerusalem shrine.

However, when it appeared that the returning exiles were determined to rebuild the Jerusalem temple, a deputation of northerners
approached Zerubbabel and the chief men of Judaea and offered to
cooperate in the rebuilding of the temple and in its worship. They
received a dusty answer: the royal authorization had been given to the
returning exiles and did not extend to the people who had remained
in the land, whether in Samaria or in Judaea. Thus the breach between
the two parts of the nation, which might have been closed had a more
conciliatory response been made to the northerners' overtures, was
destined to be perpetuated. Before we blame the returning exiles,
however, we must recall that they were a tiny community and would
have been swamped by their much more numerous neighbours of
the north had they accepted their overtures. And the new Jerusalem
community preserved certain religious ideals of great value which
could have disappeared had such an amalgamation taken place.

The northerners did not take their rebuff patiently. The Samaritans
regarded the tiny area of Judaea[2] as part of their territory, and they
made it their business to put so many obstacles in the way of the
returned exiles that the work of rebuilding the temple was soon
checked, and for fifteen years or so nothing more was done about it.
The returned exiles settled in the neighbourhood of Jerusalem; they
built houses for themselves and cultivated their lands. But a succession
of droughts and consequent poor harvests brought further dejection.

Meanwhile the Persian Empire was extending its territories more
widely. Cyrus died in battle in 530 B.C., and was succeeded by his son

---

[1] See J. S. Wright, *The Building of the Second Temple* (1958).

[2] A tiny area indeed, "stretching less than twenty-five miles in a straight line along the
watershed-ridge from north of Jerusalem to south of Beth-zur, with a total population
which can scarcely have exceeded 20,000 in 522 B.C." (W. F. Albright, *BA* 9 [1946], p. 8).

Cambyses, who in 525 invaded Egypt and added it to his realm. Cambyses's death in 522 introduced a period of civil strife, which came to an end with the accession of a member of a collateral branch of the royal house – Darius the son of Hystaspes, an able administrator who organized his farflung territories as no empire had been organized hitherto. If the civil war which had preceded his accession gave some of the subject nations cause to hope that the Persian domination would soon disappear and that they would regain their independence, they were quickly disillusioned.

The empire was divided into great areas, each governed by a viceroy or satrap who was almost a subordinate king with a court and body-guard of his own. The satrapy to which Judaea belonged comprised the territory between the Euphrates and the Mediterranean Sea, and was known in the official Aramaic of the Persian court as Abar-nahara ("Beyond the River") – a name which appears in inscriptions as well as in the Book of Ezra (4:10 ff., etc.).

The satrap had supreme control of the provincial troops, of the administration of justice and of financial affairs. There might, how-ever, be special fortresses in his satrapy manned by garrisons whose commanders were appointed by the king and were directly responsible to him. The secretary of state for the satrapy was also directly respon-sible to the Great King. In addition, there was an elaborate system of imperial inspectors, known as the "King's Eyes and Ears" who went on annual circuits through the satrapies to investigate the adminis-tration and deal with grounds for complaint. There may be an allusion to these in the explanation of the seven lamps which the contemporary prophet Zechariah saw in one of his visions: "These seven are the eyes of Yahweh, which range through the whole earth."[1] And the general administration of the empire may be reflected in the same prophet's vision of horsemen described as those "whom Yahweh has sent to patrol the earth."[2] In any case, Darius instituted an elaborate system of checks and counter-checks to forestall disloyalty and prevent maladministration.

Early in the reign of Darius a fresh impetus was given to the returned exiles to resume the work of temple rebuilding by the ministry of two prophets, Haggai and Zechariah. Both urged that the building of the temple was a necessary condition of the nation's receiving the blessing of God promised by the earlier prophets but until now with-held, so far as concerned its full outpouring. The recent disorder in the Persian world showed that God was about to act; the droughts and bad harvests which had lately befallen the land of Judah would give way to abundant rain and fresh prosperity if the people of God would only put His interests first, instead of their own. In particular, the

---

[1] Zech. 4:10.   [2] Zech. 1:10; cf. 6:1 ff.

prophets spoke encouraging words to Zerubbabel. In this prince of the house of David the hopes of many were centred; his grandfather Jehoiachin had been rejected,[1] signet ring on God's right hand though he might have been, but Zerubbabel would be restored to that place of honour.[2] He who laid the foundation stone of the new temple would complete the work and enjoy the signal favour of God.[3] Jeremiah had spoken of the day when God would raise up a worthy branch or scion of the line of David; Zerubbabel was hailed by Zechariah as "the man whose name is the Branch",[4] who "shall build the temple of Yahweh, and shall bear royal honour, and shall sit and rule upon his throne. And there shall be a priest by his throne, and peaceful understanding shall be between them both."[5] The priest here referred to was Jeshua, grandson of the last high priest of Solomon's temple, who was to be the first chief priest of Zadok's line in the restored temple.

Encouraged by the two prophets, Zerubbabel and Jeshua took the lead in resuming the work of rebuilding the temple. Their action was quickly reported to Tattenai, satrap of the province of Abar-nahara, and his subordinate governors (it may well be that the Samaritans, smarting from the rejection of their offer of assistance some years before, drew the satrap's attention to the work in the hope that it would be prohibited). Tattenai asked the Jews by what authority they were rebuilding the temple; they replied that they did so in pursuance of Cyrus's decree. Tattenai reported the matter to the Persian court, and asked that the Jews' claim be investigated. The edict in question was found among the archives at Ecbatana, the old capital of Media, which was now the summer capital of the Persian kings[6]. A rescript was accordingly sent from the court to Tattenai, telling him not to hinder the Jews in their work, but rather to give them all the assistance provided for in the original decree of Cyrus. Heartened by this further token of the favour of God, the Jews pressed on with the work, and the temple was completed and dedicated four years after its resumption, on March 12, 515 B.C. The Passover and the festival of unleavened bread were celebrated with special rejoicing in the following month. Jerusalem once more had its temple, seventy years after the destruction of the first temple by Nebuchadrezzar. It might seem a poor structure by contrast with the house "exceeding magnifical" which King Solomon built; yet the prophets assured the people that this mean

---

[1] Jer. 22:24.   [2] Hag. 2:20–23.   [3] Zech. 4:9.

[4] Cf. Jer. 23:5; 33:15. Not that Zerubbabel himself fulfilled Jeremiah's prophecy; but the fact that after the exile a prince of the house of David was governor of Judah showed that the promises made to that house had by no means been revoked.

[5] Zech. 6:12 f.

[6] The Persian kings had three capitals; the other two were Susa, the old Elamite capital (now the spring residence), and the rebuilt Persian capital of Pasargadae (the winter residence).

shrine, as it appeared to them at present, would be endowed with greater glory than had ever graced the temple of Solomon.

After the dedication of the temple Zerubbabel disappears from our records. It is commonly conjectured that he allowed himself to be manoeuvred into a false position by those who envisaged him as the one in whom the glories promised to the house of David would find their fulfilment. It is also possible that the success of the rebuilding of the temple led some to think that it would be a good thing to rebuild the walls of Jerusalem again – perhaps to guard against a Samaritan assault. Some such move may be alluded to in a vision of Zechariah in which a young man[1] who is on the point of measuring the length and breadth of Jerusalem is restrained by an angel who assures him that Jerusalem will become so populous that she will far exceed her ancient confines, and can yet safely retain the status of "unwalled villages" because Yahweh, "a wall of fire round about, and . . . the glory in the midst of her", will be a more effective protection than any walls could be.[2] In His own time God will shake all nations, remove "the great mountain" that stands in Zerubbabel's path and establish his kingdom.[3] If news of such plans, or of the exaggerated hopes which some placed in Zerubbabel, came to the Persian King's ear, he would certainly not overlook them. We cannot tell what happened, but no more is heard of Zerubbabel, and the hopes attached to the house of David find little or no place in extant Jewish literature for many a long year.

The Samaritans had not been able to frustrate the completion of the temple, but throughout the following decades they seized every opportunity to annoy their Jewish neighbours. They kept careful watch on them and if they seemed to do anything that infringed Persian law or ran counter to Persian interests, they made it their business to report it to the Persian authorities. Darius had shown his good will to the Jews, and they were unable to do much so long as he lived, but as soon as he died they sent a memorial to his son and successor Xerxes[4] (486—465 B.C.) containing a charge against the Jews of Judaea of which no details are preserved to us.

---

[1] W. F. Albright argues that Zerubbabel was "a cautious man of middle age" by this time, and so is unlikely to be the "young man" of the vision, as has sometimes been thought (*BA* 9 [1946], p. 9).

[2] Zech. 2:5.   [3] Hag. 2:21 f.; Zech. 4:7.

[4] To the reign of Xerxes the book of Esther ascribes an attempt by influential quarters at the Persian court to take hostile action against the Jews throughout the Persian Empire.

CHAPTER XIII

THE PEOPLE OF THE LAW

(465—400 B.C.)

IN THE REIGN OF THE NEXT KING, ARTAXERXES I (465—423 B.C.), AN
opportunity came to the Samaritans to lodge a really serious
complaint against the Jews. The returned exiles, at some point early
in his reign, began to rebuild the walls of Jerusalem. This was something which could not legally be done without royal authorization,
and the officials of the province of Samaria knew that no such authorization had been given. They therefore sent a letter to the court,
drawing attention to Jerusalem's seditious record in the Assyrian and
Babylonian periods, and warning the king that this rebuilding of the
wall was but the prelude to a declaration of independence. If it was
allowed to proceed unhindered, they said, Jerusalem would be a focus
of unrest and disaffection in that part of the king's domains. A rescript
came back from the court ordering that the rebuilding must cease
until the king himself might choose to decree otherwise.

At the beginning of Artaxerxes' reign there was a nationalist revolt
in Egypt, and it took six years before it was put down (460—454 B.C.).
If it was during this period that the report of the rebuilding of the walls
of Jerusalem came to Artaxerxes, we can understand that his suspicions
would be aroused, especially if he was aware that the Jewish rebellions
of earlier days, of which his informants told him, were regularly
undertaken in concert with Egypt. In any case, his rescript was received
with joy by the Samaritans, and with corresponding dejection by the
Judaeans. It may well be that the Samaritans, not content with com-
municating the royal interdict to the wall-builders, took the opportunity to demolish the part of the wall that had already been built,
knowing that no action would be taken against them for this zeal on
behalf of the king's interests.

This may explain the situation to which we are introduced in the
twentieth year of Artaxerxes (445 B.C.) when his chief cup-bearer at
Susa, a Jewish favourite named Nehemiah, received a visit from some
of his kinsmen from Judaea. When he asked how matters stood at
Jerusalem, he was told that the Jewish community there was "in great
trouble and shame; the wall of Jerusalem is broken down, and its

gates are destroyed by fire."[1] Nehemiah, a man of simple piety and single-minded resolution, confided his thoughts and actions to his personal journal, parts of which have fortunately been preserved to us in that part of the Chronicler's history which we know as the book of Nehemiah. He tells how he was so dejected himself by the news which his visitors brought that he could not conceal his sorrow when he entered the royal presence in the discharge of his normal duties. The king noticed his sadness and asked the cause – a question which alarmed Nehemiah because his private grief had no right to intrude into the presence of the king. But he spoke out: "Let the king live for ever! Why should not my face be sad, when the city, the place of my fathers' sepulchres, lies waste, and its gates have been destroyed by fire?" The king's response was encouraging: "What would you like me to do for you?" he asked. Then Nehemiah took his courage in both hands, and asked the king to send him "to Judah, to the city of my fathers' sepulchres, that I may rebuild it". Now he had burned his boats; had he gone too far? The king calmly asked: "How long will you be gone, and when will you return?"[2]

Did the king not realize that the city which Nehemiah wished to fortify was the very one whose unauthorized walls had been the object of his interdict some years before? No doubt Nehemiah was wise in not mentioning Judah or Jerusalem until he saw that the king was favourably disposed to his plea. But the king may not have been so ignorant or inconsistent. The face of affairs had changed during the last three or four years. In 448 a serious rebellion was raised against the Persian government by Megabyzus, satrap of Abar-nahara. If the Samaritan officials, Rehum and Shimshai, who had lately taken action against the Jews when they began to build the wall of Jerusalem, were involved in this rebellion, this could change the attitude of the Persian court to the status of Jerusalem. The Jews would not have joined a rebellion in which the Samaritans took part, and it may well have seemed to the king and his advisers that the elevation of Jerusalem to the status of a walled city, far from being a threat to law and order, might be expected to promote stability in that part of the empire. Rehum and Shimshai disappear from the record; their places are taken by Sanballat as governor of Samaria.

Nehemiah, then, was sent to Judaea as governor, with a specific commission to rebuild Jerusalem's walls. His commission, and the resolution and despatch with which he proceeded to carry it out, enraged Sanballat, the new governor of Samaria (whose right of supervision over Judaea was diminished if not abolished by Nehemiah's appointment), and the lieutenant-governors of the neighbouring areas – Tobiah of Ammon, Gashmu of Kedar in North-West Arabia, and the

[1] Neh. 1:3.   [2] Neh. 2:1-6.

governor of the Philistine territory. By intimidation and cajolery they tried to hinder him, but he would not be turned aside from the task, and he found such hearty and enthusiastic cooperation from all the inhabitants of Judaea that in fifty-two days the wall was erected; Jerusalem was once more a city. The completion of the work was followed by a service of dedication, marked by public thanksgiving and rejoicing and by a solemn procession round the new wall.[1]

But that was only the beginning of Nehemiah's work as governor. Who had been directly responsible for the administration of Judaea in the seventy years since Zerubbabel we do not know. But a situation had developed during the interval which called for drastic action in various directions. We do not know what answer Nehemiah gave Artaxerxes when the king asked him how long he would be away in Judaea, but in the event his first governorship lasted for twelve years.

The old curse of the land in the days of the great prophets, money-lending and the consequent reduction of insolvent debtors to the status of serfs, had appeared again. The small-holders had not only to maintain themselves by the produce of their land; they had to pay the temple tax and an imperial tax as well, and many of them were driven to mortgage their fields, vineyards and houses to their wealthier neighbours to raise the money. When they were unable to repay the loans, they were forced to sell their children into serfdom. Nehemiah called an assembly of the people and pointed out the enormity of this behaviour. He persuaded the creditors to restore the mortgaged lands free of charge and to remit the debts owed to them. They may not have done this very willingly, but at least they could not complain that Nehemiah did not show them a good example. For instead of exacting a tax from the people of Judaea to maintain his household in the style befitting a governor, as his predecessors had done, he himself regularly entertained a hundred and fifty Jews at his table at his own expense, and did what he could to redeem Jews who had been sold into slavery to foreigners. His servants, instead of being a charge upon the community, took part in public work such as the building of the wall.

But there were other features of the situation which required to be dealt with by an authority which Nehemiah did not and could not hold. The civil governor could not regulate the religious life of the people, and yet their religious life called for regulation. So, very probably at the suggestion of Nehemiah (although we have no explicit statement to this effect), another official was sent from the Persian court to Judaea. This was a priest of Aaronid descent, Ezra by

---

[1] Nehemiah's eastern wall was built farther west than its predecessor, owing to the collapse of the platform structures by which the pre-exilic city was extended eastwards. Cf. K. M. Kenyon, "Excavations at Jerusalem, 1962," *PEQ* 95 (1963), pp. 7 ff.

name, who is described in official court-documents as "scribe of the law of the God of heaven". "The God of heaven" is a title by which Yahweh is commonly designated under the Persian régime, and as "the law of the God of heaven" constituted the way of life which the Jews followed, it has been plausibly conjectured that Ezra's title marks him out as "Secretary of State for Jewish Affairs" in the imperial civil service. However that may be, Ezra was sent to Judaea by the king and his council "to make inquiries about Judah and Jerusalem according to the law of your God, which is in your hand"[1] and also to take with him a handsome contribution from the king and freewill offerings from the Jews still in Babylonia to set the sacrificial ritual in the Jerusalem temple on a more seemly and regular footing. Ezra was further authorized to appoint magistrates and judges who would teach and administer "the laws of your God" among the Jews in the satrapy of Abar-nahara.[2] The satrap of Abar-nahara was also required to give Ezra further financial support up to a fixed amount, and instructions were given that the temple staff should be exempt from tax and tribute.

Nor did Ezra set out for Judaea unaccompanied; there went with him nearly two thousand Jews from the province of Babylonia, including a considerable number of priests, Levites and temple attendants.

Ezra's task, in short, was to regulate the religious life of the Jews in conformity with a written law-book which he took with him. What the scope of this law-book was is a matter of interest for Penta-teuchal criticism, but there seems to be no sound reason why it should not have been the Pentateuch in its final recension, more or less in the form familiar to us. Jewish and Christian traditions give Ezra an important place in the formation of the Old Testament canon, but the most important feature that emerges from these traditions, is that Ezra stands at the end of the history of the Pentateuchal law of the Old Testament as Moses stands at the beginning of it. Not that Ezra was in any sense an author or creative figure such as Moses was; he was not even a legislator, but more probably an editor and codifier, and "a scribe skilled in the law of Moses which Yahweh the God of Israel had given".[3]

The official interest taken by the Persian court in the religious affairs of subject nations is illustrated by the Elephantine documents, of which more will be said later.[4] The terms of the letter addressed by Artaxerxes to Ezra do not necessarily imply a personal interest on the

---

[1] Ezra 7:14.   [2] Ezra 7:25.

[3] Ezra 7:6. "There seems no adequate reason to deny that it was known in Jerusalem generations before Ezra, but it seems highly probable that it was Ezra who introduced the complete Pentateuch into normative Jewish use and who is largely responsible for the way in which its archaic practices were adjusted to actual ritual usage in the Temple. The latter was alone a major contribution to normative Judaism" (W. F. Albright, *BA* 9 [1946], pp. 14 f.).

[4] See pp. 112 ff.

king's part; the letter would be issued by the department of state dealing with these affairs, but issued in the king's name because it was an official state document.

Ezra's mission had far-reaching results for the life of the Jews. The law-book which he carried became the officially recognized constitution of the community in Judaea and Jerusalem. From the imperial point of view Judaea was formally constituted a hierocracy or temple-state, that is to say, a community the centre of whose life was the temple, and whose constitution was founded on the constitution of the temple. The civil governor of Judaea was the representative of the imperial overlord, but the community enjoyed a considerable measure of autonomy in internal matters, raised its own taxes and struck its own coins. In these internal matters the head of the community was the head of the temple organization, the high priest. This form of sacred constitution was not unparalleled in the Persian Empire, and the system continued into the Greek and Roman periods.

The law-book was formally accepted by the people as their constitution at a public ceremony described in the eighth chapter of Nehemiah. At the beginning of the month Tishri, the people of Judaea gathered into Jerusalem, and listened to the public reading of the law-book from dawn to noon, as it was read aloud by Ezra from a wooden pulpit erected in "the square before the Water Gate" and interpreted by his assistants – perhaps for the special benefit of those people who understood Aramaic better than Hebrew. It is improbable that the whole Pentateuch was thus read; there is something to be said for the view that what was read was the Deuteronomic legislation,[1] for this is the part of the Pentateuchal law which makes special provision for its being publicly read.[2] Later in the same month came an opportunity for putting the festal requirements of the law into practice, when the occasion for keeping the Feast of Tabernacles came round. The people spent the week from the fifteenth to the twenty-second day of the month in the booths or "tabernacles" from which the feast receives its name – a thing they had not done, we are told, since the times of Joshua[3] – and throughout the week there were further opportunities of becoming better acquainted with the law-book, for it was read publicly day by day.

Part of the religious policy of Ezra (in which he had the firm support of Nehemiah) was the avoidance, as far as possible, of foreign associations, in terms of Israel's ancient covenant-law. During the years since the return from exile, there had been considerable traffic between the people of Judaea and their non-Jewish neighbours, including a good deal of intermarriage. It was plain that, if the people were to live in

[1] See L. E. Browne, *Early Judaism* (1920), pp. 185 ff.
[2] Deut. 31:9-13.   [3] Neh. 8:17.

accordance with the law-book, this tendency must be reversed; and when the Feast of Booths was over, a solemn assembly was held in which the covenant was reaffirmed by the people, led by Nehemiah and the chief personages in religious and civil life. "The Israelites separated themselves from all foreigners, and stood and confessed their sins and the iniquities of their fathers".[1] In particular, they agreed, and their leaders set their seal to a confirmatory document in which they bound themselves under oath to keep the divine law, to refuse intermarriage with Gentiles, to abstain from trade on the sabbath and generally to observe the sacredness of that day and other holy days, to leave their lands untilled and give a free release to all their Jewish debtors every seventh year, to pay a third of a shekel of silver each year for the maintenance of the temple service and to contribute tithes, first-fruits, and various freewill offerings for the same purpose.

There are some grounds for concluding that Ezra came to Judaea about 438 B.C.[2] and remained there when Nehemiah returned to the Persian court after his first term of office as governor. The extent of intermarriage with Gentiles caused Ezra great grief, but he was able to persuade many of the people who had married foreign wives to put them away, including a number of priests and Levites. It may be that many of these men had married foreign wives after first divorcing their Jewish wives; at least, this scandalous conduct is reprobated in the prophecy of Malachi which belongs to this period. It is plain that many of the other obligations to which the people bound themselves under covenant were calculated to remove abuses against which Malachi similarly inveighs, such as the neglect of the temple services.

On Nehemiah's return to assume the duties of governor for a second term, he pushed ahead vigorously with the social and civic reforms which Ezra had begun. Foreign marriages were annulled with a more peremptory procedure than Ezra had been able to adopt. It was particularly galling to Nehemiah to hear the children of mixed marriages using the speech of their mothers, from the Philistine seaboard and the lands east of Jordan, instead of the Hebrew tongue.

---

[1] Neh. 9:2.

[2] Cf. T. K. Cheyne, "Nehemiah", *Encyclopaedia Biblica* iii (1902), col. 3385; R. H. Kennett, "History of the Jewish Church from Nebuchadnezzar to Alexander the Great" *Cambridge Biblical Essays* (1909), p. 123. This involves an arbitrary emendation of "seventh" in Ezra 7:7 f. to "twenty-seventh", and represents a compromise between the traditional dating of Ezra's mission in the seventh year of Artaxerxes I (458 B.C.) and Van Hoonacker's dating of it in the seventh year of Artaxerxes II (398 B.C.). Strong arguments are presented for the traditional dating by J. S. Wright in *The Date of Ezra's Coming to Jerusalem*[2] (1958), and for Van Hoonacker's dating by H. H. Rowley in "The Chronological Order of Ezra and Nehemiah", *The Servant of the Lord and Other Essays on the O.T.* (1952), pp. 131 ff., and "Nehemiah's Mission and its Background", *BJRL* 37 (1954–55), pp. 528 ff. For an alternative compromise dating, which brings Ezra to Jerusalem in the thirty-seventh year of Artaxerxes I (428 B.C.), cf. W. F. Albright, *The Biblical Period* (1952), pp. 53, 64; J. Bright, *A History of Israel* (1959), pp. 375 ff.

Those who had brought this state of affairs about met with short shrift at his hands, no matter how exalted their station might be. A grandson of Eliashib the high priest had married the daughter of Nehemiah's old enemy Sanballat; Nehemiah expelled him from the city.[1] Another of Nehemiah's old enemies, Tobiah, had actually had an apartment in the temple precincts put at his disposal by Eliashib, who was related to him; Nehemiah threw Tobiah's furniture out of the room, and restored it to its original purpose, which was to house the frankincense and cereal offerings given to the Levites and other temple servants. This was but a symptom of the general neglect of the temple services, and Nehemiah did his best to remedy this. The disregard of the sabbath similarly caused him concern; he ordered the gates of Jerusalem to be kept shut over the sabbath to prevent tradesmen from outside coming in to sell their wares on the sacred day, and he forbade the tradesmen themselves with threats to camp outside the city over the week-end until the sabbath was past.

The combined influence of Ezra and Nehemiah succeeded in making the people of Judaea regard the written law-book as the divinely appointed basis of their way of life, and gave to orthodox Judaism a direction which it has followed ever since.

Just as an important literary activity followed Josiah's religious reformation in the seventh century B.C., in the form of the Deuteronomic historical writing, so now the new reform under Ezra found literary expression in a further rewriting of the history of Israel, the work of the Chronicler, preserved in our canonical books of Chronicles, Ezra and Nehemiah. The Chronicler outlines the earlier history, before the reign of David, in skeleton form by means of genealogical tables. The history of a temple-state must lay special emphasis on the temple, and so his history proper begins with the reign of David, who planned to build the temple, and of Solomon, who carried his father's plans into effect. The history of the schismatic northern kingdom is for the most part ignored; the writer concentrates on the southern kingdom in which the holy city and the legitimate temple stood, and makes ample use of temple archives, stressing the rôle of the Levites in the national life so much that it has been thought he was a Levite himself. In his history of the post-exilic age he has made use of the personal journals of Ezra and Nehemiah, and incorporates much valuable genealogical material. If he was not (as W. F. Albright suggests)[2] Ezra himself, he was Ezra's spiritual son, thoroughly imbued with the ideals of Ezra's reform. The state of political and religious equilibrium which the community had attained in the Persian Empire through the work of Ezra and Nehemiah is reflected throughout the Chronicler's work.

---

[1] See page 115.
[2] *J.B.L.* 40 (1921), pp. 119 f.; *B.A.* 9 (1946), p. 15; *The Biblical Period* (1952), p. 64.

CHAPTER XIV

THE JEWS IN THE PERSIAN EMPIRE
(539—331 B.C.)

THERE WERE JEWISH COMMUNITIES IN MANY OTHER PARTS OF THE
Persian Empire than Babylonia and Palestine. Special interest
attaches to those in Egypt, and particularly to one settled at the
southern border of the country.

The twenty-sixth dynasty of Egyptian kings, founded by Psamtek I,
who won his country's independence from Assyria in 654 B.C., made
greater use of foreign mercenaries possibly than any Egyptian dynasty
had hitherto done. Many of these mercenaries were Greeks, but some
were Jews. As we have seen, when a group of Judaeans fled to Egypt
after the murder of Gedaliah in 586 B.C. and forced Jeremiah to
accompany them, there were many of their compatriots in Egypt
before them, and the warning oracle preserved in Jer. 44 was addressed
to all of them. Among those addressed were some "in the land of
Pathros" – i.e. in Upper Egypt – and these in fact appear to have been
the most numerous; at any rate it was they who replied to Jeremiah's
plea with the assertion that they would continue to worship the queen
of heaven as their fathers had done before Josiah's reformation.

Of one at least of the groups of Jews settled in Upper Egypt we
are rather well informed through documents from Syene and Elephantine belonging to the fifth century B.C.[1], discovered between 1893
and 1908. Psamtek II (594—588 B.C.) employed a force of Jewish
mercenaries in a war against his southern neighbours, the Ethiopians,[2]
and at the end of the war he settled them on his southern frontier, at
the first cataract of Nile, in the fortresses of Syene (modern Aswan)
and Elephantine – a river-island known to the ancient Egyptians as
Yeb. There the colony maintained its separate existence for over
180 years. They built a temple of Yahweh at Elephantine and carried
on a sacrificial ritual there similar to the one carried on at the Jerusalem
temple. No doubt this was a contravention of the law of Deuteronomy,
which prescribes one single sanctuary, but Deuteronomy did not
envisage a Jewish community in Egypt (indeed, the very idea of
Israelites' returning to Egypt would have been clean contrary to the

[1] Cf. A. Cowley, *Aramaic Papyri of the Fifth Century B.C.* (1923); E. G. Kraeling, *The
Brooklyn Museum Aramaic Papyri* (1953). [2] *I.e.*, Nubians.

112

ideals of the Deuteronomic law). The Jerusalem temple, however, lay in ruins; and besides, the religion of these colonists was of a completely unreformed character, showing very little trace of Josiah's purifying influence. This is shown, for example, by the way in which the names of Canaanite gods and goddesses are freely combined with the name of Yahweh – or Yahu, the form in which that name appears in their documents. We find such compound divine names as Anath-Yahu, Anath-Bethel, Ishum-Bethel, Herem-Bethel. The compounds which contain the name Anath[1] remind us of the reference made by the Jews of Pathros to the worship of the queen of heaven. It may be that by the fifth century B.C. these compounds were little more than names under which various aspects of Yahweh were personalized, but the very retention of these Canaanite names in any form would have been condemned by the great prophets.

When Cambyses conquered Egypt in 525 B.C., he found the Jewish temple at Elephantine already built, and treated the colony and its temple with complete correctness – indeed, he showed less hostility to this Jewish temple than he did to some of the native Egyptian cults. Perhaps this made the Egyptians feel sore. From time to time the Persian court issued directives to the governors of Egypt authorizing certain celebrations in connection with the temple; for instance, one document contains instructions from King Darius II to the colony, sent through the governor Arsames, with reference to the celebration of the Feast of Unleavened Bread in 419 B.C. The official interest taken by the court in such religious details presents a useful parallel to a similar interest reflected in the documents preserved in the book of Ezra. This letter was written by a Jew named Hananiah, who held some position at the Persian court, possibly in the Department of State for Jewish Affairs; but it is outrunning the evidence to identify him with Nehemiah's brother Hanani.[2]

In 410 B.C. disaster overtook the temple. The governor Arsames was absent, and his place was taken temporarily by a deputy named Waidrang. With Waidrang's connivance, an anti-Jewish riot broke out at Elephantine, led by the priests of Khnub, the ram-headed potter-god, and the Jewish temple was destroyed. The Jewish colonists did their best to get their temple rebuilt, but had to engage in a protracted correspondence with various officials before permission was at last forthcoming. We gather that the Persian government exercised such control over the details of their subject-nations' religious life as well as civil affairs that even the repair of a building which had been destroyed could not be undertaken without special licence. First the Elephantine Jews sent a letter to the high priest of the Jerusalem temple,

1 Anath was a Canaanite goddess, sister and consort of Ba'al.
2 Neh. 1:2; 7:2.

asking him to use his good offices on their behalf. This letter was ignored; we can quite well appreciate that the Jerusalem high priest would not be over-eager to promote the interests of a rival temple to his own legitimate shrine in Jerusalem. The Jerusalem high priest at this time was John, one of the sons of Eliashib who had been high priest when Nehemiah entered on his first governorship.[1] After patiently waiting for two years, the Elephantine Jews gave up all hope of an answer from John. They therefore sent a letter to the governor of Judaea, a Persian named Bagoas, and they sent one in similar terms to Delaiah and Shelemiah, the two sons of Sanballat, governor of Samaria. Sanballat, Nehemiah's old opponent of thirty-five years earlier, was still at his post, but it appears that in his old age these two sons acted as his deputies.

The letter to Bagoas and the sons of Sanballat was more effective than that sent to John. A reply has been preserved in the following terms:

> Memorandum from Bagoas and Delaiah. They said to me: Let it be a memorandum to you in Egypt to speak to Arsames concerning the altar-house of the God of heaven, which was built in the fortress of Yeb formerly, before Cambyses – the altar-house which that reprobate Waidrang destroyed in the 14th year of King Darius – that it be rebuilt in its place as it was before, and that cereal offerings and incense be offered upon that altar as was done formerly.

Here we have the title "the God of heaven" applied to Yahweh just as is done in the Old Testament documents which belong to the Persian period. The Elephantine Jews had asked permission to offer burnt-offerings as well as incense and cereal offerings. Whether there is any significance in the omission of any reference to burnt-offerings in the reply we cannot say; but conceivably the offering of burnt-offerings was not permitted, because the sacrificial slaughter of certain animals would be an offence to the religious sentiments of the Egyptians of that district, and the authorities wisely decided not to give unnecessary cause for a further breach of the peace.

The temple, then, was rebuilt. But probably it did not stand for long. The death of Darius II in 404 B.C. was followed by rivalry for the succession between his two sons Artaxerxes and Cyrus, and civil war broke out, as all beginners in Greek literature know, when Cyrus invaded his elder brother's domains in 401 with an army of ten thousand Greek mercenaries. The Egyptians seized the opportunity to revolt against Persia, under a native ruler called Amyrtaeus (perhaps a grandson of the Amyrtaeus who led the revolt against Artaxerxes I in 460—454 B.C.). They succeeded in gaining their independence.

[1] Neh. 3:1; 12:23.

In 400 B.C. a dynasty came to power which venerated the god Khnub, and it is likely that the priests of Khnub at Elephantine saw to it this time that the cult of "the God of heaven" was suppressed with no opportunity of revival by grace of Persian intervention.

So ends the history of this interesting shrine which, in terms of Isaiah's prophecy, contained "an altar to Yahweh in the midst of the land of Egypt, and a pillar to Yahweh at its border".[1]

The names of the governor Bagoas and the high priest John have been mentioned above in connexion with the Elephantine temple; they figure also in a story told by Josephus[2] of unseemly conduct in the Jerusalem temple. John had a brother named Jeshua, who enjoyed the good will of Bagoas and had received a promise from him that he should have the high priesthood. A quarrel broke out in consequence between the two brothers, and John in exasperation dealt his brother a fatal blow in the sacred temple-precincts. Bagoas, in defiance of Jewish religious convention, entered the temple-precincts to restore order, maintaining that his presence there did not defile their sanctity so much as the presence of the blood-polluted John; and he imposed as a penalty a fine of fifty shekels for each lamb offered in the public daily sacrifices. For seven years this tax had to be paid.

It was about this time that something happened which made the breach between the Jews and Samaritans complete. Nehemiah tells us towards the end of his memoirs how he expelled a grandson of the high priest Eliashib for having married the daughter of Sanballat.[3] Josephus tells us how one Sanballat, governor of Samaria, gave his daughter in marriage to Manasseh, a younger son of the high priest John. It is natural to identify Manasseh with the unnamed grandson of Eliashib mentioned by Nehemiah, even although Josephus says that Manasseh's father-in-law Sanballat was appointed governor of Samaria by the last king of Persia (Darius III, 336—331 B.C.).[4] There were at least two, and possibly three Sanballats who governed Samaria in the period between 450 B.C. and 330 B.C., but Josephus is quite confused in general in his account of the kings of Persia.

In any case, this Manasseh, expelled from the temple because he would not put away his Samaritan wife, betook himself to his father-in-law, Sanballat, who welcomed him warmly. In due course permission was procured from the Great King to build a temple on the sacred Samaritan hill of Gerizim, near the ancient sanctuary of Shechem, where Manasseh was installed as high priest. Here a rival cult was established to that in Jerusalem, and it has survived to this day, based on the same law-book as that recognized by the Jews. It is remarkable

---

[1] Isa. 19:19.   [2] Josephus, *Antiquities* xi. 297 ff.   [3] Neh. 13:28.
[4] *Cf.* H. H. Rowley, "Sanballat and the Samaritan Temple", *BJRL* 38 (1955–56), pp. 166 ff.; F. M. Cross, "Discovery of Samaria Papyri", *BA* 26 (1963), pp. 110 ff.

that while the name of Ezra is execrated in Samaritan tradition (where he is regularly called '*Ezra ha-'arur*, "Ezra the accursed"), yet the law-book which he brought from Babylon was accepted at Gerizim as it was in Jerusalem. This suggests that the Samaritans knew that the authority of this law-book was higher than any that Ezra could confer on it.

In the reign of Artaxerxes III (359—338 B.C.) the Jews suffered a calamity of which we are imperfectly informed.[1] This king's reign was marked by revolts in Phoenicia and Cyprus, which were forcibly suppressed. Of these the revolt in Phoenicia comes closest to our purpose. It was led by Sidon, and supported by 4000 Greek mercenaries from Egypt. Sidon was besieged, and was at last taken by treachery, but the despairing inhabitants set their fleet and city on fire rather than let them fall into the Persian king's hands, and it is said that 40,000 Sidonians perished at this time (345 B.C.). But the Syrian domains of the Persian king in general were implicated in the revolt, and it is quite likely that Judaea was involved. For several chroniclers tell us that about this time Artaxerxes III removed a considerable number of Jews and settled them in the district called Hyrcania, south-east of the Caspian Sea. There is also some evidence that Jerusalem and Jericho were captured about this time.[2] Some scholars have magnified these events to the scale of "the third of Israel's great captivities", comparable to the deportations under the Assyrians in 732—721 B.C. and the Babylonians in 597—587, and have found here the historical setting for several passages of Old Testament scripture, such as Psalms 74 and 79 and Isaiah 24-27; 63:7-64:12.[3] But our knowledge is too scanty for such literary conclusions to be established.

The Jews lived for just over two hundred years under Persian sovereignty (539—331 B.C.). During that period they were exposed to far-reaching influences from Persia in various ways, but especially in their religious thought. The official religion of Persia from Darius I onwards was Zoroastrianism, and several features of this religion have left their mark on Judaism, without modifying the essence of the Jewish faith. Zoroastrianism was thoroughly dualistic: over against the good spirit Ahura Mazda (the "wise lord") with the other six Amesha Spentas ("immortal holy ones") who supported him in the cause of truth and light, were ranged his rival Angra Mainyu (the "hostile spirit") and the Daevas, his attendant evil spirits.[4] Judaism with

---

[1] *Cf.* L. E. Browne, *Early Judaism* (1920), pp. 202 ff.

[2] It is possible that the book of Judith, among its historical blunders, preserves some reminiscences of Persian action about this time; at any rate Holofernes, the general of "Nebuchadnezzar king of Assyria" is probably Orophernes, known as a general under Artaxerxes III.

[3] *Cf.* T. K. Cheyne, *Introduction to the Book of Isaiah* (1895), pp. xxvii, 155 ff., 358 ff.

[4] *Cf.* J. H. Moulton, *Early Zoroastrianism* (1913); R. C. Zaehner, *The Dawn and Twilight of Zoroastrianism* (1961).

its monistic theism could not and did not become dualistic, but in later Judaism the angelic attendants on the Supreme God become more definitely individualized; angels increasingly receive names and have distinct provinces of activity assigned to them. On the other hand, the hierarchy of evil powers becomes similarly defined, and their origin is traced back to the account in Gen. 6:4 of the "sons of God" who fell through succumbing to the charms of the "daughters of men". These concepts find clear expression in such a work as the book of Enoch, a body of apocalyptic literature of the closing century B.C. and first century A.D. Other characteristic Persian concepts are apparent in the book of Tobit (*c.* 200 B.C.).[1] There the angel Raphael ("one of the seven holy angels, who present the prayers of the saints, and go in before the glory of the Holy One") accompanies young Tobias in human guise under the name Azariah, and may well reflect the Zoroastrian concept of the *fravashi* – the spirit-counterpart or guardian angel.[2] More certain still is the Zoroastrian provenance of the evil spirit Asmodeus;[3] he can hardly be other than Aeshma-daeva, the "angry demon", one of the arch-fiends attendant upon Angra Mainyu.

Zoroastrianism also had a very sharply defined eschatology, from which later Jewish literature – especially apocalyptic – may have derived some of the imagery with which it depicts the day of judgment. By some scholars the extent of Zoroastrian influence in Jewish thought has been exaggerated; it has been detected even in the teaching of Jesus.[4] It must be repeated, however, that the Zoroastrian influences affected the fringes of Jewish faith and not its essence. Another noteworthy point is that our first evidence for this influence dates a considerable time after the end of Persian political domination.

In other ways the Persian period was of decisive importance for the Jewish people. When civil governorship was in the hands of a representative of the Great King, who would only occasionally be a Jew,[5] the prestige of the high priest tended to increase. He was not only at the head of the temple ritual; he became in practice head of the Jewish state in all that concerned its internal affairs, the more so as the Jewish state was now a temple-state, and this position was retained by the high priest, apart from a few exceptional intervals, throughout the era of the Second Temple.

In this period, too, the religion of Judæa tended to become more and more a religion of law, and with this was combined a policy of religious and racial exclusiveness. It is common form to deplore this tendency – so plainly contrary, as it seems, to the programme of

---

[1] Tob. 12:15.   [2] *Cf.* Peter's "angel" (Acts 12:15).   [3] Tob. 3:8.
[4] *E.g.* by R. Otto, *The Kingdom of God and the Son of Man*[2] (1943), pp. 20 ff.
[5] In addition to Zerubbabel and Nehemiah, the names of two other Jewish governors of Judaea under the Persians, Jehoazar and Ahiyo, are recorded on stamped jar-handles found in 1960 at Ramat Rahel, between Jerusalem and Bethlehem.

Israel's mission to the nations[1] – but it may be asked if it was not necessary for the time being. Perhaps the tender life of Israel's reborn faith needed to be protected by these legal barriers until it reached maturity and was able to make its own conquering way in the world in the form of Christianity. When the supreme crisis for Israel's faith arrived in the second century B.C., it is difficult to see how it could have survived apart from the strength of that spirit of exclusive devotion to the divine law which stems from Ezra's reform.

It may be in this period, too, if not indeed during the exile, that the institution of the synagogue began. Its origins are shrouded in obscurity, but it was closely connected with the reading and exposition of the sacred law. Probably it arose in places like Babylonia where there were Jewish communities isolated from the temple worship of Jerusalem. Instead of following the example of the Elephantine Jews, these Babylonian Jews instituted a community centre where the law could be read and expounded, and where a service of worship could be carried out in non-sacrificial forms, yet following as closely as possible the order of the sacrificial worship in the Jerusalem temple. As time went on, the synagogue's importance as the centre of Jewish community life was to increase, in Palestine itself as well as in remoter parts, until the day when the temple worship came to an end and the synagogue was left to perpetuate the religion and life of Judaism.

From the Persian period onwards, Aramaic gradually displaced the sister Hebrew language as the common tongue of the people.[2] In exile Aramaic had served as their *lingua franca* among an alien population, and even in Palestine it became more and more the ordinary vernacular. When they came to hear the Scriptures read, it was necessary that they should be provided with an interpretation into the language with which they were more familiar. For several centuries these interpretations or *targums* existed mainly in oral form,[3] but even so a traditional rendering tended to establish itself. It is thought by some that this is what is meant when we are told that on the day when Ezra's law-book was publicly read, the readers "read in the book, in the law of God, with an interpretation,[4] and gave the sense so that the people understood the reading."[5] It was not only the speech that was subjected to this Aramaic influence, but the writing too. Whereas

[1] Cf. Isa. 2:2 ff.; 11:10; 19: 24 f.; 56:6 f., 60:3.
[2] There was a patriotic revival of Hebrew as a result of the Hasmonaean rising in the second century B.C., and its use (alongside Aramaic) for ordinary purposes is attested in Judaea as late as the second century A.D.
[3] Portions of written Targums have been identified among the Qumran texts; see F. F. Bruce, *The Books and the Parchments*[3] (1963), pp. 134 f.
[4] Heb. *mephorash*, the equivalent of Aramaic *mepharash*, a technical term used when an imperial official read an official document off in the vernacular of the people whom he was addressing.
[5] Neh. 8:8.

Hebrew had been written formerly in an alphabet closely similar to the Phoenician script, in which the letters took various angular shapes, it came to be written from about 400 B.C. onwards in the Aramaic alphabet, an alphabet derived, like the Phoenician, from the original North Semitic alphabet, but one in which the letters had acquired a square shape. The "square" characters in which Hebrew has usually been written and printed ever since were originally Aramaic and not Hebrew. For certain purposes like inscriptions on coins, and also in some degree (presumably in more conservative schools) for the copying of sacred scripture, the Phoenician or "palaeo-Hebrew" script was retained. The Samaritans did not change their script as the Jews did; the Samaritan alphabet is a development of the palaeo-Hebrew script.

CHAPTER XV

THE HE-GOAT FROM THE WEST

(334—198 B.C.)

WHEN CYRUS THE GREAT OVERTHREW CROESUS OF LYDIA IN 546 B.C., and added the Lydian domains to his own, he brought into his empire a number of Greek settlements in the west of Asia Minor which had previously been under Lydian control. These Greeks had close ties with their kinsmen across the Aegean, who lived in independent city-states, and a revolt by the Greek settlements of Ionia against the Persians in 494 B.C. was supported by some of the states of mainland Greece. When Darius I put down the Ionian revolt, he determined to bring the states of mainland Greece into his empire as well, and in 490 sent an expedition against Athens, which had taken the lead in abetting the Ionian revolt. This expedition was worsted on the plain of Marathon. Ten years later Xerxes in person led a much larger host against Greece by land and sea, but this host too was routed by the combined states of Greece in the naval battle of Salamis (480) and the land battle of Plataea (479). An attempt was made to carry the war into the enemy's territory and liberate the Greek states under his yoke, but this attempt was not so effective as it might have been, because the city-states which had united to repel the Persian invader could not remain united in purpose when the immediate threat receded, and the Persian kings were able to profit by their endemic disunity and play off one against another. In the middle of the fourth century B.C., Philip II, king of Macedonia, having established his mastery over all the territory from Epirus to Thrace, established his mastery also over the city-states of Greece, and with the Battle of Chaeronea in 338 B.C. he completed by force and diplomacy the unification which they had never been able to achieve voluntarily. Having thus unified all Thrace, Macedonia and Greece under his rule, Philip planned to lead a united Greco-Macedonian army against the Persian Empire. He was, however, assassinated in 336 B.C. before he could achieve his ambition, and his plan was bequeathed to his twenty-year old son Alexander.

Alexander had some trouble at the outset of his reign because some of the Greeks lately subjugated by his father thought that the accession of so youthful a ruler was their signal to revolt. They were not long in discovering their mistake. Alexander was not a man to be trifled with, and he showed that he had inherited to the full his father's military and political skill. By 334 he was undisputed master of his father's empire and was ready to put his father's plan into operation. Leading his armies into Asia across the Hellespont, he paused to visit the site of ancient Troy, drawing inspiration, perhaps, from the place where Achilles, whom he claimed as his ancestor, had fought and died. Alexander had a heroic imagination himself, and had the gift of impressing the imagination of his followers. There, in the neighbourhood of Troy, he won the first of his victories over the enemy, when he defeated a Persian army at the river Granicus. This victory laid all Asia Minor open before him. A second victory won at Issus, on the Gulf of Alexandretta (333 B.C.), opened his way south into Syria. He marched south through Syria and Phoenicia, but his progress was blocked by the city of Tyre which held out against him during a siege of seven months (January–July, 332 B.C.). At last he reduced the island fortress by building a causeway to it from the mainland. The savage vengeance which he took on the city which had withstood him so long showed that the bearer of Greek culture to Asia had something of the barbarian in him too. He continued his southward road from Tyre, and the various petty states along his route, including Samaria and Judaea, paid homage to him as he went. Gaza, like Tyre, was fortified against him, but it was taken after hard fighting, and the way now lay open into Egypt, which fell into the conqueror's hands with little trouble. There, in 331, Alexander founded the great city which bears his name to this day – Alexandria. Alexandria was to play a notable part in the history of Israel for many centuries to come.

Having established his dominion over Egypt, Alexander retraced his steps. There remained a large area of the Persian Empire to conquer yet, and the Great King had raised a third army to oppose his advance. So Alexander marched north through Syria, crossed the Euphrates and Tigris, and in October, 331, he met the new Persian army at Gaugamela, in the plain of Arbela, east of the Tigris. This army, too, fell before him, and this final defeat effectually brought the Persian Empire to an end. Darius III fled east, to be assassinated by one of his courtiers, but his family and treasures fell into the hands of Alexander. Alexander continued his eastward march, occupying the Persian capitals of Susa, Ecbatana and Persepolis on his way. The burning of Persepolis, which took place at this time, has been traditionally put to Alexander's account; whether or not it was a histrionic announcement that the Greek revenge upon the Persians for their invasion of Greece and burning of Athens a century and a half before was now accomplished, it is certain that Alexander's policy henceforth was animated by quite other motives than motives of revenge on Persia. But his advance was not finished with the sack of Persepolis; he marched farther east, through Afghanistan into India, crossing the Indus and occupying the territory which we now know as West Pakistan. By this time, however, his soldiers (not unreasonably) felt that they had come far enough away from home, and that their leader and they themselves had won sufficient glory. So Alexander began to lead them back, while his admiral Nearchus sailed back from the mouth of the Indus to the Persian Gulf, exploring the uncharted waters of that part of the Indian Ocean.

Alexander died of a fever at Babylon in 323 B.C., having conquered most of the known world. He did not live to consolidate the empire he had won, and its political unity did not long outlive himself. But his conquests imposed all over the Near and Middle East a cultural unity which was to last for a thousand years.

Alexander envisaged in various ways the union of east and west under his control. Once he had conquered Persia in battle and fulfilled his token vengeance by the burning of Persepolis, he did not treat the Persians as second-class subjects or serfs. He married Statira, daughter of the last Persian king, and he similarly encouraged his generals to marry other Persian ladies. He had already married Roxana, daughter of a Scythian chief, according to Scythian rites. The men who marched behind him, having been drawn from all parts of the Greek-speaking world, began to develop a common Greek speech, not marked by the dialect peculiarities of the various cities from which they had come, and this common speech was spread all over the eastern Mediterranean and western Asia as the Hellenistic vernacular throughout the following centuries. But the outstanding feature of the Greek way of life was the Greek city, or *polis*. The old days when each *polis* was a sovereign state had been swept away by Philip's conquest, but the Greek cities retained their internal freedom and provided their citizens with all the means for what they regarded as the "good life". There they lived together, talked together in the market-place, administered civic affairs and justice, and enjoyed the amenities provided by the temple, the theatre, the gymnasium, the hippodrome (for chariot-races), the stadium (for foot-races) and so forth. One of the chief features of the cultural effects of Alexander's conquests was the rise of new cities after the Greek model wherever his armies marched and his veterans settled. Many of these were called after Alexander himself, or after his generals, or after members of their families. Among the many Alexandrias which arose at this time we must include not only the most famous of all, Egyptian Alexandria, but, far to the east, those Alexandrias whose name survives to this day in Kandahar (Afghanistan) and Khojend (Uzbekistan). In those cities Alexander's veterans and many other Greeks, traders and so forth, settled and married and brought up children, philosophized and worshipped their gods and pursued their favourite way of life. In the surrounding countryside the indigenous inhabitants pursued *their* traditional way of life, speaking non-Greek languages – Coptic, Aramaic, and others – and worshipping other deities. Yet they could not remain uninfluenced by the Greek cities in their midst; they had to learn some Greek themselves when they brought their wares to sell in the city market-place and bought products of city industry to take back home with them. It was soon realized that gods as well as men are very much like one another the wide world over, and Aphrodite was easily identified with Astarte, Athene with Anath, and the supreme god Zeus himself, Olympian Zeus, with the deity whom the Syrians worshipped as "the Lord of heaven," *Ba'al Shamen*.

Alexander's legal heirs were his half-witted half-brother Philip Arrhidaeus and his child by Roxana, unborn at the time of his death, who proved to be a boy, and was named Alexander after his father. A council of Alexander's generals appointed one of their number, Perdiccas, as guardian of the two heirs; meanwhile six other generals administered large areas of Alexander's empire as regents. In particular, Ptolemy the son of Lagus administered Egypt, Seleucus the satrapy of Babylon, and Antigonus the greater part of Western Asia. These three, with Antipater, regent of Macedonia and Greece, formed a league against Perdiccas, for they feared that his guardianship of the rightful heirs, added to his alliance with Alexander's mother Olympias and his widow Roxana, made him aim at supreme authority for himself. Perdiccas was assassinated in 321, and Antipater was named as guardian, but Antipater's death in 318 was followed by civil war in Macedonia and Greece. Within a few years Philip Arrhidaeus and his wife Eurydice had been put to death by Olympias; Olympias in turn was put to death by Cassander, son of Antipater, who controlled Macedonia and Greece, and later on Cassander also murdered Roxana and her young son Alexander. As all Alexander's legitimate heirs had thus been removed, there was no longer any need to maintain the pretence of guardianship and regency, and a scramble began for the succession. By 275 B.C. the Macedonian dynasties were reduced to three – Ptolemies in Egypt, Seleucids in Asia and Antigonids in Macedonia.

Of these rulers the two who are important for the history of Israel are Ptolemy in Egypt and Seleucus in Asia. They both founded dynasties, one of which (the Ptolemaic) lasted until 31 B.C., the other (the Seleucid) until *c*. 65 B.C., and for most of the period of their co-existence the relations between the two dynasties were generally those of cold war, when they were not engaging in open hostilities. Judaea, which lay on their common frontier, was intimately involved in their quarrels, as may be seen from the eleventh chapter of Daniel, where the relations between "the king of the north" (the Seleucids) and "the king of the south" (the Ptolemies) are outlined in the allusive language of apocalyptic.

To begin with, Ptolemy and Seleucus were friends and allies. Indeed, Seleucus had been glad to find refuge with Ptolemy and serve as admiral of his Mediterranean fleet when Antigonus drove him out of Babylon in 316 B.C. and extended his control over all Asia. But when Ptolemy and Seleucus, with Lysimachus, the ruler of Thrace, defeated Antigonus at Gaza in 313, Seleucus was able to return to Babylon, and it is from the year of his return (312 B.C.) that the Seleucid dynasty reckoned its official era. Ptolemy, however, profited by his victory to add to his empire Coelesyria (Southern Syria and Phoenicia). Antigonus was again defeated (and killed) at Ipsus in Phrygia in 301 B.C., and Seleucus became master of most of Western Asia.

Ptolemy's command of the Mediterranean coastland of Asia as far north as the Phoenician ports brought him a great accession of maritime and commercial power, the more so as he controlled Cyprus as well. His command of the land-bridge between Egypt and Asia gave him further commercial advantages by his control of the trade-routes leading north and east from the Egyptian frontier. His control of Lebanon gave him a plentiful supply of timber for his building projects in Alexandria, for the city built by Alexander was now Ptolemy's capital, and he determined to make it a worthy capital of a great empire. It was towards the end of his reign, for example, that the great lighthouse was erected on the island of Pharos, just off the Alexandrian shore, which speedily won renown as one of the seven wonders of the world.

But from our point of view, the most important feature of Ptolemy's control of Syria and Phoenicia is the fact that he was thus master of Judaea. Josephus tells how he entered Jerusalem on a sabbath day in 320 B.C., pretending that he wished to offer sacrifice in the temple, and made himself master of the city by force. At that time, too, he deported a considerable number of people from Jerusalem and Judaea, and settled them in Alexandria. There they lived as free men under their own laws, and the attractions of the new city were such that many other Jews soon made their way there voluntarily, until one of the five wards of the city was completely Jewish and they spread into one of the other wards as well. The Jewish community of Alexandria speedily became one of the most important communities of the Diaspora. They formed the most important section of the city's non-Greek population; they were accorded special privileges and had their own constitution as a sort of municipality within a municipality.

In Alexandria after one or two generations the Jews gave up the use of their old Semitic tongue and spoke Greek like their neighbours. It was for the benefit of these Greek-speaking Jews of Alexandria that the first translation of the Bible was made. The legend preserved in the *Letter of Aristeas* tells how Ptolemy II (285–245 B.C.), son and successor of the first Ptolemy, in order to complete his great library by the inclusion of the sacred books of the Jews, sent to the high priest at Jerusalem and procured from him seventy-two selected scholars who were given quarters on the island of Pharos and there translated the Pentateuch from Hebrew into Greek in seventy-two days. It is in fact true that some beginning was made with the translation of the Hebrew scriptures into Greek at Alexandria in the third century B.C., but the work was carried out in the first instance for the benefit of members of the Jewish community of the city rather than for the royal library. In due course a carefully prepared Greek version of the Pentateuch appears to have been given official authorization by the leaders of the Jewish community; the translations of the books of the prophets and the other sacred writings were carried through by private enterprise over a period of 150 years or so.

The Seleucid dynasty also built great cities, prominent among which were Antioch, fifteen miles from the mouth of the Orontes in North Syria, its seaport of Seleucia, and another Seleucia, a new city on the Tigris, some miles north of Babylon, whose ancient greatness it soon eclipsed. In these cities too Jewish merchants settled and received special privileges from Seleucus and his successors as their brethren in Alexandria did from the Ptolemies.

As for Jerusalem and Judaea, the Jews there continued to enjoy their temple-constitution under the new Macedonian overlords as they had formerly done under the Persians. Although the Seleucid and Ptolemaic armies marched against each other along the coastal road, Jerusalem and the surrounding territory were not directly affected by these wars until nearly the end of the third century.

Ptolemy I abdicated in favour of his son in 285 B.C., and died two years later. In 281 B.C. Seleucus was murdered, and his son Antiochus I succeeded him on the throne. (All the male sovereigns of the Ptolemaic dynasty bore the throne-name Ptolemy, but there was a little more variety in the names of the Seleucid monarchs.) War broke out between the two kingdoms; in 275 B.C. Ptolemy II invaded Northern Syria, but he was forced to retreat, and after an indecisive war of three or four years peace was declared. A second outbreak took place in 261 B.C., when Antiochus I had been succeeded by Antiochus II. This time it was the Seleucid monarch who took the offensive, but the outcome was equally indecisive, and at least peace was concluded in 252 B.C., and a treaty between the two rulers was confirmed by

Antiochus II receiving in marriage Berenice, daughter of Ptolemy II and his sister-queen Arsinoe.[1]

But it was this very marriage that led to a third outbreak of hostilities, for in order to marry the Alexandrian princess, Antiochus put away his existing wife Laodice, by whom he already had a son Seleucus. She procured Antiochus's death by poison in 246 B.C., her partisans murdered Berenice and *her* son, and Laodice's son ascended the throne as Seleucus II. But naturally Ptolemy III, who now reigned at Alexandria in place of his father, was bound to avenge his sister's murder and the insult offered thereby to his family; he invaded Asia, extended his domains as far north as Damascus, and carried immense booty home to Egypt. Peace was again restored in 240. An attempt by Seleucus II to invade Ptolemy's territory was repulsed with heavy losses.

When Seleucus II died in 226, he left his throne to his son Seleucus III, but three years later the new king was taken off by poison and was succeeded by his younger brother Antiochus III (223–187). This Antiochus has come down in history as "Antiochus the Great", for he extended his realm both north and south and bade fair to recover the major part of Alexander's empire for himself when he found himself checked by a greater power than his own.

In 218–217 Antiochus marched south along the coastal road, conquered the cities of Phoenicia and Philistia and reached Raphia on the Egyptian frontier. There he was met by Ptolemy IV (221–203) and suffered a disastrous defeat at his hands. He was forced to retire to his northern territories, and Ptolemy recovered at his leisure the cities which had transferred their allegiance to Antiochus. A tradition preserved in the Third Book of Maccabees tells how this Ptolemy received an embassy from Jerusalem to congratulate him on his victory and how he visited Jerusalem. This is probable enough, but the further tale of his determination to enter the holy of holies and his attempt to revenge himself on the Jews of Alexandria when he was supernaturally prevented from entering cannot be regarded as historical.[2]

Antiochus III, although foiled in his first attempt to extend his realm southward to the Egyptian border, had no thought of abandoning his plan. After spending some years in restoring order on the eastern frontiers of his empire, he resumed his attack on the Ptolemaic territories in Asia in 203, when Ptolemy IV had been succeeded by his infant son Ptolemy V (203—181 B.C.). Gaza was besieged and reduced by Antiochus's troops, and in 200 B.C. he won a decisive victory over

[1] Cf. Dan. 11:6 ("the daughter of the king of the south shall come to the king of the north to make peace").

[2] III Maccabees 1:1 ff. The latter part of the story has apparently been confused with an incident which Josephus, with greater probability, assigns to the reign of Ptolemy VIII (*Against Apion* ii. 52 ff.).

Ptolemy's general Scopas at Panion, near the source of the Jordan. As a result of this victory he gained control of all Syria and Palestine as far as the frontier of Egypt. After more than a century under Ptolemaic suzerainty, Jerusalem found itself obliged to recognize the Seleucid king as overlord (198 B.C.).

Some at least of the people of Jerusalem were well content to transfer their allegiance to Antiochus, and helped to expel the Ptolemaic garrison from the citadel. Antiochus, in his turn, confirmed the privileges which Jerusalem and the Jews had enjoyed under the Ptolemies, and granted them some reduction in the tribute which they had been accustomed to pay, and made certain contributions to the temple funds. The Sanhedrin – the council of elders – led a deputation of the citizens to greet him as he approached the city and assured him of their welcome. It looked as if Jerusalem would be at least no worse off under the Seleucids than it had been under the Ptolemies. But the events of the next thirty years were to prove otherwise.

CHAPTER XVI

ONIADS AND TOBIADS

(200—175 B.C.)

IT WAS INEVITABLE THAT UNDER THE PTOLEMAIC AND SELEUCID régimes the Jews should be exposed to the influence of Hellenistic civilization in various ways. This influence was more obvious among the Jewish communities of the great Hellenistic cities such as Alexandria and Antioch, but even in Jerusalem and Judaea it was manifest. On a higher level, the influence of Greek thought may be seen in the wisdom literature of Israel at this time. It has even been thought that a literary relationship may be detected in the similar themes occasionally treated in the pastoral idylls of Theocritus and the pastoral passages in the Hebrew Song of Songs; but this is far from certain.

At the time when Judaea passed under Seleucid control the high priest was Simon II.[1] In the contemporary Wisdom of Jesus the son of Sira (Ecclesiasticus) there is a long panegyric on Simon:

> The leader of his brethren and the pride of his people
>   was Simon the high priest, son of Onias,
> who in his life repaired the house,
>   and in his time fortified the temple.
> He laid the foundations for the high double walls,
>   the high retaining walls for the temple enclosure.
> In his days a cistern for water was quarried out,
>   a reservoir like the sea in circumference.
> He considered how to save his people from ruin,
>   and fortified the city to withstand a siege.
>
> How glorious he was when the people gathered round him
>   as he came out of the inner sanctuary!
> Like the morning star among the clouds,
>   like the moon when it is full;
> like the sun shining upon the temple of the Most High,
>   and like the rainbow gleaming in glorious clouds;
> like roses in the day of the first fruits,
>   like lilies by a spring of water,
>   like a green shoot on Lebanon on a summer day . . .

---

[1] Perhaps to be identified with Simon the Just of rabbinical tradition. According to the Mishnaic tractate called *The Sayings of the Fathers*, "Simon the Just was one of the last survivors of the Great Synagogue. He used to say 'Upon three things the world is based: upon Torah, upon the temple service, and upon the practice of charity'."

PLATE VII

Ivory carvings, being
decorative components
of couches, thrones, etc.
found in Assyria (Nim-
rud) but probably booty
from Syria and Palestine.

Left: man presenting a
sheep for sacrifice,
north Syrian style (actual
size).

Right: winged boy
holding lotus flower,
Phoenician work on
Egyptian lines.

Right: Kneeling figure
wearing Egyptian crown,
also Phoenician. Similar
carvings decorated
Israelite palaces, *cf.* p. 57,
and examples were found
in the ruins of Samaria.
Eighth or seventh cen-
turies B.C. (Courtesy,
British School of Archaeology in Iraq.)

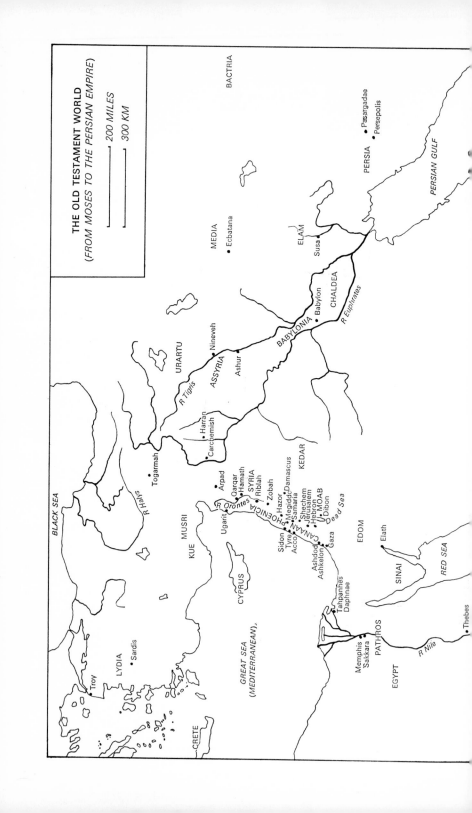

THE OLD TESTAMENT WORLD
(FROM MOSES TO THE PERSIAN EMPIRE)

200 MILES
300 KM

BACTRIA

PERSIA
• Pasargadae
• Persepolis

PERSIAN GULF

MEDIA
• Ecbatana

ELAM
• Susa

CHALDEA

BABYLONIA
• Babylon

R. Euphrates

URARTU

ASSYRIA
• Nineveh
• Ashur

R. Tigris

BLACK SEA

R. Halys

Togarmah

• Harran
• Carchemish

KUE

MUSRI

• Arpad
• Qarqar
• Hamath
SYRIA
Riblah
• Zobah

R. Orontes

Ugarit

PHOENICIA

KEDAR

Damascus

Hazor
Megiddo
Shechem
Samaria
Jerusalem
Hebron
MOAB
• Dibon

CANAAN

Dead Sea

Sidon
Tyre
Acco

Ashdod
Ashkelon
Gaza

EDOM

• Elath

CYPRUS

LYDIA
• Sardis

Troy

GREAT SEA
(MEDITERRANEAN)

CRETE

Tahpanhes
Daphnae

SINAI

RED SEA

Memphis
Sakkara

PATHROS

EGYPT

R. Nile

• Thebes

When he put on his glorious robe
    and clothed himself with superb perfection
and went up to the holy altar,
    he made the court of the sanctuary glorious.
And when he received the portions from the hands of the priests,
    as he stood by the hearth of the altar
with a garland of brethren around him,
    he was like a young cedar on Lebanon;
and they surrounded him like the trunks of palm trees,
    all the sons of Aaron in their splendour
with the Lord's offering in their hands,
    before the whole congregation of Israel...

Then Simon came down, and lifted up his hands
    over the whole congregation of the sons of Israel,
to pronounce the blessing of the Lord with his lips,
    and to glory in his name;
and they bowed down in worship a second time,
    to receive the blessing from the Most High.[1]

The reference to the work of rebuilding which went on in his day is probably to be linked with what Josephus tells of the decision of Antiochus III to repair the city of Jerusalem, and to finish the work about the temple, together with the colonnades, as a reward for the good will shown him by the people's representatives when he became their overlord.

So illustrious a high priest as Simon added lustre to the family to which he belonged, the family of Zadok, and we do not wonder that in a psalm of praise appended to the Hebrew text of Ecclesiasticus, modelled on the hundred and thirty-sixth psalm, one cause for praise should be mentioned thus:

Give thanks unto Him that chooseth the sons of Zadok for priests,
    For His mercy endureth for ever.

Simon's immediate family are frequently referred to as the Oniads – Onias being an attempt to Hellenize the Hebrew name Honi, a shortened form of Yohanan (John), borne by the great-grandfather, father and son of Simon II. The Oniads were specially respected by those in Judaea who deplored the excessive assimilation to Greek ways which they saw in other leading families of Jerusalem. Of these other families one of the most notable was the Tobiad family, to which in an earlier century Tobiah, governor of Ammon, and one of Nehemiah's adversaries, had belonged.[2] The fortunes of one branch of the Tobiad

---

[1] Ecclus. 50:1-8, 11-13, 20 f. This panegyric on Simon concludes the section of Ecclesiasticus known as "The Praise of the Elders" (which begins with 44:1, "Let us now praise famous men ... "). See p. 147, n.2.

[2] See pp. 106, 111. Cf. B. Mazar, "The Tobiads", IEJ 7 (1957), pp. 137 ff., 229 ff.

family illustrates the sort of career that was open under the Hellenistic monarchies to Jews who did not make too much conscience of faithfulness to the traditional piety of Israel.

The Tobiads were related by marriage to the Oniads. Josephus tells how Joseph, son of Tobiah, and nephew of the high priest Onias II, won the favour of Ptolemy III (247—221 B.C.), when the latter was angered by the high priests' dilatoriness in paying him the customary tribute of twenty talents. Ptolemy sent one of his courtiers, Athenion by name, as ambassador, demanding payment and threatening that if it was not forthcoming drastic steps would be taken against the temple constitution and the territory of Judaea. Joseph obtained permission from his uncle Onias, who found the responsibilities of his office onerous and distasteful, to act as his plenipotentiary. Joseph accordingly welcomed Athenion, entertained him sumptuously, and saw to it that he would take back to Ptolemy a very favourable report of the treatment he had received. Joseph journeyed to Egypt a short time after Athenion's return and found (as he expected) that Ptolemy and his queen Cleopatra were already well disposed to him by reason of Athenion's report. The collection of taxes in the Ptolemaic domains was arranged by farming the right to collect them to the highest bidders; Joseph, using money which he had borrowed from friends in the province of Samaria, outbade all other bidders for the right of farming the taxes of the king's Asian provinces. He then returned to Syria, and exercised the right which he had bought with ruthless severity, for he borrowed the services of some of the royal soldiery, and when at first the citizens of one of the Philistine towns refused to pay what he demanded, he had twenty of the wealthiest of them put to death and their property confiscated. He acted similarly at Scythopolis (Beth-shan). These grim examples effectively discouraged the other cities from withholding what Joseph demanded. He exacted so much that he not only paid the stated sum of 16,000 talents into the royal exchequer, and repaid his creditors with interest, but made handsome presents to the royal pair as well. By this mixture of unscrupulous enterprise and diplomacy he retained the right of collecting the taxes in these parts for twenty-two years. Members of his family continued to collect them after his death, and found no great difficulty in transferring their services to Antiochus after his victory in 200 B.C. Joseph's youngest son Hyrcanus, borne to him by his niece, the daughter of his brother Solymius, also won great favour at the Alexandrian court, and later carved out an independent principality for himself in Transjordan, with a fortress-palace at Araq al-Amir, from which he made constant raids upon the subjects of the Nabataean kingdom, a powerful Arabian state established in the third century B.C. with Petra as its capital.

There were other members of leading families in Jerusalem who were eager to enjoy in their own city those amenities of Greek city life which were available in places like Alexandria and Antioch. Jerusalem must also have its open-air gymnasium and theatre, its hippodrome and stadium. Other Greek ways were affected, and the Seleucid culture, by which Jerusalem became influenced after their province changed hands in 198, was of an inferior quality to that of Alexandria. Some of these trends were inimical to the true calling of Israel, because they broke down the wall of partition between Jew and Greek in the wrong way, by blurring the sharp distinction between Israel's ethical monotheism and Greek paganism. All this was abhorrent to the old-fashioned pious people of Jerusalem, but there was little they could do to check the tendency which they deplored. These pious people came to be recognized as a definite party – the *hasidim* (or Hasidaeans, as they are called in the books of Maccabees) – and although they were despised as hopelessly behind the times by the "progressive" elements in the population, the day came when they proved to be the salt of the land and the salvation of their people.

The conquests won by Antiochus III on the eastern and southern frontiers of his empire were not enough for his ambition. He set himself to expand his dominions in the north and west as well. In the course of his operations against Egypt he made an agreement with Philip V, king of Macedonia, for the partition of Ptolemy's possessions outside Egypt, of which the Aegean possessions were to go to Philip. Now this Philip had some years previously become involved in war with the Roman Republic, for in 215 B.C., when Rome seemed to lie at the mercy of the Carthaginian invaders of Italy, led by Hannibal, Philip made an alliance with Hannibal in order to acquire control of the Adriatic. The Romans did not forget Philip's attack on them at a time when they were fighting for their lives against Hannibal. In 202 Rome's second Punic War came to an end, with the decisive defeat of Hannibal on the field of Zama by the Roman general Publius Cornelius Scipio Africanus. About the same time Philip's efforts to gain control of the Aegean stirred the alarm of the Rhodians and of the king of Pergamum (whose kingdom had emerged as an independent state some sixty years previously). Both Rhodes and Pergamum sought the help of Rome against Philip, and Rome took up arms against him. In order to win the support of the Greek city-states, the Roman general Flamininus proclaimed independence for all the Greeks in 198 B.C., and defeated Philip decisively at Cynoscephalae in Thessaly in 197. Philip was restricted to his home-territory of Macedonia, and the Romans withdrew their armies from liberated Greece in 194. But some of the Greek states, united in the Aetolian League, resenting the restrictions which the Roman gift of liberty imposed on them, invited

Antiochus to come over from Asia and "liberate" Greece from her "liberators". In 192 Antiochus landed in Greece and made himself master of Euboea and part of Thessaly. Next year, however, the Romans took action against this challenge to their "Monroe doctrine" for Greece, and routed Antiochus in the historic pass of Thermopylae. They then pursued their war against Antiochus into Asia. In 190 Antiochus's fleet was destroyed in a naval engagement in the Aegean, and a large Roman army crossed into Asia under the command of Lucius Cornelius Scipio (Asiaticus), brother of the conqueror of Hannibal. The army which Antiochus raised to meet the Roman force was cut to pieces at the Battle of Magnesia (190), and Antiochus accepted the Roman conditions of peace. By the Peace of Apamea (188) he undertook to evacuate all his territories west of the Taurus range, which were divided between the Rhodians and the Pergamenes, to surrender all his elephants and most of what remained of his fleet, to agree to recruit no soldiers from Greece and the Aegean lands, and to pay an indemnity of 15,000 talents.

These terms constituted a heavy burden on the Seleucid resources. The indemnity, which was to be paid in instalments over twelve years, was the heaviest known to ancient history; and the wealthiest parts of Antiochus's empire, from whose revenues he might have raised a considerable part of the sum, were detached from him by the treaty. On his eastern frontier, too, Armenia, Parthia and Bactria, which had been tributary to him, asserted their complete independence and no longer paid him tribute or acknowledged even his nominal sovereignty. The money had to be raised somehow, and the following year Antiochus made an expedition into Susiana (the former territory of Elam) in order to plunder a wealthy temple of Bel ("Elymaean Zeus" to the Greeks). Temples were largely used as banks in antiquity, and some of them housed large stocks of treasure, but the greater the wealth that lay stored within their precincts, the greater became the temptation to some needy ruler or adventurer to ignore the sacred sanctions by which it was protected. While Antiochus was engaged in this sacrilegious enterprise, he was surprised by an attack from the local inhabitants and lost his life (187 B.C.).

He was succeeded by his elder son Seleucus IV. His younger son, Antiochus, was being brought up at Rome, for he had been sent there in accordance with the Peace of Apamea as a hostage for the full payment of the war indemnity. Seleucus now inherited the unenviable task of finding money to raise the annual instalments. The only way to do it was by increasing the taxes payable by his subjects. The inhabitants of Coelesyria, including Judaea, had reason to rue the day when they exchanged Ptolemaic suzerainty for Seleucid; even the exactions of Joseph the Tobiad, exorbitant as they were, were not so grievous as the exactions of Seleucus's tax-collectors. This is the one feature of Seleucus's reign singled out for mention in the review of Dan. 11:20, "Then shall arise in his [Antiochus III's] place one who shall send an exactor of tribute through the glory of the kingdom [Judaea]." If in the strenuous quest for money even the sanctity of temples was disregarded, there was no reason why the temple of "the God of heaven" at Jerusalem should be specially exempted. To the Jews, of course, this temple was the only temple in the world where the true God was worshipped; all other shrines were dedicated to the worship of gods that were no gods. But the Seleucid kings and their ministers could not be expected to make any such distinction.

According to the narrative of II Maccabees, Apollonius, governor of Coelesyria, had his attention drawn to the wealth that lay stored in the Jerusalem temple. His informant, we are told, was Simon, captain of the temple, probably a son of Joseph the Tobiad; Simon acted thus because of a quarrel which he had with the high priest Onias III. This may well be a partisan account. In any case, the story goes on, Apollonius reported his information to the king, and the king charged his chancellor Heliodorus to go to Jerusalem and take possession of the gold in the temple. When Heliodorus came to Jerusalem, he was courteously entertained by the high priest, and when he asked about the temple treasures, the high priest assured him that they consisted chiefly of deposits of widows and orphans, and included also money deposited there by Hyrcanus the Tobiad (who at this time had installed himself as an independent chieftain in Transjordan). Heliodorus, however, said he had to carry out the royal orders and take possession of this wealth. But when he insisted on doing so despite the protests of the priests, he was attacked by a heavenly apparition and thought himself lucky to have escaped with his life.[1] What basis of truth underlies this story we cannot be sure; a day was to come when the temple would not only be plundered but desecrated, with no supernatural intervention of the kind that is said to have checked Heliodorus in his ill-advised endeavour.

The feud between Onias III and Simon continued, and Simon lost no opportunity of poisoning the minds of the people of Judaea, and of the king's governor as well, against Onias. At last Onias decided that the only way in which he could put the matter right, and defend himself against the charges of disloyalty which Simon was continually bringing against him, was to go to Antioch himself and seek an interview with the king. To Antioch, then, he went in 175 B.C., and he was there when King Seleucus met his death, assassinated by his chancellor Heliodorus.

<hr>

[1] II Macc. 3:4 ff.

CHAPTER XVII

THE LITTLE HORN

(175—168 B.C.)

HELIODORUS'S INTENTION PROBABLY WAS TO ASSUME A NOMINAL regency on behalf of Seleucus's young son Antiochus, but in reality to exercise supreme power in the kingdom. Seleucus had a second son, Demetrius, but he had recently been sent to Rome. Seleucus's brother Antiochus had spent twelve years as a hostage in Rome, but the payment of the indemnity had fallen into arrears, and Antiochus was allowed to leave Rome only on condition that his place as a hostage was taken by his nephew Demetrius. This was arranged, and Antiochus left Rome. From Rome he went to Athens, and there he spent some time as a very popular visitor. He so won the affection of the people of Athens by his democratic ways and by the munificence which he displayed in adorning their city (as he did other cities) with gifts of temples and other buildings that they made him an honorary citizen and bestowed on him the office of Master of the Mint. While his years of exile at Rome had made him a warm admirer of Roman power and institutions, he was also a passionate champion of the Hellenistic way of life in all its aspects.

Antiochus was still at Athens when news reached him of the murder of his brother by Heliodorus. As both the sons of Seleucus were minors, Antiochus was lawful regent of the kingdom. He borrowed troops from King Eumenes II of Pergamum, and with their aid was able to put down Heliodorus. He received a warm welcome at Antioch. Once he had put down the usurping Heliodorus, Antiochus took the status not of regent but of king. His nephew Antiochus was nominal joint-king until his death some years later. This nephew ought by rights to be styled Antiochus IV, but in fact that style has always been reserved for his uncle. Antiochus's action in taking the position of joint-king with his nephew, the rightful heir, was not inconsistent with Hellenistic practice, and in fact the Pergamene king took it for granted that he would assume royal status, for when he lent him an army to attain his purpose, he also presented him with the various trappings of royalty, including a crown.

Many tales are told about Antiochus's affable and democratic ways,

THE LITTLE HORN   135

his fondness for practical jokes, his proneness for roaming the streets of his capital by night incognito, his capricious fits of generosity. Some of his subjects called him Epimanes, the "madman" – probably by a play on words on the title which he himself affected later in his reign (c. 169 B.C.), Epiphanes (or more fully *Theos Epiphanes*, "God Manifest" – for he looked on himself as an incarnate manifestation of Olympian Zeus). But he proved himself a good soldier and wise administrator. He saw the perilous state to which his kingdom had been reduced by the Peace of Apamea, and planned to keep on good terms with Rome on the one hand, but on the other to make up in other directions for the losses suffered by the terms of that Peace – in particular in Egypt and in the eastern territories of his kingdom. For our purposes, however, we have to pay special consideration to his relations with the Jews, and in these he does not appear to such advantage as he does in some of the other affairs of his kingdom.

When Antiochus established himself as king, the high priest Onias III was still at Antioch, to which he had gone to gain the ear of Seleucus IV against the calumnies of the Tobiads. But now another rival to Onias makes his appearance at Antioch – none other than his own brother Jason.[1] Jason gained the ear of King Antiochus, and assured him that, if he were made high priest in his brother's place, he would promote the cause of Hellenism in Jerusalem, and would pay a handsome sum into the royal treasury. Antiochus listened to him, and appointed him high priest instead of his brother Onias. Jason accordingly instituted a gymnasium at Jerusalem, and enrolled several of the young men of noble family in an order of *epheboi*, an athletic corporation such as was common in Greek cities. It shocked the pious party in Jerusalem to see these young men walking through the streets of Jerusalem wearing the broad-brimmed hat or *petasos*, the hallmark of the *epheboi*; is also shocked them to see the same young men engage in athletic exercises in the gymnasium – wrestling and discus-throwing – completely unclothed; worse still, some of them took steps to obscure the fact that they were circumcised. Even among the priestly families this ardour for Greek ways was spreading; some of the priests hurried through their sacrificial duties in the temple so as to attend the sports in the gymnasium as quickly as possible.

The old temple constitution of Jerusalem remained, but now those citizens of Jerusalem who were so minded might be enrolled as citizens of Antioch. This was a privilege which Jason bought from the king for 150 talents at the same time as he bought the high priesthood for himself. These "Antiochenes of Jerusalem" probably formed a distinct corporation in Jerusalem, and enjoyed the privileges normally granted to a free Greek city. It has indeed been thought that Jerusalem

[1] A Hellenized form of Joshua.

as such was given the constitution of a Greek city and had its name changed to Antioch. This would be in accord with Antiochus's practice in many other parts of his kingdom, for he founded many new cities or gave Greek civic constitutions to old cities (such as Tarsus), and many of these new foundations received the name Antioch in honour of their founder. But there is no real evidence to support the view that Jerusalem was actually given a civic constitution under the name Antioch. No doubt the granting of Antiochene citizenship to the new corporation in Jerusalem, without abrogating at this stage the old temple-constitution, was regarded as a first step towards granting Jerusalem full status as a Greek city. But there were special features in the situation of Jerusalem, of which Antiochus had not the faintest idea, which effectively barred the attainment of this goal.

Further offence was given to the pious Jews in 174 B.C. when the quinquennial games were held at Tyre in honour of the city and its tutelary deity Heracles.[1] Jason sent a deputation of "Antiochenes of Jerusalem" as sacred envoys to this festival, bearing a gift of 300 talents. Other Greek cities and corporations dedicated their gifts to Heracles himself; Jason's gift, however, was not dedicated to the pagan deity, but donated directly to the king's Tyrian fleet of triremes: even a Hellenizing high priest of Jerusalem must draw the line at open recognition of a pagan divinity. Even so, Jason's action was condemned as gross impiety by the *hasidim*. The *hasidim*, however, were unable by themselves to stem the tide of which they disapproved so heartily. But in another part of the Hellenistic world events were taking place at this time which were to have the profoundest effect on the situation in Jerusalem.

Ptolemy V, king of Egypt, died in 181 B.C. His heir, Ptolemy VI, was only a child, and Cleopatra, the boy-king's mother, acted as regent for him. Cleopatra was a sister of Antiochus IV.[2] She died in 176, and two courtiers became joint regents in her place. The new regents began to plot for the recovery of Coelesyria for the Ptolemaic throne. In 174 Apollonius, a former governor of Coelesyria under Seleucus IV, was sent to Alexandria as Antiochus's representative at a royal celebration, perhaps on the occasion of the young king's marriage, according to established custom, with his sister Cleopatra. There Apollonius, a wise and experienced statesman, got wind of the plot, and reported it to Antiochus on his return. Antiochus inspected the disputed province, to take what steps were necessary for its defence;

---

[1] Heracles was the name which the Greeks gave to Melqart, the chief deity of Tyre; see p. 44.
[2] She is "the daughter of women" in Dan. 11:17 ("he [Antiochus III] shall give him [Ptolemy V] the daughter of women to destroy the kingdom").

he paid a visit to Judaea, in which (as was quite well known) there were many people who favoured Ptolemaic rule in preference to Seleucid. Not only had they felt the weight of increased taxation since 187; the pious elements in the population felt that the Ptolemies were less likely to intervene in the Hellenizing interest than the Seleucids were; the Hellenizers, on the other hand, had begun to learn by experience that they could count on Seleucid patronage. When Antiochus visited Jerusalem (his first visit to the city, probably, since his accession), he was welcomed by Jason and his party with a torch-light procession, and no doubt he got the impression that the city as a whole was well disposed both to his own person and to the Hellenizing cause.

Next year (173) Apollonius was sent on a more distant mission; he went to Rome to present the final instalment of the indemnity due under the Peace of Apamea, and to try to renew a treaty of friendship between the Seleucid kingdom and the Roman Republic.

In 171 Jason sent his usual augmented tribute to the king, and appointed as tribute-bearer Menelaus,[1] brother of that Simon whom we have already met as captain of the temple in the reign of Seleucus IV. But when Menelaus came to Antioch, he began to outbid Jason for the high-priesthood by promising to pay Antiochus 300 talents more than Jason did. Antiochus unwisely allowed himself to be persuaded by Menelaus, and appointed him high priest. The appointment of Jason in 174 had been a high-handed irregularity, as his elder brother Onias was alive and in office, but at least Jason belonged to the legitimate high-priestly family. Menelaus, however, certainly did not belong to the house of Zadok, and it is not quite certain that he belonged to any priestly family.

Menelaus discovered that performance was more difficult than promise, for he failed to provide the additional 300 talents which he had offered as the price of the high-priesthood. Even Sostratus, military governor of the district, found it impossible to extract the sum from him. Both of them were accordingly summoned to the royal presence, and no doubt some arrangement was reached; at any rate, Menelaus was confirmed in the high-priesthood.

But Menelaus knew that he had no shadow of right in Jewish religious law to the office which he had secured by bribery; he knew that those in Judaea who had some respect for that law would continue to regard the members of the house of Zadok as true high priests. Jason knew that the sooner he withdrew himself from the jurisdiction of the man who had outplayed him at his own sordid game, the better it would be for himself; he accordingly escaped to Transjordan. Onias, who still lived at Antioch, was less fortunate. The king had to

1 Hellenized form of Menahem.

make an expedition into Cilicia to deal with disorders there, and in his absence left a minister Andronicus as his lieutenant in Antioch. Menelaus bribed Andronicus with some of the temple treasures to have Onias put out of the way, and this he did, although Onias had sought sanctuary in the sacred precincts at Daphne, five miles from Antioch. The news of the assassination of one whom they still regarded as legitimate high priest filled the pious Jews with horror, and when Antiochus returned to Antioch he punished Andronicus by degrading him from his high rank and having him executed on the very spot where he had perpetrated his murderous sacrilege. So far was Antiochus at this stage from wishing to offend the religious susceptibilities of the Jews.[1]

Menelaus himself was placed in jeopardy, for serious complaints were brought against him before the king. During his sojourn at Antioch he had left his brother Lysimachus as his deputy in Jerusalem, and Lysimachus's acts of sacrilege against the temple, by appropriating some of the sacred vessels, provoked serious riots. Three members of the Sanhedrin were deputed to go to Tyre when the king was there to urge their complaint against Menelaus. But Menelaus's bribery once again won him his own way; he was acquitted, and the three senators, as representing the party adjudged responsible for the rioting, were sentenced to death. They were looked upon by most of their fellow-Jews as martyrs who laid down their lives for the sanctity of the temple, and even in Tyre they had sympathizers, who provided them with an honourable burial in that city.

Some time in the winter of 170–169 B.C. the Egyptian government declared war on Antiochus.[2] This was an act of great folly, and actually played into Antiochus's hands. For, in spite of the restrictive clauses of the Peace of Apamea, he had in the first five years of his reign built up his military strength to very impressive proportions. Besides, the situation in Egypt, where his nephew, the reigning Ptolemy, was a child, promised to develop favourably for him, if he acted wisely – especially if he achieved his aim of establishing control over Egypt without incurring the disapproval of Rome. Rome at the moment was involved in another war against Macedonia, the Third Macedonian War (171—168 B.C.); Rome's ally, Eumenes of Pergamum, had lodged complaints at Rome against the Macedonian king Perseus (178—168 B.C.) and hostilities broke out when Perseus rejected Rome's ultimatum ordering him to disarm.

The Egyptian forces were about to invade Coelesyria, with the aim

---

[1] An alternative account is that Andronicus was really put to death for killing Antiochus IV's infant nephew, namesake and nominal colleague; see E. R. Bevan in *CAH* VIII, n. 5 at end.

[2] Diodorus, *History* xxx. 15.

of bringing it once more under Ptolemaic sovereignty, when Antiochus forestalled them by crossing the frontier first and routed them so thoroughly near Pelusium that the way into the heart of Egypt lay open before him. He advanced to Memphis, and there his nephew came to him with an embassy to discuss terms of peace. Antiochus imposed terms which confirmed Ptolemy VI as titular king of Egypt, but gave himself the real protectorate over the land. In this way he hoped to build up for himself a position of strength to the south which would compensate for his father's losses in the north, and yet to do so in such a way as not to infringe the terms of his treaty with the Romans. That treaty forbade him to attack a friend or ally of Rome, such as Egypt was, but did not prevent him from resisting aggression himself, such as Egypt had initiated. He wished to be welcomed by the Egyptians as a friend and protector, and as the champion of their royal house. A united front from the Taurus range to the Nile would not only promote the cause of Hellenistic culture in general but strengthen the Hellenistic world against the growing menace of the Parthians to the east. When Antiochus and Ptolemy concluded their treaty at Memphis in 169, it looked as if these aims were in a fair way to be realized.

But when the terms of the treaty became known in Alexandria, trouble broke out. The Alexandrians would not tolerate the idea of Seleucid overlordship, no matter how mildly the terms of that overlordship might be expressed. They repudiated the king who had made this agreement with Antiochus, together with his counsellors, and proclaimed his younger brother king in his place. In the list of Ptolemies this younger brother ranks as eighth of the name; he was given the official surname Euergetes ("Benefactor"), but was vulgarly distinguished as Ptolemy Physcon ("Pot-belly"). Alexandria prepared itself to withstand the assault which Antiochus was sure to launch against it, and so successful were its preparations that when the assault was launched (in the late summer 169) it was repulsed. Antiochus withdrew, resolved to press the siege to a successful conclusion in the next campaigning season.

The operations of this summer, and the prospective operations of the following year, demanded very heavy expenditure, especially as Antiochus's army was a very large one. But his diplomatic policy towards Egypt made it impossible for him to exact the sinews of war from what was officially a friendly country. The Alexandrian revolt had, in a way, strengthened his position; he was now the ally of Egypt's rightful king, Ptolemy VI, against his rebellious subjects. But the Egyptians would soon cease to regard him as a friend if he plundered their land.

The revenue must therefore be raised elsewhere, in his own Seleucid kingdom. The ordinary tribute, heavy as it was, was inadequate to finance large-scale military expeditions of this sort; he must lay his hand on available capital. And it was well known that capital was available in many of the temples of the kingdom, including the temple of Jerusalem. Antiochus accordingly called at Jerusalem on his way back to Antioch. Something had happened to check an attempt to appropriate the temple treasures in the time of Antiochus's elder brother, but Antiochus met with no such impediment. Far from the high priest's offering any objection now, as Onias III had done during the visit of Heliodorus, Menelaus actually escorted Antiochus in person into the sanctuary (where no Jewish layman was allowed to penetrate, let alone a pagan king), and facilitated the removal of the sacred vessels and costly dedications and ornaments, to the sum of 1800 talents.

From the viewpoint of royal policy, the robbing of a temple was not particularly serious. From the viewpoint of the custodians of any particular temple, with the people who worshipped there, such an act was a dreadful sacrilege. What he did to other temples did not much matter, but *their* temple was not as other temples were. And the Jews above all others felt like this about their temple. To Antiochus the act was simply one dictated by financial necessity; at this stage he was no more hostile towards the Jewish religion than towards the cults associated with any of the other temples which he robbed. But to the Jews, especially in the light of later events, this act of the sacrilege represented one of the earlier stages in Antiochus's proceedings against their faith and practice. The religious narrator of II Maccabees explains that Antiochus was able to accomplish his impious deed unhindered because God was angry with His people's sins and had therefore for the time being averted His face from His sanctuary (otherwise, it is implied, Antiochus would have been supernaturally repulsed even as Heliodorus had been).[1] The more secular author of I Maccabees breaks into poetry and records how

> Israel mourned deeply in every community,
>   rulers and elders groaned,
> maidens and young men became faint,
>   the beauty of the women faded.
> Every bridegroom took up the lament;
>   she who sat in the bridal chamber was mourning.
> Even the land shook for its inhabitants,
>   and all the house of Jacob was clothed with shame.[2]

It must be remembered that when we are dealing with the history of Israel Antiochus inevitably wears a different aspect from that which

---

[1] II Macc. 5:15-20.   [2] I Macc. 1:25-28.

he wears in the record of the wider Hellenistic world. From the wider point of view Judaea was a minor province of his empire; from Judaea's point of view Antiochus was the very incarnation of Belial.

Antiochus made a second expedition against Egypt in 168, but the situation was not so favourable to him as it had appeared to be when he left Egypt the previous year.[1] The two Ptolemies had come to an agreement with each other, and were now reigning as joint sovereigns together with their sister Cleopatra, who was also the wife of the elder brother. Antiochus could no longer pose as the defender of the rightful king against a usurper. If he invaded Egypt now, it would be difficult to avoid the charge of aggression. But the Romans were still engaged in the Third Macedonian War; they might be too preoccupied to intervene at the moment, and he hoped that by the time they were free to take an interest in Egyptian affairs, he would be able to present them with a *fait accompli*.

Early in the year he attacked Cyprus, which was a Ptolemaic dominion; the governor surrendered to him. In spring his army penetrated the Egyptian mainland and began the siege of Alexandria. Antiochus himself remained in Memphis, the ancient capital of Lower Egypt, and there he had himself crowned king of Egypt according to the traditional rites by the priests of Ptah. There was no longer any pretence of coming as the ally and protector of the Egyptian crown. Whereas he had scrupulously refrained from offending the population the previous year by plunder and extortion, he suffered from no such inhibitions this year; in particular, the temples of Egypt were now looted as thoroughly as the temples of Asia.

From Memphis Antiochus set out to join his besieging army at Alexandria. But now his Egyptian ambitions received a rude check. About a week before (June 22), Rome had brought the Third Macedonian War to a victorious conclusion by the battle of Pydna. Rome had not been oblivious of Antiochus's activity in Egypt, but bided her time until the Macedonian business was settled. An envoy was waiting in the Aegean Sea, ready to sail for Alexandria as soon as victory was won. This envoy was Lucius Popillius Laenas, with whom Antiochus had formed a friendship in the days of his exile at Rome. The meeting of the two outside Alexandria is one of the famous scenes of history. Laenas, instead of accepting the friendly right hand which Antiochus held out to greet an old friend, put into it a copy of the decree of the Roman senate bidding Antiochus leave Egypt at once, and told him of the Roman triumph at Pydna. Antiochus said he must consult with his advisers; Laenas drew a circle round the king in the sand and told

---

[1] I Maccabees (1:16-19) records only Antiochus's first invasion of Egypt, making no reference to the second ; II Maccabees (5:1) records only the second, but calls it the second; Daniel records both the first (11:25-27) and the second (11:29 f.).

him to give his answer before he stepped out of the circle. Antiochus had no option; he bowed to the dictation of Rome. It was little consolation for him that Laenas then consented to shake hands with him on the basis of their old friendship! The power of Rome, great as it had been in the east since Magnesia, was now paramount: within a week she had conquered Macedonia, taken Egypt under her protection, and forced the Seleucid king to submit to her dictation. Thus these three chief heirs of Alexander's empire had to acknowledge a new and superior power.

CHAPTER XVIII

THE ABOMINATION OF DESOLATION

(168—167 B.C.)

A NTIOCHUS WAS COMPELLED TO ABANDON HIS AMBITIONS IN Egypt; but no pressure was put on the Ptolemaic dynasty to abandon its ambitions in Asia. Antiochus must therefore be on his guard against any Ptolemaic attempt upon Coelesyria. And news which reached him suggested that such an attempt was already being engineered from within. Jerusalem was in revolt in the Ptolemaic interest against the discomfited king – or so it appeared.

News of the rebuff which Antiochus received from the Romans preceded his arrival back in his own kingdom, and in some places, including Jerusalem, was exaggerated into news of his death. This distorted rumour reached the former high priest Jason in his place of refuge in Transjordan. Immediately he judged that the moment had come for him to regain his high priesthood and to oust the illegitimate nominee of Antiochus. Accordingly, he gathered a band of a thousand men and led them against Jerusalem, seizing the city and temple, with the exception of the citadel, in which Menelaus was forced to take refuge. Although Jason himself had originally obtained the high priesthood by bribery and usurpation, and was a notorious Hellenizer, at least he belonged to the legitimate high-priestly family, and was on this account far more acceptable to the pious people of Jerusalem than Menelaus could ever have been, the more so as Onias, whom Jason had displaced in the first instance, was now dead. On the other hand, the pious party could not approve of the violent methods by which Jason tried to gain his ends, with the deplorable shedding of Jewish blood that they involved – or so they reasoned when his enterprise failed and he had to flee the country.

For his enterprise was bound to fail. Antiochus was not dead, but on his way back from Egypt in considerable chagrin at the rebuff he had suffered. And as he was on his way back, news came to him of the rising at Jerusalem. To him, naturally, the rising assumed the guise of a revolt against his authority – doubtless, he supposed, in favour of the Ptolemies. There were more rebels in Jerusalem than he had imagined; otherwise it would not have been so easy for Jason

to seize the city with so little trouble. He therefore sent a contingent of his soldiery against Jerusalem with instructions to put down the revolt, punish the rebels, and reinstate Menelaus. They appear to have treated Jerusalem as a rebellious city, and taking it by force of arms they wrought considerable slaughter not only among the military defenders but among the civil population as well, while many of the inhabitants were seized and sold into slavery. Menelaus was forcibly reimposed upon them as high priest, and was more unpopular than ever; in addition, a garrison was quartered in the city under the command of one Philip, a native of Phrygia, and the citizens were placed under martial law.

These measures were calculated to punish the city for having revolted. But other measures were deemed necessary to prevent a recurrence of such action. The alteration in Antiochus's fortunes made it doubly necessary to guard the parts of his kingdom in the vicinity of the Egyptian frontier; he could not afford to leave a city like Jerusalem in possession of a pro-Ptolemaic population. Judaea's former constitution as a temple-state must be abolished; a Greek city-state must be established in its place, controlled by those whom Antiochus could trust. The carrying out of this plan was entrusted to Apollonius, governor of Samaria and Judaea. He began his operations on a sabbath day, after speaking peaceably to the people; the walls were demolished (as regularly happened to a city which had revolted), a new citadel, the Acra, was erected to dominate the temple area,[1] and a garrison was stationed in it. This citadel was to serve as the acropolis for the new civic body of Jerusalem, in which the Hellenizing elements in the population were enrolled as citizens, "Antiochenes of Jerusalem." Apollonius's measures were not accomplished without bloodshed; probably there was some attempt at resistance when he began to demolish the walls, which was repressed without much care to distinguish combatants from non-combatants.

The members of the garrison in the Acra were probably given allotments of territory around Jerusalem. The former walled city was now reduced to the status of an unwalled village which it had had before Nehemiah's time.

But Antiochus was not content with this radical revision of Jerusalem's political status. Its religious organization must be revised as well. And revised it was, quite probably with the co-operation of Menelaus, the Hellenizing high priest. It had become quite clear that the core of the Jewish resistance to Hellenization lay in the Jewish religion. The Jews' religion was of an exclusive kind, unlike the religion of the other

[1] The site of the Acra is given in I Macc. 1:33; 14:36 as the "city of David." Whether this is to be identified with the original city of David south of the temple area or to be located on the western hill, looking across the Tyropoeon valley to the temple, is an unsolved problem in the archaeology of Jerusalem.

subject-nations of the kingdom, including the various temple-states. There was therefore no need to take steps against the religion of these other peoples such as were now taken against the Jewish religion. And the steps taken against the Jewish religion were drastic enough in all conscience. Orders were given that the temple ritual must be suspended, that the sacred scriptures be destroyed, that the sabbath and other festival days be no longer observed, that the strict food-laws be abolished, and that the rite of circumcision (to the Jews the sign of the covenant made by God with their ancestor Abraham) be discontinued. These steps were taken towards the end of 167, and the culminating attack on the Jewish worship came in December of that year, when a new and smaller altar was erected upon the altar of burnt offering in the temple court, and solemnly dedicated to the worship of Olympian Zeus, the deity of whom Antiochus claimed to be a manifestation. Among the Syrian subjects of the king Olympian Zeus had already been identified with the god whom they knew as *Ba'al Shamen*, "the lord of heaven"; and it was by this name (or by the corresponding Hebrew *Ba'al Shamayim*) that he was worshipped in the Jerusalem temple. Perhaps the more extreme Hellenizers among the Jerusalem Jews were content to regard Olympian Zeus or *Ba'al Shamayim* as the equivalent of Yahweh, just as in the Persian period Yahweh had been commonly known as "the God of heaven". But "the lord of heaven" to whom the new altar was erected in the temple was worshipped according to pagan forms; his cult was solemnly inaugurated with the sacrifice of animals accounted unclean by the Jewish law. The pious Jews refused to take upon their lips the name of the pagan divinity: for long they had been accustomed to regard the name Baal as a *shiqqus*, an abomination, and they transformed *Ba'al Shamayim* to *shiqqus shomem*, "the abomination of desolation", to give it its traditional rendering; "the Appalling Horror", as Moffatt aptly turns it.

About the same time the worship of Yahweh in the Samaritan temple on Gerizim was transformed into the cult of *Zeus Xenios*, Zeus the Protector of Strangers.[1]

The author of I Maccabees represents Antiochus's action against the Jewish religion as part of a policy designed to make all his subject nations practise one religion and one way of life. No doubt such a policy might have promoted the cultural unity of his kingdom; but in fact there was no need for the deliberate espousal of such a policy; the Syro-Hellenistic amalgam was developing throughout his kingdom in any case, except among the pious worshippers of the God of Israel. Nor was their resistance to religious and cultural assimilation the primary target of the king's attack; his first aim was to render them politically innocuous, and he was so ill-advised as to think he could

[1] II Macc. 6:2.

achieve this aim by abolishing their religion. He had been grossly misinformed about the strength and intensity of Jewish religious devotion, as he was shortly to discover.

The idea of centralization of the worship was abolished along with the other distinctive features of the old order; altars in honour of "the lord of heaven" were now set up throughout Judaea – in the market place of Jerusalem and in every town and village throughout the territory. The inhabitants of each place were required to sacrifice at these local altars, and severe penalties were imposed on those who refused, as also on those who persisted in observing those Jewish practices whose abolition had been decreed by the king. What followed was in effect a thorough-going campaign of persecution on *religious* grounds – perhaps the first campaign of this kind in history. To circumcise one's children, to be found in possession of a roll of the sacred law, to refuse to eat pork or the meat of animals offered on these illicit altars, were capital offences.

CHAPTER XIX

THE HASMONAEAN RESISTANCE
(167—164 B.C.)

IN SPITE OF THE ROYAL DECREE AND THE SEVERE PENALTIES ATTACHED
to its infringement many Jews refused to submit, choosing to
remain loyal to the God of Israel and His holy laws and face the
consequences. Some traditions of their sufferings have been preserved –
e.g. in the narratives recorded in II Maccabees of the aged scribe
Eleazar and of the mother with her seven sons, all of whom preferred
death to consenting to eat the abominable food urged upon them.
Their memory has been preserved not merely in Jewish but also in
Christian martyrologies; the first day of August finds a place in the
Church Calendar as the festival of the "martyrdom of the holy
Maccabees" – the name Maccabees has been attached to them for no
better reason than that their martyrdom is related in the books of
Maccabees.[1]

One important consequence of this campaign of persecution was
the stimulus thereby given to the resurrection hope. The Old Testament has but little to say about the future life. Long life in the land
which Yahweh their God gave them bulked more largely in the
eyes of most pious Israelites during the main Old Testament period
than the life of the world to come. As late as the time of Ben Sira
(c. 190 B.C.), posterity's remembrance of a good man's virtues is the
kind of immortality most worth desiring.[2] But when the persecution
broke out under Antiochus, the fear of the Lord was more likely to
lead to an early martyrdom than to length of days. The martyrs had
faith to realize that their loyalty to God could not have death and the
gloom of Sheol as its final issue. The hope of resurrection blazed up and
burned brightly before their eyes, giving them added courage to
endure their torments. Those confessors whose sufferings are related
in II Maccabees die in the confident expectation that they will rise
again in the identical bodies that are at present being maltreated, and
that their mutilated limbs will then be restored to them in wholeness.
It is probably these and others like them who are referred to by the

---

[1] For the name Maccabees see below, p. 150.
[2] This is the point of the best known passage in Ben Sira's work, beginning "Let us
now praise famous men . . ." (Ecclus. 44:1 ff). See p. 129, n.1.

author of the Epistle to the Hebrews in the New Testament when, towards the end of his list of Old Testament characters who were distinguished by their faith, he adds: "Some were tortured, refusing to accept release [which they might have won by apostasy], that they might rise again to a better life."[1] From this time forth the doctrine of resurrection came to be held as an essential article of Jewish orthodoxy (except among the Sadducees). As Jesus was later to point out, the doctrine was implicit as far back as the patriarchal period, for the God who made Himself known to Moses as the God of Abraham and Isaac and Jacob[2] is not the God of the dead but the God of the living, "for all live to him."[3] But it did not win general recognition until the period with which we are now dealing; henceforth it came to be so generally accepted that one of the titles under which God received His people's praise in their liturgy was "The Raiser of the Dead".[4]

The proscribing of their holy religion, the pollution of the sanctuary, and the apostasy of so many of their brethren proved unspeakably bitter to the *hasidim*, but it also stirred the patriotic indignation of many Jews who had not formerly been reckoned among the pious.

The reaction of the *hasidim* is illustrated by the story of a thousand of them (including wives and children) who fled from the intolerable conditions in Jerusalem to take up their abode in the caves in the wilderness of Judaea. When their whereabouts became known to the king's officers, they sent an expedition against them, and offered them amnesty if they would leave their caves. But they chose the sabbath day to make this offer, and therefore it was rejected; the law was plain on the matter: "Let no man go out of his place on the seventh day."[5] They were therefore attacked and slaughtered *en masse*; they would not violate the sabbath law by resisting their assailants.[6]

These were the true *hasidim*, manifesting the purest spirit of uncompromising loyalty to the divine law – a loyalty which despised mere considerations of personal safety. But if all those like-minded had taken this attitude of passive resistance, noble as it was, the hope of regaining religious freedom would have been slender indeed.

There were others who judged that it was not such passive resistance that the hour demanded. Chief among these latter were a priest called Mattathiah and his sons, who lived in the town of Modin, in Western Judaea. In this town, as in others, a pagan altar was set up, and the inhabitants were summoned to participate in sacrifice thereat. The king's officer, who was present to supervise and enforce parti-

---

[1] Heb. 11:35.   [2] Ex. 3:6.   [3] Luke 20:38.
[4] *E.g.*, in the words "Blessed art Thou, O Lord, the Raiser of the Dead", at the end of the second benediction of the *Shemoneh 'Esreh* (*cf.* S. Singer, *Authorized Daily Prayer Book*, pp. 44 f.).
[5] Ex. 16:29.   [6] I Macc. 2:29–38.

cipation, invited Mattathiah to offer sacrifice first, as he was a leading citizen of the place, and promised him royal favour if he would do so. But Mattathiah loudly and contemptuously repudiated the suggestion, proclaiming that he and his family would maintain the ancestral covenant though all others should apostatize. Nor was this all, for when a more pliable citizen came up to the altar to offer sacrifice, Mattathiah ran forward and killed him and then killed the officer who stood by. The altar was then pulled down, and Mattathiah uttered his war-cry: "Let every one who is zealous for the law and supports the covenant come out with me!"[1] Then with his five sons and others who joined him he left Modin and made his headquarters in the hill country of Judaea. There they heard the pitiable news of the massacre of the non-resistant *hasidim* on the sabbath, and they decided that they themselves, if attacked on that day, would resist. This dispensation from the letter of the sabbath law was necessary if any of those who refused to apostatize were to survive. There, then, at the headquarters of Mattathiah and his sons, a band of insurgents gathered, consisting mainly of those whose opposition to the king's decree was based on patriotic grounds rather than on the ideals of the *hasidim*. But it added greatly to the moral prestige as well as to the strength of these insurgents when many of the *hasidim* joined them, recognizing that, whatever their religious differences might be at other times, now at any rate they were at one in their opposition to the king's decrees and in their determination to fight for their religious freedom. A powerful guerrilla force was thus built up. Detachments appeared suddenly in the towns of Judaea, where they demolished idolatrous altars, killed Hellenizing Jews, circumcised boys whose parents, through fear of the authorities, had neglected to do so – and then disappeared as suddenly as they came. It became clear throughout Judaea that there were men in the country who were determined not to let the royal policy triumph if they could help it.

Yet it must have seemed a forlorn hope. It was one thing to organize sudden raids on the small towns of Judaea and attacks on small detachments of troops; but the royal policy was backed by powerful armies. How powerful the military forces of Antiochus were was publicly shewn in a great parade which was held at Daphne near Antioch in 166 B.C.[2] In this parade, according to Polybius, there took part 30,000 heavy-armed infantry, 6,000 light-armed infantry, 9,500 cavalry and 5,000 archers, slingers and similar auxiliaries. Antiochus himself was no mean military commander, but fortunately for the Jewish insurgents, the presence of his armies was required in other parts of his kingdom. His expulsion from Egypt made it more necessary for him to strengthen the eastern areas of his kingdom, where it was being

[1] I Macc. 2:27.   [2] Polybius, *History* xxx. 25.

menaced by the increasing power of Parthia. It was, no doubt, largely as a preliminary step to his eastern expedition that he held the review of his armies at Daphne, although its ostensible occasion was the celebration of his Egyptian victory before the Romans stepped in.

About this time Mattathiah died, urging his sons with his latest breath to persist in the good work which they had begun, putting their trust in God; he bade them make Judas their commander-in-chief but look to Simon, the eldest of the five, for wise counsel. The careers of these two show how sound the old man's judgment was.

Judas bore the surname Maccabaeus, a word which has been variously explained, but probably means "The Hammer." From it the term "Maccabees" has popularly been extended to his brothers, and their descendants, and even to the martyrs who suffered in the persecution. The family, however, is more accurately described as the Hasmonaean family, from Hashmon, an ancestor of Mattathiah. Judas quickly showed himself to be a gifted guerrilla chief, operating in an area admirably lending itself to guerrilla tactics, not only in raids on small towns and isolated detachments of the king's soldiery, but in ambushing strong military formations as well. In 166 he showed his qualities by routing two armies which were making their way against him by the hill-roads leading into Judaea. The first of these was led by Apollonius, governor of Samaria and Judaea, who himself perished in the engagement. The second, led by Seron, commander-in-chief of the royal forces in Coelesyria, was attacked in the pass of Beth-horon, leading from the coastal plain to Jerusalem, and scattered as the former one had been.

These successes brought Judas and his followers great prestige, and won them the adhesion of many Jews who had hitherto sympathized with the insurgents but judged it unwise to make common cause with them publicly. They also made it clear to the king that the Judaean resistance was much stronger than he had been led to expect. He himself was about to lead the main body of his armies eastwards to recover his lost provinces beyond the Tigris, the revenue of which his kingdom desperately needed. But he left a considerable force under the command of Lysias, who was given charge of the territory west of the Euphrates during the king's absence, with orders that he was to suppress the revolt in Judaea, deport the Jewish population and divide up the land among settlers from other parts of his kingdom.

Accordingly, in the summer of next year (165) Lysias sent a larger army than those led by Apollonius and Seron, including cavalry as well as infantry, to put down the rising once for all. They encamped at Emmaus, in the western lowlands of Judaea, to make their preparations for action against the insurgents. Slave-traders from far and wide congregated in the vicinity, ready to buy the huge haul of

Jewish captives that would be taken in the approaching battle and depopulation. Judas and his followers, on their hand, saw that the menace this time was far greater than it had been in the previous year. Material weapons and guerrilla technique were not enough; they must have recourse to spiritual resources. Accordingly, with prayer and fasting, they solemnly renewed the ancient ritual of the holy war.[1] For this purpose they gathered at Mizpah, where Samuel centuries before had called the people of Israel to repentance and rededication for a holy war against the Philistines.[2] There Judas and his followers consecrated themselves, fulfilling as far as they could the provisions laid down in the ancient law. Having then made every preparation to fight the next day, they committed the course of their endeavour to God.

That night Gorgias, one of the commanders of the Seleucid army, detached a contingent of infantry and cavalry from the main body and (guided by some of the Hellenizing party in the Acra) led it against the Jewish forces, to attack them in the morning. But Judas and his men struck camp by night, and in the morning came suddenly upon the remainder of the king's army, still encamped at Emmaus, and threw them into confusion by the suddenness and violence of their attack. The king's men fled from their assailants to the security of the cities of the Philistine seaboard. And when the troops under Gorgias, returning from their vain quest for the army of Judas, saw the smoke from their burning camp at Emmaus and the army of Judas drawn up in battle order in the plain, they too took fright and fled to the Greek cities.

It is the more to the credit of Judas as a leader of men when we recall that four hundred years and more had gone by since the Jews had taken part in any real fighting. Yet in spite of their complete lack of experience Judas's inspiring genius led them to one victory after another.

Lysias, the viceroy, had failed completely to carry out his commission against the insurgents. But another attempt must be made, and in the autumn of the same year (165) he himself marched south with an even greater force of foot and horse. This time he decided to attack Judas from the south, and not from the west; accordingly he encamped at Beth-zur, on the border of Judaea and Idumaea, four miles north of Hebron. Judas's late success had naturally augmented the number of his followers too, but they were far fewer than Lysias's host. Yet a surprise attack was again launched against the royal army, and once more the royalists were dispersed with much loss of life. Lysias returned to Antioch.

It was plain that other measures must be adopted than direct assault. Lysias opened peace negotiations with Judas, with the consent of

[1] Cf. Deut. 20:1–9.　　　　[2] See p. 23.

King Antiochus. No more soldiers could be spared, because so many were required for the king's eastern expedition. Judas was invited to send ambassadors to Antioch to discuss terms of peace, and he sent two of his lieutenants named John and Absalom. The Hasmonaean terms included a complete removal of the ban on Jewish worship, and as this would involve a rescission of the royal decree it was referred to the king. But early in 164 a Roman embassy made its way from Alexandria to Antioch, to investigate rumours of anti-Roman activity on the part of the Seleucids, in violation of the Peace of Apamea.[1] The leaders of this embassy consented very readily to press the Jewish claims at the court of Antioch; any opportunity of weakening the Seleucid power a little further by encouraging an independent attitude in its subjects was welcome to them. At a conference held in Antioch, between the Seleucid government and the Roman ambassadors, to which Antiochus himself returned from the east, both Jewish parties were represented, the Hellenizers by Menelaus and the insurgents by John and Absalom. It was clear by this time to Antiochus that the policy of banning the Jewish religion was proving calamitous to his own cause – that instead of promoting peace and order in the south-western parts of his kingdom it had actually produced the opposite effect. Accordingly the ban was withdrawn: the persecution decree was rescinded; the Jews were free once more to practise their religion according to the tradition received from their fathers. But Menelaus was probably confirmed in the high-priesthood and it was stipulated that he must retain control of the temple.[2]

Peace terms or no peace terms, however, neither the nationalists nor the pious people in Judas's following could be content to leave the temple under the control of one whom they abhorred as a traitor and an apostate. The withdrawal of the Syrian armies left two military forces in Judaea, the garrison in the Acra and Judas's guerrilla band. All that the garrison could do was to provide protection to those Hellenizing Jews who sought refuge among them from the vengeance of Judas and his men; they were impregnable in their fortress but were not strong enough to take any military initiative against such seasoned veterans. Judas therefore determined to occupy the temple area and cleanse it of its pollutions. A detachment was sent to engage the attention of the garrison in the Acra, so that the work of cleansing the temple might be carried out without hindrance. The idol altar and other installations of paganism were carried forth and dumped in an "unclean place"[3] (possibly in the Valley of Hinnom). The altar of

[1] Polybius, History xxxi. 1:6.
[2] Some informative documents relating to these negotiations are preserved in II Macc. 11:16–38.
[3] I Macc. 4:43.

burnt offering had been defiled by the erection of "the abomination of desolation" upon it and by the blood and fat of abominable sacrifices which had dripped down on to it; it was therefore dismantled. Failing some special revelation, they did not know what the proper procedure was for this altar thus polluted, so they stored the stones of which it was composed in a convenient place in the temple area until a prophet should appear to give a divine response concerning this matter. A new altar of unhewn stones was set up in place of the polluted altar; the holy place and holy of holies were repaired, the sacred furniture was renewed and placed in the proper position; the seven lamps were lit, incense was burned on the incense-altar, shew-bread was placed on the holy table, the curtains were hung in due order before the holy place and between it and the holy of holies. Then, on the 25th day of Kislev, the third anniversary of the day when the abominable sacrifice was offered on the altar of Olympian Zeus, the daily burnt offering was resumed on the new altar in the temple court. By this the temple was formally rededicated to the service of the God of Israel according to the holy law, and the dedication festival was prolonged, amid great rejoicing, throughout eight days, in imitation of the feast of Tabernacles which fell two months and ten days earlier.

Since that day the dedication of the temple by Judas has been commemorated year by year in the eight-days' festival of Hanukkah, commonly known as the "Feast of Lights" from the Jews' practice of lighting candles or lamps in their houses during the festival.[1]

At the same time the temple hill was fortified to serve as a counter-citadel to the Acra, and Beth-zur was also fortified as a frontier outpost against attacks from Idumaea.

[1] This feature of the festival is admittedly older than the rededication of the temple. II Macc. 1:18 ff. explains it as a commemoration of the alleged recovery in Nehemiah's time of the sacred altar-fire which fell from heaven at the dedication of Solomon's temple; but it probably goes back to an ancient celebration of the winter solstice. No doubt we have here an instance of a very common phenomenon in religious history – the adaptation to a new purpose (e.g. to the commemoration of an important historic event) of a festival already in existence. When such a development takes place, many of the former features will survive, but take on a new significance, and it is the new significance and not the original derivation that is the important thing, as a consideration of the festivals of the Christian year will show.

CHAPTER XX

JUDAS MACCABAEUS

(164—160 B.C.)

THE DEDICATION OF THE TEMPLE, ALTHOUGH NOT PROVIDED FOR BY the truce, might in itself have been accepted by the Seleucid authorities as a *fait accompli*. But the fortification of the temple hill over against the Acra indicated that Judas and his followers were not content with the restoration of religious freedom, or even with the restoration of the temple to its former ritual. With the end of 164, in fact, a new phase of the struggle is introduced. The struggle had begun because the religious heritage of Judaea was attacked. It had succeeded in defending and preserving that heritage. But it continued in order to win a greater measure of political freedom as well. The guerrilla successes won by Judas's army over enemy forces greatly superior in manpower and equipment suggested to the insurgent patriots that further successes might be gained and further aims realized by the same means. The *hasidim*, who had joined the militant patriots because they could see no other way of regaining their religious liberty, tended to be satisfied when that goal had been reached; not so the Hasmonaeans.

In other parts of Palestine and in Transjordan there were Jewish communities, some of which were minorities living in the midst of populations which were not only alien to them but actively hostile. The year 163 saw the inauguration of a new phase of Judas's activity designed to help these Jewish minorities – a campaign of concentration, aimed at bringing them under armed guard from the exposed positions in which they lived and settling them in Judaea, in territory under the control of Judas and his armies. This policy would not only be beneficial to the Jewish communities thus rescued from an unfriendly environment; it would strengthen Judas's hand in Judaea, for those who owed their security to his enterprise would be likely to support him in other things.

In particular, attacks on the Jewish communities of Transjordan and Galilee led to appeals for help by these communities to Judas. Judas and his brother Jonathan made an expedition to Transjordan, in the course of which they attacked several Greek cities and rescued many of their kinsfolk and brought them under escort to Judaea. While these two brothers were thus engaged in Transjordan, Simon, the eldest of the brothers, led a similar campaign in Galilee. An attempt by the deputies who had been left in command of the forces in Judaea to attack Jamnia, in western Palestine, was repulsed with much loss of life; the author of I Maccabees ascribes the failure of this enterprise to the fact that its authors were not Hasmonaeans – not "of the seed of those men, by whose hand deliverance was given unto Israel."[1] But Judas and his brothers, on their return, led raids into the Idumaean and Philistine territory to strike the terror of Jewish armed might into their inhabitants. At Marisa, in Idumaea, they clashed with a small force under the governor of that region, and defeated it. But it became known that even among the followers of Judas there were some whose religious practice was far from orthodox; among the garments of those Jews who fell at Marisa were found pagan amulets from Jamnia. (This, says the writer of II Maccabees complacently, was why they fell in battle; but he could not know how many of the survivors possessed similar idolatrous tokens.[2]) Judas was deeply shocked, and had a special sin-offering presented in the temple on behalf of the fallen, to make posthumous expiation for their guilt, that they might not miss the resurrection of the righteous.

While the Hasmonaeans were engaged in these expeditions outside the Judaean frontiers, Antiochus's expedition in the eastern part of his kingdom, which he was conducting with a skill that brought good hope of success, was brought to an end by his death at Gabae (the modern Isfahan) in May, 163 B.C.[3] Before his death (which may have been due to phthisis) he sent a letter to the people of Antioch[4] nominating his nine-year-old son Antiochus as his successor. This was a change of policy, for it had been generally understood that his nephew Demetrius, son of Seleucus IV, would succeed to the throne. Demetrius might have been content to be heir to his uncle, but the nomination of the boy Antiochus as his father's successor meant that Demetrius's chances of ever becoming king were reduced to vanishing-point unless he did something about it. Not only so, but Antiochus nominated as guardian and regent during his son's minority a high court official named Philip, a member of the Order of Kinsmen, who was with the king at the time. But the young Antiochus had been left in Antioch, under the guardianship of the viceroy Lysias, and Lysias was not minded to relinquish his twofold authority. The dying king's dispositions therefore made for disunity within his kingdom, as the events of the following years made plain. This disunity in the Seleucid

[1] I Macc. 5:62. [2] II Macc. 12:40.
[3] See M. B. Dagut, "I Maccabees and the Death of Antiochus IV Epiphanes", *JBL* 72 (1953), pp. 149 ff.
[4] II Macc. 9:19 ff., omitting "Jews" in verse 19.

state contributed very considerably to the success of the Hasmonaean cause.

When news of the king's death came to Antioch, Lysias ignored the nomination of Philip as guardian and regent, and proclaimed the younger Antiochus king – Antiochus V (Eupator) – with himself as regent. The news of the king's death also reached Jerusalem, and encouraged Judas to lay siege to the Acra, with its Seleucid garrison, the bulwark of the Hellenizing party. Menelaus and his friends sent word to Antioch, and Lysias led an army south. The dedication of the temple and fortification of its precincts, even if it exceeded the terms of the truce of 164, might be overlooked; but aggression against a royal fortress must be repelled. At Beth-zechariah, six miles north of Beth-zur, Judas, having raised the siege of the Acra, met the royal army. This time it was Judas who was defeated; for the first time in an action in Judaea the royal army used elephants. Eleazar, Judas's brother, judging from the rich ornamentation of the howdah on one of these elephants that it carried the young king himself, gave the elephant a mortal thrust from beneath and was crushed in its fall – all to no purpose, for it was not the king's elephant after all.

The Hasmonaean fortress at Beth-zur was surrendered to the king's forces, who put a garrison in it; the fortified temple hill was then besieged and was like to be speedily reduced by famine. But news came to Lysias that Philip, the legal regent, had returned from the east, and was in occupation of Antioch. Lysias therefore offered the Hasmonaeans easy terms of surrender, which were accepted. These terms included a confirmation of the grant of religious freedom made by Antiochus IV in the agreement of the preceding year (together probably with an amnesty for the Hasmonaean breaches of that agreement), and the restoration of the temple to the Jews in accordance with their ancient practice. Thus the Hasmonaean rededication of the temple was in effect legalized. But the temple was to be used as a temple, not as a fortress; the fortifications recently erected by the Hasmonaeans were now demolished. Lysias made yet another concession: he realized that Menelaus was completely unacceptable as high priest, and that no stable peace could be hoped for so long as he remained in office. He therefore deposed him, and nominated as his successor a priest named Alcimus, who was at least of the lineage of Aaron although he did not belong to the Oniad family. The Hasmonaeans presumably undertook to recognize Lysias's nominee, and in general to follow a policy of 'live and let live' with the Hellenizers. Peace was concluded on these terms, and sacrifice was offered for Lysias in the temple on his departure.

Lysias then returned to Antioch and ejected Philip, who escaped to Egypt and received asylum from Ptolemy VI.

Philip was not the only person of note from Asia to seek refuge in Egypt about this time. Another was Onias, son of the murdered high priest Onias III. This younger Onias, by the laws of primogeniture, was the rightful high priest of Jerusalem, but his claims had been ignored in favour of Lysias's nominee Alcimus. He therefore betook himself to Egypt and obtained permission from Ptolemy VI to build a Jewish temple at Leontopolis, after the fashion of the Jerusalem temple. There the Jerusalem ritual was duplicated, and there the legitimate Zadokite high priesthood was perpetuated by Onias IV and his successors for two hundred and thirty years.

Demetrius, son of Seleucus IV, had been in Rome since 176 B.C. He had gone there to replace his uncle Antiochus as a hostage for the payment of the indemnity of Apamea, and remained there after the indemnity was paid. Now that Antiochus IV was dead, Demetrius asked the Roman senate to allow him to return and reclaim his rightful heritage. But the senate refused; as they saw the situation, the Seleucid kingdom would be weaker and more divided under the uncertain minority of the boy-king Antiochus Eupator than it would be under an able ruler like Demetrius – for Demetrius, who was now twenty-three, gave ample promise of being an able ruler if the opportunity offered.

The Roman senate intended to exploit the weakness of the Seleucid kingdom to their own advantage. The Treaty of Apamea had forbidden the Seleucids to possess a navy or employ a force of elephants in their army. These terms had not been kept to the letter, and the Romans had apparently turned a blind eye to the situation. But in 162 a commission of three arrived in Syria from Rome to inspect the affairs of the Seleucid kingdom, and they enforced the destruction of the navy and the hamstringing of the army elephants. When Lysias protested, they threatened to send Demetrius back to Antioch. But the populace were enraged by the high-handed Roman action, and in the naval port of Laodicea one member of the commission, Octavius, was murdered by a Syrian. Lysias sent an embassy to Rome to dissociate himself from all complicity in the murder.

The arrival of this piece of news at Rome suggested to Demetrius that his opportunity had come. The senate still refused to let him go, but he escaped on board a ship of Carthage bound for Tyre, largely by the aid of his friend the historian Polybius, who was himself resident as a hostage at Rome, and who relates the story of the escape. With sixteen companions Demetrius landed at Tripolis in Syria, and the army immediately went over to him. The loss of the fleet and the elephants had completely alienated them from Lysias. They offered to put Lysias and the young Antiochus into Demetrius's hands, but he wished to avoid all direct responsibility for putting them to death. "Do not let me see their faces", he said.[1] So the army took the hint, and killed them.

Demetrius I was now established in the kingdom. In the northeastern part of his empire Timarchus, satrap of Media, proclaimed himself independent ruler: but elsewhere for the time being Demetrius appeared to have no rival.

The Hellenizers in Jerusalem sent an embassy to him, led by the new high priest Alcimus, complaining of the hostility of Judas Maccabaeus and his followers, who among other things prevented Alcimus from discharging his high-priestly duties in the temple. The king sent Bacchides, whom he had made governor of the lands west of the Euphrates, to Jerusalem with soldiers to install Alcimus by force if necessary.

It was the Hasmonaean party that was most opposed to the idea of Alcimus's functioning as high priest, and one may wonder if already the idea of securing the office for themselves had not occurred to the family. Perhaps, however, they were simply opposed to the idea of accepting a high priest nominated by the Seleucids, even if he were of the seed of Aaron. But the *hasidim* were disposed to accept him. Religious freedom had already been secured, and in their eyes the Hasmonaean intransigence bade fair to endanger that recovered freedom. They were accordingly prepared to welcome Alcimus. But the Seleucid authorities made no distinction between the Maccabaean insurgents and the *hasidim* who had accepted the military command of the insurgents. Accordingly when a delegation of scribes (who now appear as a well-defined caste) waited on Alcimus, he spoke them fair and promised to do no harm to them or the *hasidim* in general; but in the operations designed to install Alcimus in office sixty *hasidim* were seized and killed. Bacchides succeeded in imposing Alcimus on the people, but with so much brutality that Alcimus's position was fatally compromised even in the eyes of those who had been inclined to accept him. For not only did Bacchides attack open partisans of Judas, but he even put to death a number of deserters from Judas's ranks who had gone over to him. Leaving part of his troops in Jerusalem as a bodyguard for Alcimus, Bacchides returned to Antioch.

Bacchides's ruthlessness had the effect of strengthening Judas's position. Judas continued to make raids on the towns of Judaea and attack members of the Hellenizing party, together with those who deserted from his ranks, desiring to lead a quiet life. At last Alcimus went to Antioch and asked for further help. Demetrius had just left for Media, to put down Timarchus. Bacchides, who was left in charge in the west (as Lysias had been when Antiochus IV went east),

[1] I Macc. 7:3.

had few troops to spare, but he instructed Nicanor, commander in Judaea, to do what he could, but to try to avoid an engagement, and rather to enter into negotiations with Judas and try to keep him in play until the king came back with his army from the east.

Nicanor, who had previously had experience of Judas's military prowess, entered into negotiations with him and a warm personal friendship sprang up between the two men. They appeared together in public, and Nicanor persuaded Judas that it was time for him to settle down, marry, and bring up a family. This development, however, was not at all to the liking of Alcimus, who lodged a further complaint at Antioch, protesting that Nicanor was fraternizing with the enemy leader instead of attacking him. Orders therefore were sent to Nicanor to take Judas alive. Judas got wind of Nicanor's new orders and eluded him. Nicanor, exasperated at this frustration of his plan, went to the priests and threatened to demolish the temple and replace it by a temple in honour of Dionysus unless they handed over Judas to him or gave information leading to his arrest.

Hearing that Judas was in the region of Samaria, Nicanor went out to attack him, but at Adasa, in the same pass of Beth-horon where an earlier Seleucid army had met defeat, the army of Nicanor was defeated and he himself fell in battle. The head and right hand of Nicanor were struck off and brought back to Jerusalem, and nailed up in full view of the temple which he had threatened to destroy. Alcimus fled to Antioch (161 B.C.).

The anniversary of the victory of Adasa was kept as a festival, under the name Nicanor's Day. It fell on Adar 13 (March 9), the day before the festival of Purim. It was indeed a very considerable victory, the last which Judas was to win.

At this point the narrative of I Maccabees places the conclusion of a treaty between Judas and the Romans.[1] A delegation had been sent by Judas to Rome (probably in 161) and the Roman senate consented to enter into treaty-relations with Judaea. The Romans were always glad to help to weaken the Seleucid power. They had assured Timarchus that they had no objections when he proclaimed himself an independent king in Media; they now encouraged Judas and his followers in their aspirations after independence. Neither Timarchus nor Judas need expect any tangible support from Rome; but a treaty with Rome greatly increased their prestige in the eyes of their fellow-countrymen and neighbours.

Demetrius was completely successful in his campaign against Timarchus; Timarchus himself was captured and executed (161/0). Demetrius therefore was able to return home, and in the late spring of 160 he could spare a strong body of soldiers to march into Judaea and

[1] I Macc. 8:1 ff.

avenge the defeat and death of Nicanor. Another battle was fought in the Pass of Beth-horon, and in this battle the Judaeans were crushed and Judas himself was killed.

Judas had proved himself a guerrilla genius, an inspiring leader of men, and a man of immense personal courage and daring. While he lacked those qualities of statesmanship which his brothers after him exploited to further the cause for which Judas had fought, it is unlikely that they would ever have had the opportunity of exploiting their diplomatic qualities if Judas had not first shown his military qualities to such good purpose. No wonder that when he fell men said: "How is the mighty fallen, the saviour of Israel!"[1] For it appeared that all the work he had achieved was undone. Alcimus was reinstated in the temple as high priest, and the Hellenizing party was established in power. Those who had been known as partisans of Judas were sought out and punished, although here it must be said that they were simply receiving the treatment that Judas had meted out to the Hellenizers when opportunity offered. But the most important of Judas's achievements stood; the temple had been rededicated to the ancient form of worship, religious freedom had been restored to the Jewish people, and there was no idea of repeating the policy of religious persecution which Antiochus had followed for a few years with such ill success.

[1] I Macc. 9:21.

Darius I, king of Persia, receiving a Median subject, while his son Xerxes (Ahasuerus) stands behind. Sculpture from the Treasury at Persepolis.
(Photograph, Oriental Institute, University of Chicago.)

PLATE VIII

Letter written in Aramaic on leather. On the outside (above) is the address to the official of Arsham, Persian governor of Egypt *c.* 450–425 B.C., from his master in Babylon or Susa. Found in Egypt. The royal decrees and letters recorded in Ezra would have had a similar appearance.
(G. R. Driver, *Aramaic Documents* pl. 12, reproduced by permission of the Clarendon Press and the Bodleian Library, Oxford.)

PLATE IX

Stretch of stone wall
recently uncovered on the
east side of the Temple
Enclosure in
Jerusalem, perhaps part
of Zerubbabel's
building (pp. 103 ff).
The masonry is com-
parable with Persian walls
in Phoenicia and Iran.
The Herodian wall abuts
it with a straight joint
at the left of the picture.
(Courtesy, Howard
Peskett.)

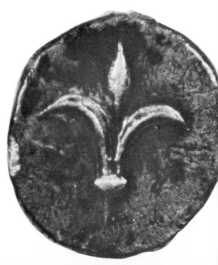

Coin issued by Jewish authorities in
Jerusalem under Persian rule.
Inscribed *Yehud* in Old Hebrew.
Silver, diameter 0·35 inch approx.
(Hyman Bessin Collection, Israel
Museum, Jerusalem.)

CHAPTER XXI

INDEPENDENCE WON

(160—128 B.C.)

WITH THE DEATH OF JUDAS THE CAUSE WHICH HE HAD LED SEEMED lost. True, the temple had been restored to its proper use as the shrine of Yahweh, and the pious Jews were free to practise their ancestral religion, but for the rest it looked as if the situation would now revert to what it had been before Antiochus IV began his ill-starred intervention in the religious life of Judaea. That it did not so revert was due in part to the refusal of a hard core of Hasmonaean partisans to accept such a settlement, and in part to further dissension over the Seleucid throne, which played into the hands of these partisans.

JONATHAN

Judas's brother Jonathan was invited to take his place as insurgent leader. Jonathan was not such a military genius as Judas, but he had greater prudence and diplomatic capacity. He was not the man to throw himself against superior numbers when there was no prospect but certain defeat. He succeeded in reviving the dejected spirits of his followers, in avoiding the attempts of Bacchides to take him by surprise, and in taking military action against a hostile tribe in Trans-jordan, who had captured and killed his brother John.

West of the Jordan, Bacchides imposed a strict military control over the land by fortifying several strategic points and manning them with garrisons. He also took steps to ensure the good behaviour of the leading citizens of Judaea – especially those of Hasmonaean sympathies– by holding their sons as hostages in the Acra in Jerusalem.

Alcimus's high-handed activites as high priest in Jerusalem provoked increasing resentment among the Jews, but a measure of tranquillity followed his death in 159. He was the victim of a paralytic stroke which befell him while he was engaged in dismantling the wall around the inner court of the temple, and the author of I Maccabees has no diffi-culty in discerning a direct divine judgment in this visitation.[1] No immediate appointment was made in his place. Demetrius, after the

[1] I Macc. 9:55 f.

hostile reception received by Alcimus, probably decided that there was a better chance of peace in Judaea if no successor was appointed to him.

As the situation now appeared quieter, Bacchides returned to Antioch. Two years later (157), Jonathan felt strong enough to strengthen his position in Judaea. Bacchides was summoned by the Hellenizers to deal with him, but he came off worst in an encounter with Jonathan and his followers east of Bethlehem. After this clash Bacchides and Jonathan concluded a truce; prisoners were returned by both sides, and (probably under the terms of the same agreement) Jonathan was allowed to set up his headquarters at Michmash. For the next five years there was peace in Judaea.

But a disturbing element was introduced into the Syrian scene in 152 B.C. There landed at Ptolemaïs[1] a young man, commonly known as Balas, who gave himself out as Alexander Epiphanes, the younger son of Antiochus IV. It is very difficult to decide whether his claim was genuine. His coinage gives him a marked facial resemblance to Antiochus IV – but were his features on the coins modified to lend colour to his claim? On the other hand the house of Demetrius and its supporters held him to be a mere pretender, a low-born adventurer from Ephesus. But he secured the recognition and support of Ptolemy VI of Egypt, who resented Demetrius's interference with his domains in Cyprus. Ptolemy also saw here an opportunity to gain a position of power in the Seleucid realm, and promised Balas one of his daughters in marriage.

Balas, however, had the support of a greater power than Egypt. The rulers of Cappadocia and Pergamum, annoyed by Demetrius's intervention in the affairs of Asia Minor, decided to put Balas forward in opposition to him, and to win Rome's support for their venture. They succeeded by careful intrigue in procuring from Rome a senatorial decree which authorized Balas to secure the throne, and it was with this backing that Balas landed in Syria in 152.

Balas saw that he could strengthen his position considerably if he could win Jonathan and his veteran guerrilla force over to his side. He therefore came to an understanding with Jonathan. In return for Jonathan's support, he not only permitted him to maintain an independent military force in Judaea, and enrolled him in the order of the "King's Friends", but actually undertook to recognize him as high priest of the Jews, and presented him with the golden tiara and purple robe which went with this quasi-royal dignity.

But see how the earlier Hasmonaean ideals have been forgotten! Antiochus IV began his policy of intervention in Jewish religious affairs, which ultimately led to the Hasmonaean rising, by deposing and appointing Jewish high priests. Now a Hasmonaean accepts the

[1] The Greek foundation on the site of the ancient Acco.

high priesthood from a man whose title to bestow it is based on his claim to be the son and successor of that same Antiochus.

Demetrius had attempted to gain Jonathan's co-operation as soon as Balas landed at Ptolemaïs, but Balas, having little to lose and much to gain, could afford to make a much higher bid than Demetrius and Jonathan accepted Balas's overtures. All the same, he profited by Demetrius's overtures too, for the Hellenizers in the Acra, seeing that both sides were eager for Jonathan's support, surrendered to him the hostages whom they held and could do nothing to prevent him when he began to rebuild the temple wall, demolished by Lysias in 163, and the city wall, demolished by Apollonius in 168. The garrisons which Bacchides had placed throughout Judaea evacuated their citadels, and only the Jerusalem Acra and Beth-zur remained in their hands.

Finding that Jonathan had accepted Balas's terms, Demetrius appealed to the whole Jewish nation, Hasmonaean sympathizers and Hellenizers alike, offering them extraordinary privileges, increases of territory and remissions of tax and tribute, if they would support him. But he was too late: Jonathan and his friends, now entrenched in a position of unrivalled strength in Judaea, stood fast by their treaty with Balas.

Balas and Demetrius met in battle in 150 B.C.; Demetrius was defeated and lost his life. Ptolemy VI then came to Ptolemaïs to greet his victorious vassal (for Balas was little more), and to give him his daughter Cleopatra in marriage. Jonathan was now summoned to Ptolemaïs to attend the court of the two kings (150 B.C.). Balas raised him to the higher rank of "First Friend" and appointed him governor of the province of Judaea. Thus the civil strife in the Seleucid realm turned out for a speedy accession of good fortune to Jonathan, who now combined the chief religious, military and civil power in Judaea. The Hellenizing party lodged complaints against this bestowal of royal favour on the Hasmonaean leader, but their protests went unheeded.

Balas appears to have been as affable and popular as his putative father; but unlike him he took no care to defend the eastern frontiers of his kingdom against the Parthians. This possibly helped to alienate his subjects' good will.

When Demetrius fell in battle against Balas, he left two sons, Demetrius and Antiochus, in the island of Cnidus. In 147 the younger Demetrius arrived in the land of his fathers with the backing of a body of Cretan mercenaries led by Lasthenes. He established control over a good part of Phoenicia and Syria, but when his governor Apollonius demanded the submission of Balas's friend Jonathan, Jonathan offered him battle near Ashdod and defeated him. As a result of this action Joppa and a number of the cities of the Philistine seaboard fell into Jonathan's hands, and he received further marks of distinction from Balas, including probably the governorship of all Coelesyria.

Ptolemy VI, however, watched from Egypt this fresh outbreak fo civil war in Syria, confident that this progressive weakening of the Seleucid power could only work to his own advantage. When he judged the situation ripe for intervention, he marched into Asia, as though to aid his son-in-law Balas against Demetrius II. Jonathan, as governor of Coelesyria, escorted him as far as the northern boundary of that territory, but when Ptolemy crossed the frontier he seized the coastal cities of Northern Syria and transferred his support – and his daughter – from Balas to Demetrius, on condition that Coelesyria should revert to the Ptolemaic empire, to which it had belonged before the Battle of Panion fifty years before. Demetrius could not refuse Ptolemy's offer, although it involved the loss of an important part of his ancestral kingdom and the acknowledgment of Ptolemy as virtually his overlord. But when Ptolemy and Demetrius joined battle with Balas in the plain of Antioch and defeated him, Ptolemy was mortally wounded. Balas sought safety in flight, but he was assassinated, and his head was sent to the victors. Ptolemy lived long enough to see this grisly trophy; but he reaped no advantage from it, for he died a few days later.

Demetrius II thus got rid of his rival and his overlord at one stroke, and reigned as undisputed ruler over the Seleucid realm (145) without having to give up Coelesyria to Egypt.

Now the Hellenizing party in Judaea, who had resented the favours heaped by Balas on Jonathan, hoped for better things from Demetrius II. They thought they had a good opportunity to accuse Jonathan before Demetrius, because during the fighting in North Syria, Jonathan tried to reduce the Jerusalem citadel, with its Seleucid garrison. Demetrius summoned Jonathan to Ptolemaïs, and there Jonathan was able to gain from Demetrius a continuation of the privileges which he and his followers had received from Balas. He was confirmed in the dual office of high priest and governor of Judaea, and was enrolled among Demetrius's "First Friends", as he had formerly been enrolled among Balas's. He on his side had to give up his siege of the Acra, and consent to the continuance of Seleucid garrisons there and at Beth-zur. Demetrius was wise enough to recognize that Jonathan could be of great value as a supporter, whereas he could be a powerful and dangerous enemy.

But Demetrius was not to be allowed to enjoy his new-won power for long without interference. He took the unwise step of dismissing the mercenaries by whose aid he had won his power, and these disbanded troops were only too ready to follow a new commander.

Nor was this the only step taken by the new king – or rather by his commander-in-chief and adviser the Cretan Lasthenes – which speedily made him very unpopular. In Antioch itself he alienated the sympathies of a large section of the civic population by his severe measures against the supporters of Balas. An insurrection broke out in the capital, and to crush this rising Demetrius called on Jonathan for help. Jonathan sent 3,000 men, who co-operated with the king's Cretan mercenaries and wrought such destruction in the city with fire and sword that the insurgents soon laid down their arms and threw themselves on the mercy of the king.

Once the insurrection was quelled, however, Jonathan did not receive from Demetrius the further rewards to which he considered himself entitled for his timely help. Accordingly, when a new claimant to the Seleucid throne appeared, Jonathan was ready to transfer his support to the newcomer.

When Balas was assassinated, after his defeat by the forces of Ptolemy VI and Demetrius II, he left his infant son Antiochus in the care of an Arabian chief. A former officer of Balas, named Trypho, saw that he could exploit the disaffection caused by Demetrius's disbanding of the Syrian mercenaries by whose aid he had secured the kingdom. He therefore persuaded the Arabians to transfer the infant Antiochus to his care and proclaimed him king as Antiochus VI (Epiphanes Dionysus). Acting in the infant king's name, Trypho was able to gather to his standard the disbanded troops together with an elephant-force which Ptolemy VI had left behind him when he died of his wounds, and to seize Antioch and many other cities (145 B.C.). Demetrius retained control of Cilicia, one or two coastal cities, and the eastern part of the Empire. But Trypho secured the support of Jonathan, when he confirmed him in his previous privileges, increased his territory as governor of Judaea and made his brother Simon military commander of the coastal area from the Egyptian border to the "Ladder of Tyre". Jonathan and Simon both engaged in military operations in support of Trypho. Simon reduced the fortress of Joppa, which was occupied by a pro-Demetrius garrison. Jonathan, however, sustained a heavy reverse at the hands of Demetrius's forces in Galilee, nor had he much greater success in operations in Coelesyria in 144, although he enriched himself by a raid on an Arab tribe.

But Jonathan and Simon's support for Trypho was for them merely a means of strengthening their own cause, and Trypho recognized this very well, especially when the two brothers strengthened the fortifications of Jerusalem and other districts which they held. Trypho found it convenient to use them for a time, until their independent action threatened his plans. For Trypho, too, had ambitions of his own. So long as it was expedient to act in the name of the infant king,

Trypho was content with the status of regent, but his ambition was to secure the royal name and the royal power for himself.

He was unable to invade Judaea and give battle to the Hasmonaeans with any hope of success, but had recourse to treachery instead of force. He invited Jonathan to Ptolemaïs, and arrested him there. He reaped no advantage from this stroke, however, for Jonathan's followers immediately acclaimed Simon, the oldest (and only survivor) of the Maccabaean brothers, as Jonathan's deputy.

So when Trypho invaded Judaea, Simon met him with a force which made Trypho decide to negotiate rather than to fight. He pretended that Jonathan was being held as hostage for the payment of money, but when the ransom-money was paid over, Jonathan was not set free but shortly afterwards put to death. His body then was given up and interred in the family sepulchre at Modin, where a splendid monument was erected for the brothers and their parents.

Jonathan, during his seventeen years' career as leader (160—143 B.C.) showed neither the the military genius of Judas nor the wise statesmanship of Simon. His successes were due mainly to the skill with which he played off one rival claimant to the Seleucid throne against another, and to the unscrupulous way in which he transferred his support from this claimant to that. His readiness to accept honours, and above all the high-priestly dignity itself, from the Syrian rulers, marked a sad departure from the ideals of the earlier days of the struggle for liberty. His wider diplomacy – e.g. the renewal of the alliance with Rome and the conclusion of a treaty with Sparta (on the basis of an alleged racial affinity)—brought more prestige than any effective increase of strength to his people's cause. So long as the Seleucid kingdom remained united, he achieved little against it; only when its period of dissension began with the arrival of Alexander Balas in 152 was he able to attain greater power and freedom by exploiting these dissensions.

SIMON

In view of Trypho's hostility, Simon, who was now undisputed leader of the Jews, entered into negotiations with Demetrius. Demetrius was only too glad now to have the Jews as allies in his fight against Trypho, and agreed that they should henceforth be free from the payment of tribute to the Seleucid exchequer. The rescript in which this decree was embodied dates from May, 142 B.C. and was in effect a charter of Jewish independence. What Judas had fought for, and Jonathan had furthered by diplomacy, Simon now secured. "In the 170th year [of the Seleucid era] the yoke of the Gentiles was removed from Israel."[1]

[1] I Macc. 13:41.

In the same year (142) Simon renewed the alliance with Rome and Sparta, and the Roman senate wrote to Demetrius, to Ptolemy VIII of Egypt, and to other eastern Mediterranean rulers, announcing its recognition of Judaea's independence under Simon and forbidding them to make war against him or to collaborate with his enemies. Perhaps Demetrius did not intend to honour his agreement with Simon any longer than he could help. But Simon, having secured the agreement, showed himself as effective in action as in negotiation, for later in 142 he reduced the Seleucid fortress of Gazara (the ancient Gezer), and in May 141 he reduced the Jerusalem Acra, which had been continuously held in the Seleucid interest since Apollonius fortified it in 167 B.C. Both citadels were now garrisoned by Simon with his own followers. But no reprisals appear to have been taken against the Hellenizing Jews who for many years had enjoyed the protection of the Acra. What their fate would have been if Judas had captured the Acra may be surmised from the punishment which he meted out to Hellenizing Jews elsewhere; but it was part of Simon's wisdom to unite the Jewish nation under his leadership and not perpetuate old dissensions.

The last vestige of Seleucid ascendancy was thus removed from Judaea. Nor could Demetrius do anything to prevent Simon's action, for in 141 he marched east against the Parthians, who had made considerable encroachment on Seleucid territory in Mesopotamia. Probably he hoped also, by strengthening his position in the east, to act more effectively in due course against Trypho in the west.

But in 139 Demetrius was taken prisoner by the Parthians, who kept him in honourable captivity for ten years. Trypho now cast off all pretence of being merely the regent for the infant Antiochus VI; he had himself proclaimed king by his soldiers, and not long afterwards made away with the boy-king, who had been useful to him for a time, but had now served Trypho's purpose sufficiently.

Trypho, however, did not enjoy his ill-gotten authority for long. Demetrius II had a brother, Antiochus, who had lived for several years in Asia Minor. Antiochus, hearing of his brother's capture, collected a mercenary force, and marched against Trypho. Trypho's troops deserted to him, or rather (in the first instance) to Cleopatra, wife of Demetrius II, who was living at Seleucia and now invited Antiochus to marry her[1] and reign in his captive brother's place as Antiochus VII (Sidetes). Trypho was chased from one refuge to another until at last he was captured and compelled to commit suicide.

Meanwhile Simon received signal honours from his grateful people for the independence and peace which he had won for them. At a meeting of the popular assembly of the Jews in September, 140 B.C.,

[1] He thus became her third husband. She had first been married to Balas.

it was decreed, in consideration of the patriotic achievements of Simon and his brothers, that he should be formally appointed commander-in-chief of the army, ethnarch or governor of the nation, and high priest. Simon had taken over from Jonathan, along with the chief civil and military functions, the high-priesthood which Jonathan had first received from Alexander Balas. But it was no longer fitting that the high priest of an independent nation should hold his sacred office by the gift of a foreign monarch, and so it was now bestowed on Simon by popular vote. To be sure, he did not belong to the ancient Zadokite line, but it was no longer practicable to reinstate the Zadokites in the high priesthood, and so Simon was made hereditary high priest ("high priest for ever") until such time as the will of God might be declared in the matter by the mouth of "a trustworthy prophet".[1] For the present, at any rate, prophecy was believed to have ceased out of Israel.

Simon thus combined in his own person the supreme civil, military, and religious dignities, and of all the members of the Hasmonaean line none merited the triple honour so much as he did. As ruler of an independent state he had the right to mint his own coinage; if he did not avail himself of this right it was perhaps because there were no facilities for minting money in his territory.[2]

When Antiochus VII arrived in Syria in 139 to take up arms against the usurper Trypho he was glad to enlist the aid of Simon. But as Trypho's cause weakened, Antiochus adopted a more high-handed attitude towards Simon, and at last (early in 138) sent a message to him demanding either the surrender of the strongholds he had taken – Joppa, Gazara, and the Jerusalem Acra – or else a monetary payment to compensate for the loss which Simon's tenure of them meant for the royal exchequer. Simon denied the king's right to make any such demands in respect of Judaean territory, but offered 100 talents for his tenure of Joppa and Gazara. Antiochus treated this offer as an insult, and sent one of his captains, Cendebaeus, military commander of the coastal territories, to attack Judaea. Cendebaeus took up his headquarters at Jamnia from whence he invaded Simon's territory and built a forward military base near Azotus (the ancient Ashdod).

Simon's son, John Hyrcanus, who had been placed in command of Gezer, reported the situation to his father. Simon appointed John and his brother Judas to take the necessary measures against Cendebaeus, and they inflicted such a heavy defeat on him in the plain of Azotus

[1] I Macc. 14:41.
[2] Coins bearing the inscription "Simeon prince of Israel" and celebrating the "liberation of Israel", formerly assigned to this period, are now known to date from the second Jewish revolt against Rome, under Simeon ben Kosebah (A.D. 132—135).

that Judaea had no more trouble from the Seleucids for three or four years.

In 134 Simon was assassinated at a family banquet by his son-in-law Ptolemy son of Abubus, whom he had appointed commander of Jericho. Ptolemy's motive seems to have been desire for personal power; he hoped to take Simon's place as ruler of the nation. To do this, of course, he had also to remove Simon's sons. He seized two who were with their father at the time of his assassination and kept them in custody in the fortress of Dok, near Jericho, and sent messengers to Gazara to seize John Hyrcanus. But news of the murder reached John before Ptolemy's envoys; he was ready for them when they came and killed them on their arrival. Then he led a force east to Ptolemy's fortress of Dok and laid siege to it. Ptolemy, seeing that his cause was hopeless, killed John's brothers and mother, whom he had held captive in the fortress, and escaped to Cappadocia.

JOHN HYRCANUS

John Hyrcanus was now acclaimed by the people as his father's successor in all his offices. But the first six years of his rule were troubled. For the disorder which followed Simon's untimely death gave Antiochus VII an opportunity to invade Judaea and besiege Jerusalem. John held out for a year, but in the end was compelled to ask for terms. The terms imposed included the repayment of tribute, as well as arrears of tribute for the years of independence, the demolition of the walls of Jerusalem, and the surrender of hostages (133 B.C.).

For five years, then, Judaea was once more tributary to a Seleucid overlord. But in 128 Antiochus VII went on a campaign against the Parthians, and fell in battle with them. Demetrius II, his brother, who had been held in Parthian captivity for ten years, was set free and came home to re-occupy the throne in Antioch. But the Seleucid power was by this time so thoroughly reduced that Judaea was able to regain complete independence without fear of further intervention from that quarter.

CHAPTER XXII

THE HASMONAEAN DYNASTY

(128—65 B.C.)

JOHN HYRCANUS

IN THE SEVENTH YEAR OF JOHN HYRCANUS, THEN, THE INDEPENDENT state of Judaea was securely established. Forty years had gone by since Antiochus Epiphanes had abolished the old constitution of Jerusalem and the surrounding territory as an autonomous temple-state within the empire. The self-sacrifice and devotion of the *hasidim*, the strategic genius of Judas and the statesmanship of Simon – combined, it is true, with the increasing dividedness and weakness of the Seleucid imperial power – had won for the Jewish people more (to all outward appearance) than they had lost at the hands of Antiochus. No wonder, then, that the early years of independence and security under John Hyrcanus, before the Judaean commonwealth was rent by inner conflict, took on the features of a miniature golden age in the eyes of later generations. The ancient venerable offices of prophet and priest and king seemed to be combined in him. "He was esteemed by God worthy of the three greatest privileges", says Josephus,[1] "the government of his nation, the dignity of the high priesthood, and the gift of prophecy, for God was with him and enabled him to know and foretell the future." He celebrated his nation's regaining of independence by the issue of a bronze coinage inscribed "John the high priest and the commonwealth of the Jews."

But the *hasidim*, or some of them at least, continued to view the Hasmonaean retention of power with disfavour. According to a story preserved by Josephus,[2] an open breach came between John and these people at a banquet to which he invited them. At the banquet he assured them of his veneration for their principles and of his desire to please God in everything, which he knew to be their desire too. If, however, they saw him unwittingly infringe the divine law in any point, he begged that they would point it out. At this one of the guests, Eleazar by name, told him that if he wished to do the will of God perfectly, he should relinquish the high priesthood and content himself with the civil and military leadership of the nation. The ostensible

[1] *Antiquities* xiii. 299.   [2] *Antiquities* xiii. 289 ff.

ground for this demand was a rumour that not long before John's birth, in the reign of Antiochus Epiphanes, his mother (the wife of Simon) had been held captive for a time by the king's officials. Under these circumstances John's legitimacy, it was suggested, could not be above suspicion, and as legitimacy of birth was an indispensable qualification for the priestly office,[1] John was urged to relinquish his sacerdotal dignity. There is no reason to suppose that the rumour was well founded. John himself interpreted the whole business as an attempt to undermine his position, and broke with the party to which Eleazar belonged. This marks the emergence of the Pharisaic party[2] as an opposition group to the Hasmonaean dynasty – a position which they retained for half a century. As the Hasmonaeans later became less popular, so the popularity of the Pharisees increased. On the other hand, John received the support of another group in the national senate or Sanhedrin whom we know under the name of the Sadducees. Whatever the origin of the name may be – there is some ground for thinking that it primarily meant members of the council[3] – it came to be explained as derived from the Hebrew word meaning "righteous". For the next fifty years, then, the Sadducees retained control of the Sanhedrin, which served as the council of the rulers of the Hasmonaean dynasty, and lent their support to the dynasty.

John Hyrcanus profited by the successive dynastic quarrels which progressively weakened the Seleucid power to extend his own power. His ambition plainly was to restore the kingdom to the limits which marked it in the great days of the united Israelite monarchy, under David and Solomon. To the south he warred against the Idumaeans, who had been such a thorn in the side of the Judaeans since the dark days at the end of the southern monarchy. He subjugated them, and compelled them to accept circumcision and thus be formally incorporated as members of the Jewish nation. One result of his action was that the members of one Idumaean family were to become a sharper thorn in the side of the Jews than ever they had been before.

In Transjordan John conquered the Greek city of Medeba. To the north of his own realm he took hostile action against the Samaritans. The Jews were now in a position to take more than ample vengeance on them for all the vexatious pin-pricks they had endured at their hands since the return from exile. Shechem was captured, and the hated schismatic shrine on Gerizim was demolished (c. 108 B.C.).

---

[1] This is implied in Lev. 21:7, 13 f. TB *Qiddushin* 66a (*cf.* Josephus, *Antiquities* xiii. 372) puts the incident in the reign of Alexander Jannaeus (103–76 B.C.).

[2] The common interpretation of the word "Pharisee" derives it from Heb. *pārash*, "separate"; *i.e.* they were "separatists" who withdrew from their alliance with the Hasmonaeans. But see a different account in T.W. Manson, *The Servant – Messiah* (1953), pp. 16 ff.

[3] T. W. Manson, *op. cit.*, pp. 12 ff.

The city of Samaria, now a Greek foundation, availed itself of its strong position to resist a siege for long, as it had done against the Aramaeans and Assyrians in the days of the monarchy, but after a year he stormed it and destroyed it, enslaving the population. The Seleucid king Antiochus IX (Cyzicenus), son of Antiochus VII, tried to intervene in defence of Samaria, but desisted when the Romans warned him off. For John had renewed the agreement with Rome made in the time of his father.

Nor did John stop short with the reduction of Samaria, but continued his campaign northwards as far as Scythopolis (the ancient Beth-shan), which he also took.

John's judaization of the Idumaeans could not be repeated with Samaritans. For the Samaritans were circumcised Israelites already, and very conscious of their ancient feud with the Jews. Far from their conquest leading to a rapprochement between the two groups, it embittered the Samaritans still more. John might raze their temple to the ground, but he could not deprive Mount Gerizim of its sacred character, and it continued to be the Samaritans' holy place. For two generations the Samaritans chafed under the Hasmonaean domination, until at last the Roman conquest of Palestine freed them from the Jewish yoke.

ARISTOBULUS I

The work of conquest which John had carried forward so well was continued by his son and successor Aristobulus (104—103 B.C.) who in the course of a short reign of one year overran a good part of Galilee and forcibly judaized some of the Gentile groups living there, as well as the Ituraeans in the foothills of Lebanon. No doubt there were several Israelite enclaves in Galilee, remaining there from the days when the area became an Assyrian province in 732 B.C. They must be distinguished from the *Jewish* colonists in Galilee whom Judas Maccabaeus brought back to Judæa in 163 B.C.[1] It may be that in the post-exilic age these Israelite enclaves had been influenced by Jerusalem in matters of religious belief and practice; at any rate Galilee, after its conquest by the Hasmonaeans, did not feel any such opposition to Judaea as Samaria did, and in fact in the Roman period the Galilaeans tended to be even more zealous Jewish patriots than the Judaeans themselves were. The part which Galilee plays in the gospel narrative gives the conquest and judaization of that region a special interest.

The fact that Aristobulus is commonly known by this Hellenistic name is significant. The dynasty which had risen to power in a patriotic

[1] See pp. 154 f.

reaction against Hellenistic domination tended increasingly to be assimilated to the external and material features of Hellenism, especially on the cruder side, while showing itself the insensate destroyer of all the better elements in Hellenistic culture in the areas which, stage by stage, they brought under their own sway. A further instance of this assimilationist tendency is the fact that Aristobulus was the first member of the Hasmonaean family to take the title "king" (Greek *basileus*) instead of "ethnarch", with which his father and grandfather had been content, and to wear the royal diadem. This was no doubt intended to raise his prestige among his Gentile neighbours; at home he styled himself by his Jewish name Judah, as is shown by the coins of his reign, which bear the Hebrew legend: "Judah the high priest and the commonwealth of the Jews".

Aristobulus, on his accession, threw his step-mother and half-brothers into prison. His fraternal affection was exclusively concentrated on his full brother Antigonus. As a result of a plot against Antigonus, Aristobulus unintentionally gave orders for his death; and this is said to have so preyed upon his mind that it hastened his death (which appears to have been due to phthisis).

ALEXANDER JANNAEUS

Aristobulus's widow bore the double name of Salome[1] Alexandra: like other members of the family, she had a Hellenistic name conjoined with her Jewish name. She is the most outstanding woman in the history of the Hasmonaean dynasty. When her husband died, she released his half-brothers from prison, and gave her hand in marriage to one of them, Alexander Jannaeus, whom she also enabled to take his late brother's place as king and high priest. (As she had borne no children to Aristobulus, her marriage to his brother conformed with Jewish law[2].) The new king and high-priest had the usual combination of Hellenistic and Jewish names; alongside his Hellenistic name Alexander he bore the Jewish name Jannaeus. This is a slightly Hellenized form of Hebrew *Yannai*, an abridged form of Jonathan, the name he bears on his coins. Some of his coins bear the legend "Jonathan the high priest and the commonwealth of the Jews"; others have more simply "King Jonathan" in Hebrew and "King Alexander" in Greek.

A more unlikely character for the high priesthood than Jannaeus could hardly be imagined. The master ambition of his whole reign was military conquest and territorial expansion. While his pursuit of this policy involved him in many reverses, yet on the whole he achieved

---

[1] In a Qumran text her Jewish name appears in the fuller form *Shelom-sion* ("peace of Zion").
[2] For the "levirate" marriage see Deut. 25:5 ff. *Cf.* p. 198.

his ambition to a remarkable degree, but at a ruinous cost to all that was worth while in the spiritual heritage of his people.

Shortly after his accession to power (103 B.C.) he laid siege to the ancient seaport of Ptolemaïs, in the north-west of Palestine. The inhabitants called upon the aid of Ptolemy Lathyrus, a member of the royal house of Egypt, who was at this time ruler of Cyprus. His aid was effective, for Jannaeus was forced to raise the siege and conclude a truce with Lathyrus. But at the same time he plotted against him by entering into an agreement with Lathyrus's mother Cleopatra III (Thea), who had driven her son from the Egyptian throne in order to enjoy supreme power herself, and invited her aid against Lathyrus. When Lathyrus heard of Jannaeus's double dealing, he invaded Jannaeus's domain, inflicted an annihilating defeat on the Jewish army in an engagement on the Jordan, and then swept down the coastal road into Egypt. By this time, however, his mother Cleopatra had mustered the reinforcements she had undertaken to send to Jannaeus's assistance. Her troops repelled Lathyrus's army from Egyptian soil and drove it into Gaza; but they went on and occupied the whole of Jannaeus's realm, and had Cleopatra been so minded, she might have once more incorporated Palestine in the Ptolemaic empire as it had been before 198 B.C. To such straits had Jannaeus's rashness brought his kingdom. Fortunately for him, Cleopatra disregarded those of her advisers who urged her to annex Palestine, and followed the advice of her Jewish commander-in-chief, Ananias, who advised her that it would be better to strike a treaty with Jannaeus. Lathyrus withdrew his army to Cyprus again, Cleopatra's forces returned to Egypt, and Jannaeus's patrimony was under his control once more.

He now turned to Transjordan and reduced two Greek cities in that area – Gadara and Amathus. Then he marched west to the Philistine seaboard and took the cities of Raphia (near the Egyptian frontier), Anthedon, and Gaza. Gaza, as usual, held out for a long time against the besieging army, but was at last reduced in 96 B.C., after a year's resistance, and was completely destroyed. No doubt in his operations in this region Alexander felt that the proximity of his Egyptian ally was a safeguard against intervention from Cyprus or anywhere else.

But his appetite for conquest and destruction was insatiable; he crossed the Jordan once again and tried to conquer the southern part of Transjordan – the territory formerly occupied by the Ammonites and Moabites. Here, however, he ran into fresh trouble. The Nabataean Arabs[1] regarded the territories which Jannaeus was now attacking as part of their sphere of influence. They were already, in fact, suspicious of Jannaeus's intentions, and before the fall of Gaza there had

[1] See p. 130.

been some word of their sending help to the besieged city. They did not send it in time, however, but now that Jannaeus was on their own borders they ambushed his army and practically wiped it out. Jannaeus himself barely escaped with his life and fled home to Jerusalem.

But during the ten years or so which had elapsed since he began to reign, he had thoroughly alienated many of his subjects. While he was a member of a Jewish dynasty, his rule was more oppressive than the rule of many of their Hellenistic overlords had been. The opposition of the Pharisees to the dynasty was hardening, and the Pharisees influenced the bulk of the common people. The first occasion on which something like open rebellion broke out against him, according to Josephus,[1] was once at the Feast of Tabernacles, when as high priest he was officiating in the temple court. As he was about to offer sacrifice, the people began to pelt him with the citrons which they carried as festal tokens, adding insulting words to their action. Alexander sent mercenary troops among them, and 600 were slaughtered. Further light may be thrown on this narrative by a tradition preserved in the Talmud,[2] which tells how an unnamed Sadducee poured out the customary libation of water on the ground and not (as the Pharisees preferred) on the altar, and was pelted with citrons by the people in consequence.

The spectacle of the king posting home to Jerusalem as a fugitive from the Nabataeans suggested to his opponents at home that their opportunity had come. They raised a rebellion against him, and for six years (94—88 B.C.) Jannaeus was compelled to fight against his own subjects with mercenary troops from the Hellenistic territories around: an ironic situation for a scion of the Maccabees! When the insurgents felt their cause weakening, they too called in Hellenistic aid; they invited the Seleucid king, Demetrius III (Eukairos), to help them. With his aid they defeated Alexander in battle near Shechem; his mercenaries were dispersed, and he himself had to seek refuge in the hill country. But this was the turning point in his military fortunes. The sight of a Jewish king driven to wander as a fugitive in the mountains after defeat at the hands of Seleucid forces awakened the patriotism of many of his subjects, including some six thousand of those who had originally rebelled against him. Having repented of their revolt, they put themselves under Alexander's command, and with this new army he expelled the Seleucid forces from his country and reduced the remnants of the rebellion.

Having thus re-established his control over his kingdom, he returned to his capital, taking the leaders of the die-hard rebels with him as captives. There he took a grim revenge. Eight hundred of them were crucified in full view of the royal palace, where the king and his

[1] *Antiquities* xiii. 372 f.   [2] TB *Sukkah* 48b.

concubines feasted their eyes on their torments; and while they were still alive on their crosses, their wives and children were brought out and butchered before their eyes. This terrorism was effective; the remainder of his opponents in Jerusalem and Judaea were so appalled by his actions that eight thousand of them fled to be out of his reach. "Truly an unlovely man", says Dr. Snaith, "though he was High Priest and King. He had no more trouble in the land for the rest of his reign."[1] No more trouble, at least, so far as his own subjects were concerned. The Seleucids and Nabataeans were yet to give him a few more anxious moments. In 86 B.C. the last effective Seleucid king, Antiochus XII (Dionysus), led an army against the Nabataean king Aretas II, and passed through Judaea on his way, in spite of Jannaeus's attempt to bar his way. Aretas, however, defeated and killed the invader, and profited by his victory to extend his own territory as far north as Coelesyria and Damascus. The remainder of the Seleucid kingdom was overrun and annexed by Tigranes, king of Armenia. The Nabataean kingdom thus became the strongest and most menacing power in the neighbourhood of Alexander's realm. Aretas followed up his success against the Seleucids by an attack on Jannaeus; he invaded Judaea and defeated him at Adida, which commanded the road from Jerusalem to Joppa. Jannaeus was compelled to sue for peace, and had to make concessions to persuade Aretas to withdraw from Judaean soil. All this, however, did not deter him from further military adventures, and in the following years he campaigned in Northern Transjordan and reduced several of the Greek cities of the Decapolis – Pella, Dium, Gerasa, Gaulana, Seleucia and Gamala.

In the closing years of his reign he suffered from ill-health which, however, put no check on his military activity. When at last he died in 76 B.C., he had won control of a realm west and east of Jordan practically coterminous with the territory claimed in earlier days by the twelve tribes of Israel. But he had won it at too great a cost. The ideals which lent such glory to the early days of the Hasmonaean rising were trodden underfoot. The spectacle of a high priest who spent most of his time in the congenial pursuit of military expansion was unedifying and a betrayal of Israel's highest traditions. That a Hasmonaean king should use pagan mercenaries against his own Jewish subjects was naturally felt to be monstrous; if later his own subjects enlisted the aid of a Seleucid ruler against Jannaeus, it was after he had set them this bad example. His way of life was modelled on that of the unworthier and cruder Hellenistic princelings of Western

---

[1] N. H. Snaith, *The Jews from Cyrus to Herod* (1949), p.48. This incident is probably referred to in the Nahum commentary found in Cave 4 at Qumran, which interprets Nahum 2:11 f. of "the raging lion, who ... took vengeance on the 'seekers after smooth things' [Pharisees?] by hanging them up alive, which was never done in Israel before" (*cf.* my *Second Thoughts on the Dead Sea Scrolls*[2] [1961], pp. 78 f.).

Asia; how little he cared for the really valuable elements in Greek civilization was shown by the ruthless vandalism displayed in the destruction of the Hellenistic cities which he besieged and took one after another.

SALOME ALEXANDRA

When he died, he bequeathed his kingdom not to one of his sons but to his wife Salome Alexandra, to whom he indeed owed it in the first instance. She was now sixty-four years old, but proved herself an able and prudent ruler for the nine years of her reign. According to Josephus,[1] Jannaeus on his deathbed advised her to come to terms with the Pharisees. Whether he did so or not, she certainly brought the Pharisees into her council and paid careful heed to their advice, so much so that rabbinical tradition pictures her reign as a golden age. Whether tradition is right in representing her as the sister of Simeon ben Shetach, a notable Pharisaic teacher of the period, is uncertain. The Pharisees endeavoured to secure satisfaction for the persecution they had endured under Alexander Jannaeus. In particular, they procured the execution of several of the men who were believed to have influenced Alexander to crucify his eight hundred Jewish captives in 88 B.C. But the Sadducean party, anxious lest their opponents should go too far in their reprisals and wipe out the old aristocracy of Judaea (which was closely bound up with the Sadducees) made representations to the queen, using the good officies of her younger son Aristobulus, and the Pharisees' plans for further vengeance were checked.

In its foreign relations, Judaea was relatively quiet during Alexandra's reign. By diplomatic approaches she was able to stave off a threatened invasion by the Armenian king Tigranes, when he came south to besiege Ptolemaïs in 69. Her younger son Aristobulus led an expedition against Damascus, but it was quite unsuccessful.

HYRCANUS II AND ARISTOBULUS II

Alexandra had borne two sons to Jannaeus – Hyrcanus and Aristobulus. Of these Hyrcanus, the elder, was a quiet and unambitious man, whereas his brother was cast in the same mould as his father and his uncle, Aristobulus I, whose name he bore. When Alexandra assumed the sovereignty by her husband's bequest, she could not (being a woman) succeed him in the high-priesthood, and she appointed her elder son Hyrcanus to this office (perhaps because she knew that with his pacific character he would not exploit his prestige as high priest

[1] *Antiquities* xiii. 401.

to the detriment of his mother's queenly authority). Her younger son Aristobulus she entrusted with a military command.

But Aristobulus, with the support of the Sadducees, waited for an opportunity to gratify his ambitions and emerge from the obscurity in which he chafed while his mother reigned. When she died in 67 B.C. his plans were ready for immediate implementation. The legitimate successor was Hyrcanus, who was already high priest. But Aristobulus gathered an army and advanced against Hyrcanus. In an engagement near Jericho so many of Hyrcanus's followers deserted to Aristobulus that Hyrcanus had to flee for safety to Jerusalem, and there he surrendered to his brother, conceding to him not only the kingly power but the high-priesthood as well, on condition that he might continue to live unmolested as a private citizen in possession of his personal estate.

This arrangement was probably a relief to Hyrcanus, who had no taste for the responsibilities and hazards which high office carried with it. But he was not to enjoy his retirement undisturbed. There was another ambitious man in the country, in whose eyes Hyrcanus appeared as the perfect tool for the achievement of his ambitions. This man was Antipater, an Idumaean by birth, whose father (also called Antipater) had been governor of Idumaea under Alexander Jannaeus and Alexandra. Possibly he himself had succeeded to his father's post. At any rate, Antipater was one of those men who are wise enough in their generation to realize that it is much more important to have the substance of power than its titles. His idea was that Hyrcanus should regain the titles of power in order that he himself, as the power behind Hyrcanus's throne, should enjoy the substance.

Antipater, therefore set himself to win the friendship and confidence of Hyrcanus, and at the same time to build up a party of opinion in Judaea in support of the claims of the rightful heir (despite that heir's personal disinterest) against the "usurper" Aristobulus. He also secured a confederate in Aretas III, the Nabataean king. Then he began to rouse Hyrcanus's apprehension by repeatedly insisting that, in spite of his undertaking to be content with a private life, his brother would not feel safe as long as he was alive. For a time Hyrcanus was disinclined to listen to him, and would not believe that his life was in such danger as Antipater represented. At last, however, Antipater's urgent warnings had their effect, and Hyrcanus was persuaded to leave Jerusalem secretly and accept the hospitality offered by Aretas at his capital, Petra.

Aretas undertook to support Hyrcanus in recovering the throne of Judaea; in return he was to receive twelve cities on the Nabataean border which Alexander Jannaeus had taken. Aretas sent a large army with Hyrcanus and Antipater against Aristobulus, and heavily defeated him. Many of Aristobulus's followers immediately went over to Hyrcanus's side, and Aristobulus had to flee to Jerusalem and fortify himself in the temple area (65 B.C.). There he was besieged by the forces of the other party, and their Nabataean allies.

But the face of Western Asia was at this moment undergoing a swift and radical change, and the control of affairs in Judaea was no longer to rest in Hasmonaean hands.

CHAPTER XXIII

THE ROMAN CONQUEST

(200—37 B.C.)

BY 200 B.C. THE CITY OF ROME HAD NOT ONLY ESTABLISHED ITS supremacy in Italy but had emerged victorious from a life-and-death struggle with Carthage, on the opposite shore of the Mediterranean Sea. With their conquest of Hannibal the Romans were indisputably the leading power in the western Mediterranean. They then imposed their suzerainty over the Macedonian king, who had lent his aid to Hannibal, and assumed the rôle of protectors of the city-states of Greece. When Antiochus III of Syria intervened in the affairs of Greece in 192 B.C., the Romans, as protectors of Greece, made war against him, and defeated him decisively at Magnesia in Asia Minor two years later. Antiochus had to withdraw from western Asia Minor, and the greater part of that territory was added to the kingdom of Pergamum, which was closely allied to Rome. The mounting prestige of Rome is clearly seen in the incident of 168 B.C., when the word of a Roman emissary, Popillius Laenas, was sufficient to turn Antiochus Epiphanes back from his projected assault on Alexandria.[1] It was natural, too, that when Judas Maccabaeus revolted against Antiochus Epiphanes he should enter into diplomatic relations with Rome, as also did his successors Jonathan, Simon and John Hyrcanus.

In 146 B.C. Carthage was finally destroyed by the Romans and the former Carthaginian territory became the Roman province of Africa. In the same year a rising in Greece was crushed by the Romans, who reduced the southern part of the Balkan Peninsula to the status of two Roman provinces – Macedonia in the north and Achaia in the south. Thirteen years later, Attalus III, the last king of Pergamum, died, and bequeathed his kingdom to the Roman senate and people. They decided to accept his bequest, and the realm of the Attalids now received a new status as the Roman province of Asia – the first Roman possession on the continent of Asia.

To the north-east of this province, however, there arose an ambitious monarch whose aim was to found a new empire for himself in Asia Minor and surrounding territories. This was Mithridates VI,

[1] See pp. 141 f.

180

last and greatest ruler of the Arsacid dynasty which had dominated Pontus, in northern Asia Minor, since about 300 B.C. His ambition brought him into collision with the Romans, who not only controlled the province of Asia but were bound by treaty to those neighbours of Mithridates who had most cause to fear his expansionist policy. In 88 B.C. he launched an attack on the Roman administrators and settlers in the province, with general support from the native provincials, who had found the taxation and extortion of the Roman governors intolerably oppressive.

The Romans at once sent armies against Mithridates, but what with the Pontic king's skill and the distractions caused to the Romans by civil war in Rome itself, the war between the two dragged on for twenty-five years.[1] At last, in 66 B.C., the Roman general Pompey was given command of operations against Mithridates, and he drove the king out of Asia Minor in a single campaign. Mithridates fled to the northern shore of the Black Sea and took his own life in 63. Having conquered Mithridates, the Romans were now faced with the necessity of reorganizing the whole political structure of Western Asia. Tigranes, king of Armenia, Mithridates' son-in-law, who had annexed a good part of the former Seleucid territory, submitted to Rome in 66 B.C. and was secured in his own kingdom, and in part of the territory he had conquered in Western Mesopotamia. Pompey sent his lieutenant Scaurus into Syria to settle the affairs of that area, where the last remnant of Seleucid rule had collapsed altogether.

Scaurus, arriving in Damascus, received news of the civil strife raging in Judaea, and made his way there to see if the matter could be exploited in the Roman interest. Both parties sought his favour, offering him large sums of money by way of persuasion. Scaurus decided to support Aristobulus's cause, and ordered Aretas to raise the siege. Aretas knew that he could not afford to disregard a Roman order, and withdrew. Scaurus returned to Syria, and Aristobulus profited by the new situation to pursue Aretas on his homeward march and launch a surprise attack on his army. Six thousand Nabataean troops were killed, according to Josephus,[2] and among them was a brother of Antipater, Phallion by name.

Aristobulus determined to make hay while the sun shone, and to win Pompey's favour as well as that of Scaurus. He sent the great general a golden vine, which was in due course dedicated at Rome in the temple of Jupiter on the Capitoline hill. In 63 B.C., Pompey, having

[1] During those years Mithridates engaged in vigorous anti-Roman propaganda throughout Western Asia (cf. Sallust, History, fragment iv. 69.1–23); echoes of it can be recognized in the portrayal of the "Kittim" in the Qumran commentary on Habakkuk (see Second Thoughts on the Dead Sea Scrolls[2] [1961], pp. 71 ff.).
[2] Antiquities xiv. 33. As so often with Josephus's numbers, the 6,000 can be considerably reduced.

reduced the northern parts of Syria, came to Damascus. There he was waited upon by Aristobulus and Hyrcanus, pleading their rival causes, and also by a deputation from the Jewish people, petitioning him to abolish the Hasmonaean monarchy and restore the old temple-constitution. Pompey listened to these representations, and bade the petitioners be patient until he imposed a settlement. First he intended to send an expedition against the Nabataeans, to teach them the lesson he thought they needed.

Aristobulus, however, whose cause had formerly been favoured, incurred Pompey's suspicion by his behaviour on his return to Judaea. He accompanied Pompey so far on his expedition against the Nabataeans, but left him and fortified himself in the citadel of Alexandrion, in the Jordan valley. Pompey decided to postpone his Nabataean venture and turned back to deal with Aristobulus. Aristobulus was compelled to hand over to Pompey the fortress of Alexandrion, but went to Jerusalem to prepare resistance there. When Pompey arrived outside Jerusalem, Aristobulus thought better of the matter and gave himself up. But Aristobulus's adherents in the city were determined to resist the Romans; Hyrcanus's partisans, on the other hand, viewed the Romans as allies. The latter were able to get control of the city proper, and opened its gates to Pompey's army (April–May). But the resistance party established themselves in the temple area, which occupied a naturally strong position and was separately fortified. Here they held out for three months against the Roman besiegers. At last the Romans succeeded in forcing an entrance from the north side of the temple area, and amid great slaughter the whole area fell into their hands. It is recorded as worthy of special mention that the priests in the temple court went on with their sacrificial duties as though nothing untoward were happening, and were cut down in great numbers. The capture of the temple took place on a sabbath day in July or August (rather than – as Josephus[1] says – on the Day of Atonement, which fell in October).[2]

Pompey visited the captured area and inspected it all thoroughly, even insisting on entering the holy of holies, despite the horrified protestations of the priests, for into this innermost shrine only the high priest might enter, and that only once a year, on the Day of Atonement, bearing the blood of the special sacrifice offered on that day. But the attempts to prevent Pompey from going in made him all the more determined to see what it was they were trying to hide from him; for curious rumours went abroad among the Gentiles about what was kept in the Jewish holy of holies, some of them grotesque, some

[1] *Antiquities* xiv. 66.
[2] See M. B. Dagut, "The Habbakuk Scroll and Pompey's capture of Jerusalem," *Biblica* 32 1951), pp. 542 ff.

of them sinister. When Pompey went in, however, he found exactly nothing. But the enormity of his sacrilege (in Jewish eyes) was not forgotten.

Those responsible for the resistance were severely punished. Judaea was deprived of the Greek cities in the coastal plain, Samaria and Transjordan which had been annexed by the Hasmonaean rulers; her control was also lifted from the Samaritan community of Shechem and its neighbourhood. Thus reduced to a purely Jewish state, Judaea was made tributary to Rome. Hyrcanus was confirmed in the high-priesthood and in the leadership of the nation, but he was not allowed to have the title of king. He was placed under the general supervision of Scaurus, now appointed governor of Syria. Aristobulus and his family, together with many other Jews, were taken to Rome to grace Pompey's triumphal procession in 61 B.C. Many Jews who were taken to Rome as slaves at this time were later emancipated, and formed the main nucleus of the rapidly expanding Jewish colony in Rome.

Roman intervention in Syria would have meant in any case the loss of Judaea's independence. But if the folly of civil strife had not played so completely into Roman hands, she might have retained a much larger measure of autonomy than Pompey allowed her. As it was, the freedom so laboriously won by the earlier Hasmonaeans, and the empire built up by their successors, vanished almost overnight, and the Jews found themselves under the domination of more powerful and ruthless masters than the majority of their Hellenistic overlords had ever been.

Roman rule was not without its benefits to Judaea. It brought a few years of peace after the civil strife between Hyrcanus and Aristo-bulus, and if the people had to pay heavy tribute, at least they were spared the hazards of aggressive campaigns such as those into which Alexander Jannaeus had led them. Nor was it really a bad thing that the Greek cities and other non-Jewish areas which they had conquered should be withdrawn from their control.

Now that Hyrcanus was confirmed in the high priesthood, his sponsor Antipater stood by him and determined to exploit this new situation to his own advantage, and also (it must be admitted) to the advantage of Judaea. From the Roman conquest onwards, it was the settled policy of Antipater and his family to support the Roman power in Western Asia. The individuals who exercised that power might change from time to time, as indeed they did, but Antipater's support was not lent to them as individuals but to the empire which they represented.

Scaurus, governor of Syria, followed up the campaign against the Nabataeans which Pompey had broken off in order to lay siege to

Jerusalem. Antipater seized the opportunity to help him by sending provisions for his army. Then Antipater offered his services as mediator between Aretas and Scaurus, and when Scaurus agreed to withdraw if Aretas paid an indemnity of three hundred talents, Antipater stood surety for the payment of the money.

Hyrcanus's brother Aristobulus II, who graced Pompey's triumph in Rome in 61 B.C., was liberated after the triumph, but had to live in Rome with his family. Both Aristobulus and his two sons, Alexander and Antigonus, caused considerable trouble in Judaea for several years to come. In 57 B.C. one of the two young princes, Alexander, who had escaped when his father and other members of his family were taken to Rome, fomented a rising in Judaea. He gained control of three Hasmonaean citadels west and east of Jordan. But Aulus Gabinius, newly appointed proconsul of Syria, put down the rising and captured Alexander. Alexander's mother pleaded with Gabinius for her son's release, which he granted when the fortresses held by Alexander were yielded up to the Romans.

Gabinius now reorganized the administration of Judaea. Hyrcanus was deprived of all political authority and left with nothing but the high-priesthood. Judaea was divided into five administrative areas, based respectively on Jerusalem, Gazara, Amathus (east of Jordan), Jericho, and Sepphoris (in Galilee). These five areas were placed more directly under the jurisdiction of the governor of Syria.

If the purpose of this reconstruction was to discourage further national risings, it was not achieved. For in the following year (56 B.C.) Aristobulus himself, having escaped from his "free custody" in Rome with his other son Antigonus, arrived in Judaea and tried to raise another revolt. This was immediately put down. Aristobulus fled to the fortress of Machaerus east of Jordan, where he held out for some time. At last he was taken, and sent back to Rome, but his family were given their freedom. Alexander and Antigonus therefore remained in Palestine, and there, undeterred by the failure of the two previous attempts, Alexander staged another revolt in 55. This time he thought he had a favourable opportunity, for Gabinius, instead of carrying out the wishes of the senate in Rome and marching against the Parthians farther east, abandoned his Parthian campaign almost as soon as it was begun in order to help the Egyptian ruler Ptolemy XII (Auletes) to regain his throne, from which he had been driven by a popular revolt. His reversal of plan was due partly to orders received from Pompey (who was at this time in conflict with the senate) and partly to a large bribe offered him by Ptolemy. Gabinius did in fact restore the deposed monarch to his throne, and on this campaign received aid from Hyrcanus and Antipater in the form of grain, money and men. Alexander's attempted rising was quickly put down in an engagement near Mount Tabor. But Gabinius's disobedience to the senate led to his recall and impeachment for treason. He was succeeded as proconsul of Syria in 54 B.C. by Marcus Licinius Crassus. Crassus was at this time one of the three most powerful men in the Roman world. Indeed, it is noteworthy from 63 B.C. onwards how many of the names most eminent in general Roman history figure in the history of Judaea and the neighbouring territories. Syria and Judaea lay on the eastern frontier of Roman power in that area, and not far to the east the powerful Parthian empire was established on the Euphrates. The later Seleucids had come to grips with the Parthians, and and had not come off the better in their encounters. Now the Romans had taken the place of the Seleucids as the imperial power in Western Asia, and they judged it necessary at the outset to teach the Parthians a lesson that would discourage them from any ideas of interfering with the new Roman sphere of influence. Gabinius had not carried out the senatorial policy against the Parthians, but Crassus came determined to take the field against them.

In 56 B.C., Pompey, Crassus and Julius Caesar, who had strengthened their position in the Roman world four years earlier by forming the coalition known as the First Triumvirate, renewed their coalition in the teeth of senatorial opposition, and arranged that Pompey and Crassus should share the consulship, the chief magistracy at Rome, for 55 B.C. (Caesar, who had been proconsul of Gaul since the end of his tenure of the consulship in 59 B.C., had his proconsulship prolonged for five years more.) When their consular year expired, Pompey chose Spain as his proconsular province (but administered it by deputy and stayed in Rome himself), while Crassus chose Syria, and went to that province in hope of winning military glory for himself such as his partners in the triumvirate had already won.

Crassus spent the winter of 54–53 in his province collecting money for a campaign against the Parthians projected for the following year. He made depredations on several temples in Syria, including the Jewish temple at Jerusalem. In 53 he led an army of 35,000 men across the Euphrates, but at Carrhae (the Harran of the Old Testament) his legions were caught at a disadvantage by the Parthian cavalry and archery, and utterly routed. Crassus himself was killed.

The news of his defeat and death was the signal for a fresh revolt in Judaea, led this time by one Pitholaus. But it was quickly put down by the new governor of Syria, a staff-officer of Crassus named Cassius; Pitholaus himself was killed and a large number of his followers were sold into slavery. Cassius also, in 51 B.C., prevented the Parthians from following up the victory of Carrhae and invading Syria.

The death of Crassus had serious consequences for the triumvirate of which he had been a member. Before long the two survivors,

Pompey and Caesar, became increasingly identified with opposing causes in the Roman state. The senate, whose scurvy treatment of Pompey after his return from the east had led him to make common cause with Caesar and Crassus, now found itself obliged to look to Pompey for protection. In 49 B.C. civil war broke out between the two sides. Caesar gained control of Rome and Pompey crossed the Adriatic. Caesar released Aristobulus from custody in order that he might take a lead in anti-Pompeian activity in Syria, where Pompey's party was in power, but before Aristobulus could leave Rome on this mission he was poisoned by Pompey's partisans. About the same time his son Alexander was also put to death at Antioch by orders of Metellus Scipio, proconsul of Syria from 49 to 48 B.C. Metellus was Pompey's father-in-law[1] and acted on Pompey's instructions.

The whole situation was resolved, however, by Caesar's victory over Pompey at the battle of Pharsalus in Thessaly early in 48. Pompey fled to Egypt and cast himself on the hospitality of the young king Ptolemy XIII. But a defeated statesman is sometimes an embarrassing guest, especially when his conqueror is on the way, and Ptolemy's ministers rid themselves and their royal master of the embarrassment by assassinating Pompey as soon as he landed. When the news of Pompey's death reached Judaea, many people there remembered how fifteen years before he had captured the temple area and forced his way into the holy of holies, and they considered his death a condign act of divine judgment, deferred indeed, but none the less sure.

Caesar was now the dominant power in the Roman world. Antipater, whose steadfast policy was to support the representatives of Roman power in the east, soon found an opportunity to win the favour of Caesar as he had previously assisted Pompey's lieutenants.

Caesar followed Pompey to Egypt hoping to take him alive and probably to display his magnanimity towards him. But he arrived too late for this. There were, however, a few matters in Alexandria which claimed his attention; in particular, there was a dispute between the boy-king Ptolemy XIII and his sister-queen Cleopatra which Caesar settled in a manner which aroused the resentment of Ptolemy's ministers. They attacked Caesar and blockaded him and his army of three thousand men in the palace quarter of Alexandria throughout the winter of 48—47 B.C.

Relief to the beleaguered force was organized by a Pergamene named Mithridates, who raised a scratch force to go to Caesar's help, and by Antipater, who organized supplies for Caesar and his men. Thus relieved and reinforced, Caesar fought and won a pitched battle against the followers of Ptolemy XIII. The young king himself was

---

[1] In 60 B.C. Pompey had married Caesar's young daughter Julia; her untimely death in 54 did much to loosen the bonds uniting the two men.

killed; his brother was put on the throne with the title of Ptolemy XIV, but from now on the chief power in Egypt was exercised by his sister Cleopatra, with whom Caesar had established close personal relations.

Caesar now returned to Rome by way of Judaea, Syria and Asia Minor. He rewarded Antipater's timely aid (which had been sent in the name of Hyrcanus) by making him a tax-free Roman citizen with the title of procurator of Judaea. Hyrcanus was confirmed in the high-priesthood and given the title ethnarch of the Jews, despite the plea of Antigonus, the surviving son of Aristobulus, that this twofold dignity belonged by right to himself as the lawful Hasmonaean successor. Hyrcanus was allowed to rebuild the walls of Jerusalem, which Pompey had dismantled, and numerous other concessions were made to the Jews, including a reduction in tribute. Gabinius's constitution imposed on Judaea in 57 was thus superseded by one which allowed the Jews a considerable measure of autonomy.

Antipater now had an established position for himself in the Jewish state. He celebrated it by appointing two of his sons, Phasael and Herod, military prefects of Judaea and Galilee respectively. Galilee was particularly troubled by brigandage, and Herod, who at this time was twenty-five years old, displayed remarkable energy in tackling the problem. But when he captured a brigand chief named Hezekiah and had him executed on the spot, he incurred the enmity of the Sanhedrin in Jerusalem, to whom alone the authority to inflict such a penalty belonged. Herod was summoned to appear before the Sanhedrin and stand his trial for this illegal act. He appeared, attended by a show of force which he hoped would intimidate the Sanhedrin; and Hyrcanus, who as high priest was *ex officio* president of the court, adjourned proceedings indefinitely. The majority of the court seemed bent on condemning Herod, regardless of the consequences, and Hyrcanus knew that the consequences could only involve bloodshed and civil strife.

Herod was therefore able to depart unscathed. He now received a considerable access of power, for the proconsul of Syria, Sextus Caesar, impressed by his energy in Galilee, appointed him also military prefect of Coelesyria.

Sextus Caesar, however, was assassinated in 46 at the instigation of a Pompeian, Caecilius Bassus, who made himself master of Syria with Parthian help. Julius Caesar sent an army to Syria, which drove Bassus into Apamea and besieged him there. But the siege was still going on when the assassination of Caesar himself on the Ides of March in 44 B.C. threw the Roman world into the melting-point again.

The assassination of Caesar led to a fresh outbreak of civil war between the party which followed the leading assassins, Brutus and Cassius, and the partisans of Caesar, led by Caesar's former lieutenant Mark Antony and Caesar's grand-nephew and adopted son Octavian.

Cassius had already been nominated proconsul of Syria by Caesar and he now proceeded thither. He had already had experience of the province as an officer in the ill-fated army of Crassus; it was he, as we have seen, who warded off Parthian encroachment on the Roman territory after the disaster of Carrhae in 53. The rival Roman forces in Syria desisted from their quarrel and joined Cassius.

The death of Caesar was a great blow to the Jews, who had received extraordinary favours at his hand, and no doubt hoped for more. The conduct of Cassius formed a great contrast to Caesar's, for he was bent on raising a huge sum of money to defray the expenses of his impending campaign against Antony and Octavian, and Judaea had to make its contribution. Some cities which did not raise sufficient were treated with exemplary severity; their inhabitants were sold as slaves. But for the present Cassius represented Roman power in the area, and thus Antipater, true to his undeviating policy, supported him, raising seven hundred talents towards his campaign. Cassius was grateful; he renewed Herod's appointment as military prefect of Coelesyria which had previously been conferred by Sextus Caesar.

In 43 Antipater met his death. One Malichus, who aimed at gaining the control of Judaea which Antipater now enjoyed, bribed the butler of Hyrcanus II to poison him as he was dining with Hyrcanus. Herod seized an early opportunity of avenging his father's death.

Next year the rival Roman armies met at Philippi in Macedonia. Victory went to Antony and Octavian, and Brutus and Cassius both committed suicide in the hour of defeat.

After Cassius's departure for the war a state of anarchy broke out in Judaea. The ruler of Tyre grabbed some Galilaean territory. There was a further attempt by Antigonus, the surviving son of Aristobulus, to seize power, but this was thwarted by Herod.

The immediate result of the battle of Philippi was that all the Roman lands in the east came into the control of Antony. The sons of Antipater, who had supported Cassius, had to tread delicately, the more so as more than one deputation from the Jewish aristocracy denounced Phasael and Herod to Antony. But Antony knew well enough that Antipater and his family had not supported Cassius for partisan reasons but because he was for the time being the local representative of Rome. He remembered his friendly relations with Antipater when he had been on Gabinius's staff in Syria fifteen years before, and he knew that he could count on the loyalty of Phasael and Herod, and control Judaea more effectively through them than in any other way. He therefore appointed them joint tetrarchs[1] of Judaea (41 B.C.) – an appointment which terminated Hyrcanus's political authority. But Hyrcanus's political authority had for long been but nominal; the prestige of the high-priesthood was enough for him.

Antony tried to win the favour of the Jews by emancipating those of their number who had been sold into slavery by Cassius and by forcing the Tyrians to hand back the territory they had seized after Cassius's departure. But in fact Antony proved an oppressive over-lord; Judaea, in common with the other eastern provinces which he controlled, had to pay enormous taxes to maintain his extravagant standard of living.

Antony spent the winter of 41–40 B.C. in Egypt as the guest of Cleopatra, under whose spell he had fallen more wholeheartedly than Julius Caesar had ever allowed himself to do. From there he went to Italy and patched up a truce with Octavian, for the rivalry between the two victors of Philippi had reached a point where a fresh outbreak of civil war seemed inevitable.

During his absence Syria was invaded by the Parthians under their king Orodes and his son Pacorus. With the Parthians marched a renegade Roman officer, Labienus, who had gone to the Parthian court as ambassador of Brutus and Cassius, and remained there after their death. Labienus was able to win over most of the Roman troops in Syria. As for Judaea, Antigonus was at last able to wear the crown of his Hasmonaean ancestors, for he had allied himself with Parthia when he saw no hope of receiving satisfaction from Rome. His uncle Hyrcanus was imprisoned and had his ears cropped to prevent him from ever again becoming high priest (such bodily mutilation was a disqualification for the priestly office). Phasael committed suicide in prison; Herod escaped to Rome.

For three years, then (40–37 B.C.) Antigonus governed Judaea as king and high priest. In 39 Ventidius Bassus, whom Antony had sent to take charge of the situation, defeated Labienus and his troops and drove the Parthians from Syria. When they tried to return next year they suffered a crushing defeat at his hands, the crown-prince Pacorus being among the fallen. But Ventidius did not interfere with Antigonus; he left him at peace in Judaea on condition that he paid tribute. Ventidius returned to Rome to receive a triumphal welcome.

But in Rome something else had taken place which was to change the whole complexion of Judaean affairs. Herod arrived there late in the year 40, and met Antony and Octavian. They both recognized the

---

[1] Originally a Macedonian title, denoting a ruler of a fourth part of a kingdom, "tetrarch" was used in Roman times to denote the ruler of any part of a province; it was an inferior title to "ethnarch".

services which Herod could render to the Roman cause in the east if he were restored to a position of power, and by their good offices Herod was declared king of the Jews at a meeting of the Roman senate. A week later he left Rome for the east, in order to recover the kingdom without which his title would be a hollow mockery.

The reconquest of his kingdom was not an easy task, and the Roman forces in the vicinity were none too co-operative at first. He took Joppa and relieved Masada, a fortress on the south-west shore of the Dead Sea, where his family had been living under siege conditions for a year. In 38 he conquered Galilee, and left it in charge of his brother Joseph while he went to have a further interview with Antony, who had now returned to Syria and was at present at Samosata. During his absence his supporters in Galilee were attacked and worsted by Antigonus, and Joseph was killed. Galilee revolted from Herod, and had to be reduced again. Then a defeat inflicted by Herod upon part of the army of Antigonus in Samaria brought all Palestine except Jerusalem under his control. In 37 he proceeded to the siege of Jerusalem, in which he had the support of Sosius, one of Antony's lieutenants, who came with a large army. After a siege and piecemeal reduction of nearly three months the whole city was in Herod's hands and Antigonus was sent to Antony in chains. Herod had much ado to prevent his Roman allies from unrestrained looting and massacre in his newly-won capital. Only when he paid them a large bribe could they be persuaded to depart. Sosius took Antigonus in chains to Antioch, and there Antony, at Herod's desire, ordered him to be beheaded. It was the first occasion, men said, on which the Romans had inflicted capital punishment on a king.

CHAPTER XXIV

THE REIGN OF HEROD

(37—4 B.C.)

FOR THIRTY-THREE YEARS HEROD REIGNED AS KING OF THE JEWS, displaying uncommon political genius throughout. Josephus has preserved for us a detailed account of these years, derived largely from the work of Herod's court historian, Nicolas of Damascus, and in part from other sources less friendly to Herod than Nicolas was.

Herod's kingdom covered all Palestine and a good part of Transjordan. He governed this territory with the official title of *rex socius*; in theory he was an independent king, enjoying an alliance with the Roman state. In fact, he was bound to respect and carry out the will of the Roman people in all his policies; otherwise he might soon have found himself dethroned. But he recognized clearly what the proper course for a ruler in his position was, and he made it his settled policy (as it had been his father's before him) to support whichever party or individual represented Roman power in the Near East at any one time. He did this so faithfully that, when Antony was overthrown by Octavian in 31 B.C., the latter did not penalize Herod for his former support of Antony; Octavian recognized that Herod could be as useful to his interests in those parts as he had been to Antony's. It was greatly to the Roman advantage to control a difficult strategic territory like Judaea indirectly through a loyal allied king; they reaped many benefits from this arrangement, and the inevitable odium attached itself to Herod.

Herod started off with two great disadvantages in his relations with his subjects. He was not of pure Israelite lineage, but a scion of the hated Edomites, although he and his family were Jewish by religion. Secondly, he had attained his power at the expense of the native Hasmonaean dynasty; he had, in fact, made his claim to the Judaean throne effective by the overthrow and execution of a Hasmonaean king. The later Hasmonaeans had been oppressive enough, but now that they had fallen from power, their misrule was largely forgotten and people remembered only that they had won independence for the Jews and ruled them as a native line of kings.

In order to add an air of legitimacy to his kingship, Herod married at the outset of his reign Princess Mariamne, who was a Hasmonaean

191

on both sides, since her father was Alexander, elder son of Aristobulus II, while her mother, Alexandra, was the daughter of Hyrcanus II. Her father had died by poison in 48 B.C., at the outbreak of the civil war between Pompey and Caesar; her mother was very much alive and united with her desire to be revenged on Herod for the despite done to her family a strong ambition for her children which over-reached itself and brought them disaster instead of the eminence at which she aimed.

Before marrying Mariamne, Herod put away his former wife Doris, by whom he had a son called Antipater, after his father. His marriage with Mariamne, however, was not merely a political marriage on his side; he appears to have cherished a passionate affection for her. She, however, cherished a continual resentment against this union with a man of inferior birth who was, moreover, the supplanter of her own family in the royal estate. In due course she bore to Herod two sons, Aristobulus and Alexander, and two daughters, Salampsio and Cypros.

The execution of Antigonus caused a vacancy in the high-priestly office, which Herod filled by appointing to it an obscure priest of the Babylonian Jews named Hananel. But Herod's mother-in-law insisted that her own son Aristobulus was the rightful heir to the high-priest-hood, and Herod yielded to her importunity and deposed Hananel in favour of the seventeen-year-old Aristobulus. Shortly afterwards, Aristobulus was drowned while disporting with some other youths in a swimming-pool. It was widely believed that his drowning was not accidental; that Herod had persuaded the boy's companions, while they were ducking one another playfully in the pool, to hold Aristo-bulus's head under the water just a little too long: and Herod's tears as he attended the funeral of his young brother-in-law did nothing to dispel this popular belief. Hananel was restored to the sacred office which he had so lately vacated, and retained it for six years (36—30 B.C.).

The Aristobulus episode brought international complications with it. For the first six years of his reign Herod had to reckon with the insatiate ambitions of his neighbouring ruler to the south-west, Queen Cleopatra of Egypt, last monarch of the Ptolemaic dynasty. Cleo-patra hoped to regain that control of Palestine which the first rulers of her dynasty had exercised, and anything that could weaken Herod's position was eagerly welcomed by her. Herod's position was rendered the more delicate because of her increasing personal ascendancy over Antony, who continued to be the dominant Roman in the Near East until 31 B.C. And, to complicate matters, Alexandra was in correspond-ence with Cleopatra to Herod's disadvantage; indeed, one account of Herod's alleged murder of the young Aristobulus ascribes his action to his discovery of a plan by Alexandra to escape to Egypt with her

Part of a leather scroll from the Dead Sea caves containing several psalms, the columns shown cover Psalm 119: 128–142, 150–164. Hebrew script of the first century B.C. or A.D. (the Divine Name is written in the older form of script, right column line 10, left lines, 2, 7, 11).
(Photographs, The Shrine of the Book, Hebrew Museum, Jerusalem.)

PLATE X

Fragments of a leather scroll containing the Minor Prophets in a Greek version, c. A.D. 100. Found near the Dead Sea. The influence of Greek culture and language gave rise to more than one rendering of the Hebrew. The portion shown is Zechariah 8:19-9:4, with the Divine Name retained in Old Hebrew script right column, lines 3, 5.

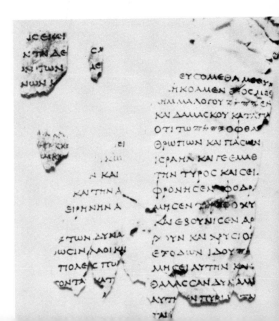

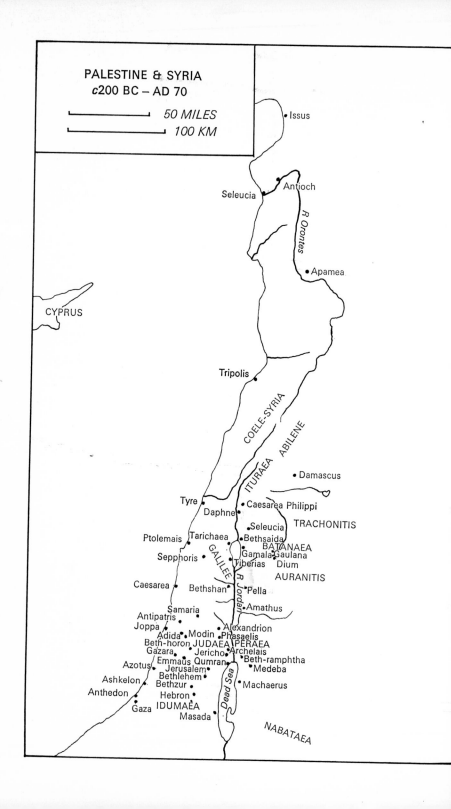

PALESTINE & SYRIA
c200 BC – AD 70

50 MILES
100 KM

Issus

Antioch
Seleucia

R Orontes

Apamea

CYPRUS

Tripolis

COELE-SYRIA

ITURAEA ABILENE

Damascus

Tyre
Daphne
Caesarea Philippi

Seleucia

TRACHONITIS

Ptolemais Tarichaea
Bethsaida
BATANAEA
Sepphoris
Gamala Gaulana
Tiberias Dium

GALILEE

Caesarea
Bethshan
Pella

R Jordan

AURANITIS

Amathus

Samaria
Antipatris
Joppa
Alexandrion
Adida Modin Phasaelis
Beth-horon JUDAEA PERAEA
Gazara Jericho Archelais
Emmaus Qumran
Beth-ramphtha
Azotus
Jerusalem
Medeba
Ashkelon Bethlehem
Bethzur
Machaerus
Anthedon
Hebron
Dead Sea
Gaza IDUMAEA
Masada

NABATAEA

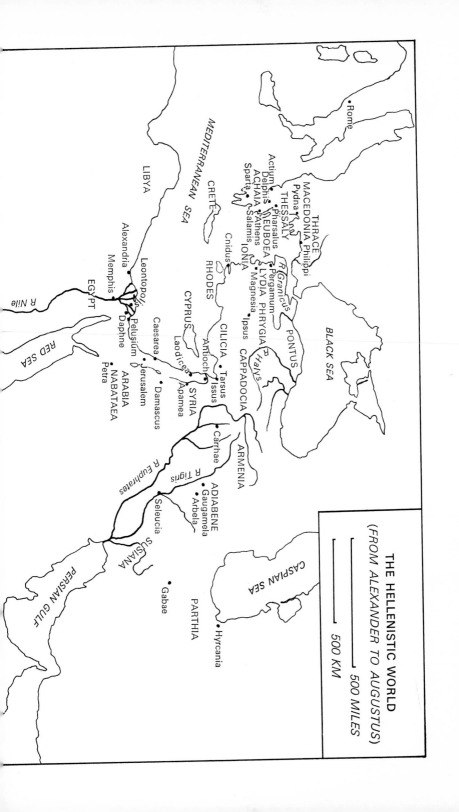

THE HELLENISTIC WORLD
(FROM ALEXANDER TO AUGUSTUS)

500 MILES

500 KM

Rome

MEDITERRANEAN SEA

LIBYA

CRETE

THRACE
MACEDONIA
Philippi
Pydna
THESSALY
Pharsalus
Actium
Delphi
EUBOEA
ACHAIA
Sparta
Athens
Salamis
IONIA
LYDIA PHRYGIA
Magnesia
Pergamum
Cnidus
R Granicus
PONTUS
BLACK SEA
R Halys
Ipsus
CAPPADOCIA

RHODES
CYPRUS
CILICIA
Tarsus
Issus
Antioch
Laodicea
Apamea
SYRIA
Caesarea
Damascus
Jerusalem
Petra
NABATAEA
ARABIA
Alexandria
Memphis
Leontopolis
Pelusium
Daphne
EGYPT
R Nile
RED SEA

Carrhae
ARMENIA
R Euphrates
R Tigris
Seleucia
Arbela
Gaugamela
ADIABENE
SUSIANA
PERSIAN GULF
CASPIAN SEA
PARTHIA
Gabae
Hyrcania

Silver tetradrachm of Antiochus IV; obverse head of Antiochus as Zeus; reverse Zeus seated, inscription 'Of king Antiochus, god manifest (*epiphanes*), bringer of victory.' Actual size. *Cf.* pp. 135, 145.
(Dept. of Coins and Medals, British Museum.)

Copper coin of John Hyrcanus showing two horns of plenty with a pomegranate and inscribed 'Yehohanan the High Priest and the Council of the Jews' in Old Hebrew script. The issue of coins carried great prestige, and was an effective means of propaganda. *Cf.* p. 170.
(Dept. of Coins and Medals, British Museum.)

PLATE XI

Bust of Pompey the Great, 106–48 B.C. Carved *c.* 60 B.C. (Ny Carlsberg Glyptotek, Copenhagen). See p. 181.

Inscribed stone block from the Roman theatre at Caesarea bearing the words 'Tiberieum . . . Pontius Pilatus . . . prefect of Judaea . . .' This is the only monument recovered with Pilate's name and title on it. (Courtesy, Professor Bastiaan van Elderen.)

THE REIGN OF HEROD

son and seek Cleopatra's aid to put him on the throne of Judaea. The idea of ruling Judaea through the young Hasmonaean as her vassal would not be uncongenial to Cleopatra.

When Aristobulus was drowned, Alexandra besought Cleopatra to do what she could to avenge his death, and Cleopatra persuaded Antony to call Herod to account. Herod was summoned to appear before Antony at Laodicea in Syria, but was acquitted of the charge of murder – partly (some said) as a result of lavish bribery, and partly because (as Antony told Cleopatra) "one must not investigate too closely the official acts of a king, lest he ceases to be really a king".[1]

But Herod's return from Laodicea to Jerusalem was followed by fresh trouble. Uncertain of his reception by Antony, he had placed Mariamne in the charge of his uncle Joseph, with strict instructions to put her to death should he himself not return alive. This was a symptom of his jealous love for Mariamne. In his absence, Joseph told Mariamne of her husband's instructions with a view to convincing her of the intensity of his love for her. Naturally, she was not favourably impressed by this way of showing conjugal love, and reproached Herod with it on his return. His suspicious nature immediately concluded that there must have been criminal relations between his uncle and Mariamne, or he would not have divulged this secret to her; Joseph was accordingly executed for his imprudence.

The circumstances of Herod's early days made him naturally suspicious, and his political and domestic circumstances alike fostered this tendency, until it reached the point of madness. Inevitably the reaction which his suspicions provoked in others gave him further grounds for suspicion, and his domestic life especially became increasingly wretched.

Cleopatra was never able to realize her designs against Judaea completely, although she used her influence over Antony to acquire the revenues of some of the richest parts of Herod's kingdom, such as Jericho and its environment. She also did her best to foment strife between Herod and his eastern neighbour, the Nabataean king Malichus, in the hope that they would weaken each other so that she might play the part of *tertia gaudens*.

The civil war between Octavian on the one hand and Antony and Cleopatra on the other, however, put an end to her ambitions and her career. Defeated by Octavian's forces at the sea battle of Actium in Western Greece in 31 B.C., Antony and Cleopatra fled back to Egypt and both committed suicide there the following year to avoid falling into the victor's hands and being compelled to grace his triumphal procession in Rome.

Octavian was now left the undisputed master of the Roman world.

[1] Josephus, *Antiquities* xv. 76.

Herod had to adjust himself to this new turn of events, and did so skilfully. Shortly after Actium, he was summoned to appear before Octavian at Rhodes. This summons he obeyed with some trepidation, as he was well known to have been Antony's friend. But he told Octavian that he was prepared to serve him as loyally as he had hitherto served Antony, and Octavian, realizing the worth of such a proved friend and ally of Rome, confirmed him in his kingdom and sent him back. In the following year, after Antony and Cleopatra's death, he went to Octavian in Egypt, and received from him the territory of Jericho, which Cleopatra had seized; the Greek cities of Hippos, Gadara, Samaria, Gaza, Anthedon, Joppa and Strato's Tower were also added to his realm.

The removal of Cleopatra and the good will of Octavian enabled Herod to breathe more freely in his political life, but there was no improvement in his domestic life. His suspicions led to the execution of the aged Hyrcanus II on the eve of his voyage to Rhodes to meet Octavian after Actium; Hyrcanus was a most unambitious man himself, but so long as he lived, Herod felt, there was the danger that others might use him, former king as he was, as their tool to Herod's disadvantage. Again, lest he should not return alive from his interview with Octavian at Rhodes, he left instructions for the safe keeping and death of Mariamne, and the leakage of these jealous directions led on his return to the immediate death of her guard, Sohaemus. Herod's mother Cypros and his sister Salome did their malicious best to foster his suspicions against Mariamne herself, and the unhappy queen was executed in 29 B.C. In the following year her mother Alexandra was also put to death.

Some years later, when time had softened, although it could never remove, his mad longing for Mariamne, Herod married another lady of the same name, the daughter of a priest named Simon, son of Boëthus. In order that he might not have a commoner as queen, he ennobled the second Mariamne's father by raising him to the high-priesthood, which dignity he enjoyed from 23 to 5 B.C.

Herod pacified the territories on his north-eastern frontier in the interests of Rome, and the grateful emperor added these territories to his kingdom – Trachonitis, Batanaea and Auranitis in 23 and Ituraea in 20 B.C.

He furthered the emperor's cultural policy by his vast building enterprises. Old cities were refounded and new cities were built; temples, hippodromes and amphitheatres were constructed – not only in his own realm but in foreign cities as well, in Athens for example. In his own kingdom he rebuilt Samaria and renamed it Sebaste, after the emperor (*Sebastos* is the Greek equivalent of the Latin *Augustus*, the title by which Octavian was known from 27 B.C. onwards).

He also rebuilt Strato's Tower on the Mediterranean coast and equipped it with a large artificial harbour, calling the new foundation Caesarea, also in the emperor's honour. The work occupied some twelve years, from 22 to 10/9 B.C. Other settlements and strongholds were constructed here and there throughout the land, many of them bearing names in honour of members of his own family, such as Antipatris (on the road from Jerusalem to Caesarea), Cypros (at Jericho), and Phasaelis (west of the Jordan). At Jerusalem he built a royal palace for himself adjoining the western wall (c. 24 B.C.). North-west of the temple area he had already rebuilt the Hasmonaean fortress of Baris and renamed it (after Antony) Antonia. But the greatest of all his building enterprises was the reconstruction of the Jerusalem temple. This grandiose project was begun early in 19 B.C. A thousand Levites were trained as builders, and they carried out their work in such a way that the sacred offices of the holy place were never interrupted while it was going on. The great outer court was enclosed, and surrounded by colonnades; the whole area was beautified with splendid gateways and other architectural structures until the temple became renowned throughout the world for its magnificence:

> far off appearing like a mount
> Of alabaster, topped with golden spires.

The main work of reconstruction was completed within Herod's lifetime, but the finishing touches were not put to it until A.D. 63, only seven years before its destruction.

Other forms of culture were patronized at Herod's court; among these historiography is outstanding, for Herod's court chronicler, Nicolas of Damascus, wrote a *Universal History* in 144 books. This work included a detailed record of Herod's career, which Josephus used as a principal source for this part of his history.

But even the trouble which Herod took to ingratiate himself with his subjects by his expenditure on the temple did not win their good will. His Edomite ancestry was never forgotten; if he was a Jew by religion and patronized the Jewish religion at Jerusalem, that did not deter him from patronizing paganism in other cities by the buildings which he erected there; his wiping out of the Hasmonaean family could not be forgiven.

Nor did his family trouble come to an end with the death of his Hasmonaean wife and her relatives. There was friction between his several wives, between them and his own blood-relations (especially his sister Salome), and between their respective families. His two sons by the first Mariamne, Alexander and Aristobulus, were his designated heirs. As descendants to the Hasmonaeans, through their mother Mariamne, they were acceptable to the people in general.

As befitted their rank and expectations, they received a special education, much of it in Rome. When they came of marriageable age, Aristobulus married Berenice, daughter of Herod's sister Salome, and Alexander married Glaphyra, daughter of King Archelaus of Cappadocia.

These two brother were tempted to consider themselves a cut above their half-brothers, Herod's sons by other wives, and gave themselves airs. This naturally did not commend them in the eyes of their step-mothers and half-brothers, who were in any case disposed to resent their privileged position. But their bitterest enemy was Antipater, Herod's firstborn, son of his original wife Doris. Antipater believed that he ought to be his father's heir, and thought that if the two sons of Mariamne could be got out of the way, his ambition might be fulfilled. He set himself therefore to poison their father's mind against them, making him believe that they were plotting against his life in order to gain his royal power. And, of course, it was conceivable, especially to Herod's guilty and suspicious conscience, that they did intend to take vengeance in this way for their mother's death. The first time that dissension broke out between them and their father, through Antipater's machinations, a reconciliation was effected by the emperor, and they were formally restored to their father's favour. But Antipater set to work again, and at last they were put on trial before their father for conspiracy and treason, and sentenced to death. The emperor's ratification of the death sentence was sought and obtained. It was perhaps on this occasion that Augustus remarked, with a play on two similarly-sounding Greek words, and a jesting allusion to the Jewish aversion from pork, that it was safer to be Herod's pig than his son.[1]

Antipater derived little advantage from the success of his scheming. Three years later he himself fell a victim to his father's suspicion in the same way, and was executed by Herod's order only a few days before Herod's own death (4 B.C.).

[1] A play on Gk. *hys*, "pig", and *hyios*, "son".

CHAPTER XXV

THE SONS OF HEROD AND THE
EARLY PROCURATORS

(4 B.C.—A.D. 37)

HEROD LEFT A WILL IN WHICH HE DIVIDED HIS KINGDOM BETWEEN three of his sons – Archelaus and Antipas, the sons of his Samaritan wife Malthace, and Philip, his son by one Cleopatra of Jerusalem – and bequeathed to his sister Salome the revenues of three wealthy cities of his realm.

The most important part of his kingdom, Judaea, fell to Archelaus, who was faced immediately with the task of crushing a riot in the temple courts of Jerusalem. Having put down the riot, he set out for Rome, in order to secure the emperor's ratification of his father's will – for as Herod had in practice ruled by grace of Augustus for the past twenty-seven years, his sons could enter into their heritage only by the same grace.

But ambassadors from the Jews of Judaea also arrived in Rome to urge that Archelaus be not appointed to succeed his father, but that rather Judaea should enjoy its former temple-constitution and internal autonomy under a governor appointed by the emperor.[1]

Archelaus, however, found an advocate in Nicolas of Damascus, and the emperor disregarded the pleas of the Jewish delegates. Archelaus was confirmed as ruler of Judaea (with Samaria), and his brothers Antipas and Philip, who had also come to Rome to press their claims, received their respective shares of the inheritance – Antipas receiving Galilee and Peraea (southern Transjordan) and Philip receiving the territory north-east of the Sea of Galilee. None of them, however, received the royal title; Archelaus was nominated ethnarch, and Antipas and Philip had to be content with the minor title of tetrarch.

Salome received the revenues of Jamnia, Azotus and Phasaelis, with a castle at Ashkelon and a legacy of half a million shekels.[2]

---

[1] In this situation some have seen the background of the Parable of the Pounds in Luke 19:11 ff., where a nobleman, who goes into a far country to receive for himself a kingdom and to return, incurs the hatred of his subjects, who send a delegation after him refusing to have him as their king.

[2] When she died in A.D. 10 she bequeathed her property to Livia, the wife of Augustus.

During the brothers' absence in Rome, further riots and risings broke out in Palestine. Herod's death, in fact, was the signal for innumerable disorders throughout his kingdom. One of these centred on Sepphoris in Galilee, where Judas, son of that brigand-chief Hezekiah whom Herod had executed forty-five years before, seized the arsenal and armed his followers. So serious were these risings that Quintilius Varus, imperial legate of Syria, intervened to put them down, and he made a stern example of the leaders, two thousand of whom were crucified alongside the roads, in order to warn the population that revolts in Rome's sphere of influence would not be tolerated.

ARCHELAUS

Archelaus – designated Herod the Ethnarch on his coins – has the worst reputation of all the sons of Herod. He had all his father's vices with none of the compensating qualities of competent statesmanship.

He continued his father's policy of appointing and deposing high priests at will: during his brief rule of nine years (4 B.C.—A.D. 6) he appointed three – Eleazar son Boëthus (4—3 B.C.), Jesus son of Seë (3 B.C.—A.D. 6) and Joazar son of Boëthus (A.D. 6).

He gave offence to the religious susceptibilities of his subjects by marrying Glaphyra, a Cappadocian princess, who had formerly been the wife of his brother Alexander (executed in 7 B.C.). The ancient Israelite institution of the levirate marriage[1] allowed such a marriage only where the deceased brother had left no children, but as Glaphyra had borne children to Alexander, this institution could not be invoked in the present instance.

Archelaus continued his father's building policy: he restored the palace at Jericho, which had been damaged in a rising soon after Herod's death; he built an aqueduct to water the palm-groves north of Jericho; he founded a city some six miles north of Jericho, which he called Archelaïs, after himself.

But his severity led to further protests; at last a deputation of the Samaritan and Jewish aristocracy went to Rome to lodge complaints against him before Augustus, and to warn the emperor that Archelaus's continued rule in Judaea would certainly cause a full-scale revolt. Augustus summoned Archelaus to his presence, and banished him to Vienne, in the Rhone valley. He had no desire to maintain a petty ruler in office when his subjects were so disaffected. Henceforth Judaea (with Samaria) was to have the status of a third-class province of the Roman Empire, governed by a procurator appointed by the emperor.

[1] See p. 173.

THE EARLY PROCURATORS

The procurators of Judaea were usually drawn from the equestrian order – the second rank of Roman society – and were subject to the general supervision of the legates of Syria. But it was only under exceptional circumstances that the legate intervened in the affairs of Judaea. In practice the procurators held independent military and political command.

Their official residence was at Caesarea, where Herod's palace served as their praetorium or official headquarters. Only occasionally did they reside at Jerusalem – for example, during the great pilgrimage-festivals of the Jewish year, when extraordinary precautions were necessary for the maintenance of public order.[1]

Now that Judaea was to be a Roman province, its tribute was payable directly to Rome. It was necessary, therefore, that its yield of tribute should be officially assessed, and for this purpose a census was held in A.D. 6, under the supervision of Quirinius, the legate of Syria. The idea of paying tribute directly to a heathen ruler was offensive to many pious Jews, and two bolder spirits, Judas and Sadduq, led a revolt against Rome. This Judas – variously called Judas of Gamala (in Transjordan) and Judas the Galilaean – is mentioned in the speech of Gamaliel reported in Acts 5:37, as having led a rising "in the days of the enrolment". He and Sadduq contended that God alone was Israel's true king, and that to Him alone (through His approved representatives in Israel) should tribute be paid.

The rising was suppressed, but its ideals were perpetuated in the party of the Zealots, which kept the spirit of revolt against Rome alive throughout the next two generations, until the banked-up fires blazed out at last in the rebellion of A.D. 66. The name Zealots which they took was probably intended to place them in the tradition of Phinehas in the early days of Israel's history[2] and of Mattathiah and his sons in more recent times,[3] all of whom displayed zeal for the honour of God's name in Israel.

When the census had been completed and the provincial tribute assessed, the first procurator, Coponius, arrived to take up office. Between A.D. 6 and his death eight years later, Augustus appointed three successive procurators of Judaea – Coponius (A.D. 6—9), Marcus Ambivius (A.D. 9—12) and Annius Rufus (A.D. 12—15). His successor Tiberius, on the other hand, during his reign of twenty-three years (A.D. 14—37) appointed two only – Valerius Gratus (A.D. 15—26) and Pontius Pilate (A.D. 26—36). This was in keeping with Tiberius's

---

[1] Hence Pilate was in residence at Jerusalem at the time of the arrest, trial and execution of Jesus, because it was Passovertide.
[2] Num. 25:7-13; Ps. 106:30 f. [3] I Macc. 2:24-28.

policy of leaving provincial governors in office for a considerably longer time than Augustus had done.

When he was asked on one occasion why he acted thus in view of the notorious rapacity of provincial governors, Tiberius replied by telling the story of a wounded man who lay by the roadside, covered with blood-sucking insects. A kindly passer-by began to brush away the insects, when the wounded man stopped him. "Leave them alone", he said; "these flies have already sated themselves with my blood and are causing me no more annoyance. But if you drive them away a new lot of hungry flies will take their place and begin to suck my blood all over again."[1]

One of the ways in which the early procurators of Judaea enriched themselves was by the appointment and deposition of high priests. When Quirinius organized the new province of Judaea in A.D. 6, he deposed Archelaus's last nominee, Joazar the son of Boëthus, from the high-priesthood, and replaced him by Annas the son of Seth (who figures in the passion narrative of the Fourth Gospel[2]). Annas occupied the office for nine years, but when Valerius Gratus became procurator in A.D. 15 he set him aside in favour of Ishmael son of Phabi. Valerius, in fact, appointed four high priests during his procuratorship; Ishmael was followed in quick succession by Eleazar (a son of Annas), Simon son of Kami, and then by Joseph Caiaphas (son-in-law to Annas). The last-named, best known today for the leading part he took in the trial and condemnation of Jesus, held the high-priesthood for eighteen years (A.D. 18—36); no other Jewish high priest retained office for so long after the death of Herod's father-in-law, Simon son of Boëthus, in 5 B.C. The fact that Caiaphas was not deposed by Pilate when he became procurator in A.D. 26, but continued to hold office throughout Pilate's governorship, suggests that it was more profitable for Pilate to confirm him in office than to replace him by another. When Pilate was removed from office in A.D. 36, Caiaphas was removed from the high-priesthood by Vitellius, imperial legate of Syria, who replaced him by two sons of Annas – first Jonathan, and then, a year later, Theophilus. In these circumstances it is clear why only a few very wealthy priestly families, such as those of Annas and Boëthus, could afford to buy and retain the sacred office. It is not surprising that the high-priesthood no longer commanded popular respect.

Of the early procurators of Judaea, the one of whom we know most is Pontius Pilate. This is not only due to the part he plays in the New Testament narrative, as the judge who tried Jesus and sentenced Him to death by crucifixion, but to the fairly full account of his ten years' governorship which Josephus has given us in the eighteenth book of his *Jewish Antiquities*. Philo, the Jewish philosopher

---

[1] Josephus, *Antiquities* xviii. 174 f.   [2] John 18:13, 24: *cf.* Luke 3:2; Acts 4:6.

of Alexandria, has also left us a description of Pilate as "inflexible of nature, stubborn and harsh."[1] But it may be accounted one of the ironies of history that the only pagan writer to mention him (the Roman historian Tacitus) merely names him as the judge who sentenced Christ to death.[2]

Whether intentionally or not, Pilate consistently offended Jewish public opinion. Early in his governorship he attempted to bring military standards, bearing the emperor's image at their crossbar, into Jerusalem, although, out of consideration for Jewish objections to such images (in the light of the Second Commandment), imperial policy had ordained their removal from the standards before entering the holy city. Pilate's attempt to disregard this concession almost precipitated a revolt, and he was forced, with a very ill grace, to yield to the Jews' insistence that the images be removed.

Similar offence was caused when he fixed golden votive shields, bearing the emperor's name, to the walls of Herod's palace in Jerusalem. These shields, having been dedicated to a pagan deity, were obnoxious to Jewish sentiment, and a Jewish deputation waited on Tiberius and assured him that Pilate's placing of them there was due not to reverence for the emperor but to his desire to annoy the Jews. The emperor ordered the shields to be taken down.

Pilate's great service to Jerusalem was the construction of an aqueduct from the southern highlands to augment the city's water-supply. But this very benefit led to further trouble between the procurator and the Jewish authorities. No institution in Jerusalem benefited so much from the new water-supply as the Temple did, and Pilate probably thought himself quite justified in demanding that the temple treasury should make a contribution to the expense of building the aqueduct. But the priests and people were horrified at the suggestion. The temple treasury was a sacred fund, which (they held) should not be used for such a secular purpose as defraying the cost of an aqueduct. Pilate insisted; but his insistence came within a hairbreadth of touching off another riot.

St. Luke's Gospel contains a reference to some Galilaeans "whose blood Pilate mingled with their sacrifices".[3] We have no other certain reference to this incident, but presumably these were pilgrims who had come to Jerusalem to attend one of the great festivals, and were involved in the temple court in a riot which was suppressed by Roman soldiers from the neighbouring fortress of Antonia. In the same context of Luke we have a cryptic reference to eighteen men on whom the tower of Siloam fell.[4] Perhaps a group of rioters had

---

[1] In his report of a letter written to the Emperor Gaius by Herod Agrippa I (Philo, *Embassy to Gaius*, 301).
[2] Tacitus, *Annals* xv. 44.   [3] Luke 13:1.   [4] Luke 13:4.

installed themselves in this tower in the south-east of Jerusalem which was undermined and overthrown upon its defenders.

Pilate was recalled to Rome in A.D. 36 in consequence of a hasty action taken against a crowd of Samaritan pilgrims. The sacred vessels of the Mosaic tabernacle were believed by the Samaritans to have been buried on Mount Gerizim ever since the Israelite settlement in the land. A self-styled prophet announced that on a given day he would locate and exhibit these vessels. A large crowd converged on the holy hill, and Pilate, suspecting a seditious intention, sent a detachment of troops against them. They were dispersed with great loss of life. The Samaritan leaders sent a complaint to Vitellius, legate of Syria, who ordered Pilate to go to Rome and answer for himself there before Tiberius. About the time of his arrival in Rome, however, Tiberius died (March, A.D. 37), and Pilate was replaced by a new procurator.

Tiberius was succeeded on the imperial throne by his grand-nephew Gaius (better known by his nickname Caligula), whose brief reign of four years was of considerable importance in its effect on Jewish affairs. But before we consider the events of his reign we must go back and outline the fortunes of the remaining heirs of Herod the Great.

PHILIP THE TETRARCH

Philip, "tetrarch of the Ituraean and Trachonitid regions",[1] governed those territories north-east of the Lake of Galilee which had been pacified by his father in the years 23—20 B.C. He was a milder character than either his father or brothers. Panion, the capital of his tetrarchy,[2] he rebuilt and named Caesarea in honour of the Emperor: it was called Caesarea Philippi (i.e. Philip's Caesarea) to distinguish it from other cities of the same name (especially his father's foundation of Caesarea on the Mediterranean coast of Judaea). According to Josephus, he traced the subterranean course of the Jordan between this city and Phiale. He also rebuilt Bethsaida ("Fishertown") on the shore of the Lake and called it Bethsaida Julias, in honour of Julia, the daughter of Augustus.

He married Salome, daughter of his brother Herod Philip by Herodias.[3] (Herodias herself was the daughter of Aristobulus, one of Herod's two sons by Mariamne: marriages between uncle and niece were remarkably common in the Herod family.)

Philip stamped the likeness of Augustus – and later of Tiberius – on the coins of his principality. He was the first Jewish ruler to do such a thing, but his subjects were largely of Gentile stock and would have no objection to a practice which Jews would have resented.

Philip had the reputation of a moderate and lenient ruler. He rarely left his tetrarchy, and made the administration of justice within

[1] Luke 3:1.   [2] See p. 127.   [3] See p. 203.

its frontiers his personal responsibility. According to Josephus, when he visited the various parts of his territory, he took his judgment-seat with him, and judged on the spot any cases that were submitted to him, pronouncing sentence of acquittal or condemnation promptly, so that none could complain that justice was delayed.[1]

When he died in A.D. 34, his tetrarchy was added to the province of Syria; but three years later, when Gaius became emperor, it was given to another member of the Herod family.

HEROD ANTIPAS

Antipas – "Herod the tetrarch" of the Gospels – ruled Galilee and Peraea for over forty years. Readers of the New Testament remember him chiefly as the ruler who imprisoned and executed John the Baptist. Luke reports Jesus' reference to him as "that fox" and describes Jesus' brief appearance before him in Jerusalem in A.D. 30 which led to the restoration of friendly relations between Antipas and Pilate.[2]

Antipas was the ablest of Herod's sons. Like his father he was a great builder: Tiberias, on the Lake of Galilee, was built by him in A.D. 22 and named in honour of the Emperor Tiberius. He rebuilt and fortified Sepphoris in Galilee (it had been destroyed by Varus when he crushed the rising of Judas the son of Hezekiah in 4 B.C.); in his Transjordanian territory of Peraea he strengthened Beth-ramphtha to defend the area against the Nabataean Arabs, and called it first Livias (after the Empress Livia), and later Julias (after the Princess Julia).

His wife was the daughter of the Nabataean king Aretas IV (9 B.C.– A.D. 40). He divorced her, however, in order to marry Herodias, who was not only the daughter of his late half-brother Aristobulus but also the wife of another half-brother, Herod (sometimes referred to as Herod Philip[3]). He fell in love with Herodias on one occasion when he was lodging with her and her husband, and arranged to marry her as soon as he could make the necessary arrangements for putting away Aretas's daughter. The Evangelists tell how John the Baptist denounced the marriage of Antipas and Herodias as unlawful.[4] But John was not the only person to disapprove of these doings; King Aretas, very naturally, took offence at the insult offered to his daughter, and some years later he seized an opportunity to declare war on Antipas, and inflicted a heavy defeat on him (A.D. 36). Josephus says that many of the subjects of Antipas believed that this disaster befell him as a divine retribution for his behaviour towards John the Baptist.

---

[1] Josephus, *Antiquities* xviii. 107.   [2] Luke 23:7 ff.
[3] Called "Philip" in Mark 6:17 (cf. Matt. 14:3); this son of Herod was a private citizen and is not to be confused with Philip the tetrarch. See p. 202.
[4] Matt. 14:4; Mark 6:18; Luke 3:19. There may also be a reference to Herodias in Jesus' ruling in Mark 10:12, that if a man's wife "divorces her husband and marries another, she commits adultery."

CHAPTER XXVI

HEROD AGRIPPA AND THE JEWS

(A.D. 37—44)

AMONG THE CHILDREN OF ARISTOBULUS, ILL-FATED SON OF HEROD the Great and Mariamne, who was executed at his father's instance in 7 B.C., was one called Agrippa, probably because of Aristobulus's friendship with the Roman statesman of that name. At the time of his father's execution Agrippa was four years old. He was sent to Rome with his mother Berenice, and was brought up in close and friendly contact with the imperial family. But he became so heavily involved in debt that in A.D. 23 he had to retire to Idumaea. Through the influence of his sister Herodias, however, who had lately come to live with his uncle Antipas as his wife, Agrippa received a home and a pension at Tiberias. But he quarrelled with his uncle, and at last, in 36, was able to return to Rome. Soon after his return he offended the Emperor Tiberius, and was imprisoned.

But the death of Tiberius in the spring of 37 marked a reversal of Agrippa's fortunes, for he enjoyed the friendliest relations with Gaius, who succeeded Tiberius as emperor. Gaius released him from prison immediately, and recompensed him with a chain of gold equal in weight to the chain of iron with which he had been fettered. But that was but a drop in the bucket compared with the further favours which the new emperor showered upon Agrippa. He gave him the territory over which his uncle Philip had ruled as tetrarch until his death three years previously, and the territory of Abilene to the north of that, which had formerly been the tetrarchy of Lysanias.[1] With these territories he gave him the title of king.

Herodias, his sister, now urged her husband Antipas to ask Gaius to raise his title from tetrarch to king. For over forty years Antipas had ruled Galilee and Peraea and had incurred the ill-will of many of his neighbours by acting as the emperor's faithful spy and informer in that part of the world. It would be but a small requital for long and thankless services rendered to Rome if he were now, at the end of his days, to receive the royal style. If Gaius had so readily bestowed

[1] Cf. Luke 3:1.

it on his spendthrift boon-companion Agrippa, surely he would recognize Antipas's more solid claims to equal honour.

So Herodias argued, but Antipas was inclined to leave well alone. However, at her insistence, he set out for Rome to make his request, and it proved to be his undoing. Instead of receiving what he asked for, he lost the position he already enjoyed. For Agrippa satisfied his grudge against Antipas by poisoning the emperor's mind against him. He suggested that Antipas was conspiring with the Parthians against Rome, and pointed out that his arsenal at Tiberias contained armour enough to equip 70,000 men. Antipas was accordingly deposed and sent into exile. The emperor offered to treat Herodias as the sister of his friend Agrippa and not as the wife of his enemy Antipas, and gave her permission to live on a private estate of her own; but she chose rather to accompany her husband into exile. The regions of Galilee and Peraea, which Antipas had ruled so long, were now added to Agrippa's kingdom (A.D. 39).

Agrippa played an important part in imperial policy towards the Jews during the reign of Gaius. When he was on his way from Rome to his kingdom in Palestine in A.D. 38, he paid a visit to Alexandria in Egypt at a time of high tension between the Greek and Jewish inhabitants of that city.

Under the Ptolemies there had been little trouble between the Greek and Jewish inhabitants of Alexandria. The Jewish inhabitants flourished until they occupied two out of the five wards of the city.[1] They constituted a corporation within the city, enjoying a large measure of autonomy, and governed by a Jewish ethnarch.

In the closing years of the Ptolemaic dynasty, the Alexandrian Jews, partly influenced by the example of Antipater and Herod in Judaea, favoured the Romans. They supported Julius Caesar in 47 B.C., and later they supported Octavian (Augustus) against Cleopatra and Antony. Julius Caesar granted them many privileges, and these were confirmed by Augustus. In 30 B.C. Augustus arranged through the Roman prefect of Egypt that responsibility for Jewish affairs in Alexandria should be entrusted to an elected senate, consisting (like the Jerusalem Sanhedrin) of seventy-one men. This senate was to be independent of the civic administration of Alexandria.

The Alexandrian Greeks resented this exceptional favour shown to the Jews; they resented also the contemptuous attitude with which they themselves were regarded by the Romans. "We used to hear about Alexandria", said Cicero in 63 B.C.; "now we are getting to know it. That is the place where all the juggling tricks, all the frauds

---

1 Philo (*Flaccus* 6, 8) estimated that in A.D. 38 there were a million Jews in Egypt; even if we make a substantial deduction from this estimate, their numbers were certainly very considerable.

in the world, come from ..."[1] It was inevitable that this resentment should find violent expression when the opportunity offered. Such an opportunity offered when Gaius became emperor in A.D. 37.

The Roman prefect of Egypt at the time of Gaius's accession was a man called Flaccus, who had taken part some time previously in an attack on Gaius's mother Agrippina. He was naturally afraid of Gaius's vengeance. The Alexandrian Greeks were well aware of this, and they approached Flaccus, promising to send favourable reports of his administration to Rome if he would take their part against the Jews of Alexandria (who at this time had been making a bid for full status as Alexandrian citizens). Flaccus agreed, and embarked little by little on an anti-Jewish policy, discriminating against Jews in the law-courts and so forth. He also neglected to transmit to the emperor the loyal address which the Alexandrian Jews had drawn up to congratulate him on his accession.

It was at this juncture that Herod Agrippa broke his journey at Alexandria. The Jews of the city greeted his visit as a godsend. They begged him to make a public procession through the city with his bodyguard. This, they hoped, would impress the Alexandrians, who already knew of the close friendship between the emperor and the Jewish king. Agrippa unwisely acceded to their request. The Alexandrian populace reacted by getting up a counter-parade, in which a local idiot named Carabas ("Cabbage") was dressed in royal robes, with mock crown and sceptre. They paid their homage to this poor fellow in the public gymnasium, hailing him with cries of *mari* (Aramaic for "my lord").

The civic leaders were horrified at what the mob had done. They knew that Agrippa would not forgive this insulting parody of his royal dignity, and that he would use his influence with Gaius to have it avenged. They therefore took hasty action with a view to putting the Jews in the wrong in Gaius's eyes. Gaius was known to take his divinity very seriously. The civic leaders, therefore, with Flaccus's connivance, decided to place portraits of the emperor in the local synagogues. They knew that the Jewish authorities would immediately remove them, and their intention was to represent their removal as a mark of disloyalty to the emperor – this in spite of the fact that respect for the Jews' objections to "images" had always marked Roman policy towards them.

The plan was set afoot; at the same time, the prefect passed an edict providing that Jewish privileges in Alexandria should be strictly confined to the letter of the existing law. A long time previously, for example, the Alexandrian Jews had been granted as a privilege the right of residence in one of the city wards. Therefore, although their numbers

[1] *Pro Rabirio Postumo*, 35.

were now much greater, it was ruled they they must all reside within that one ward. Those who lived in other wards were evicted; their houses and shops were plundered; their synagogues were destroyed. Many had to take refuge outside the city.

But the anti-Jewish passion of the city mob, thus enflamed, could not be held in check. Acts of violence multiplied until, on the emperor's birthday, thirty-eight members of the Alexandrian Jewish senate were publicly flogged in the theatre; other anti-Jewish spectacles were enacted in the same place for the delectation of the populace. The civic leaders were dismayed by the excesses to which their policy had given rise, and they hastened to Rome to exculpate themselves, laying all the blame on the wretched Flaccus. Flaccus was found guilty of treason, sentenced to confiscation and banishment, and soon afterwards executed.

With his arrest (which took place on the Day of Atonement in A.D. 38, a significant coincidence in Jewish eyes) order was restored for the time being, and some alleviation of the plight of the Alexandrian Jews was granted. But they did not recover the full enjoyment of the privileges which had been theirs before the riots. A delegation of five leading Jews of the city, headed by the philosopher Philo, went to Rome in the following year to petition Gaius for the full restoration of their former privileges. Gaius, however, gave them no satisfaction. He found fault with them for failing to recognize his divinity, saying that it was all very well to offer sacrifices for him (as was done daily in the Jerusalem temple), but he expected his subjects to offer sacrifices to him.

This subject was specially present to the emperor's mind just then, because of a crisis which was beginning to develop in Judaea. At Jamnia, in western Judaea, the Gentile population set up an altar in the emperor's honour; the Jewish inhabitants of the town pulled it down. When Gaius heard of this, he retaliated by ordering that his statue should be erected in the temple at Jerusalem. He knew that the Jews would resist this order fiercely, so he commanded Petronius, the governor of Syria, to march to Jerusalem with two legions to enforce the order.

Consternation broke out in Judaea and throughout the Jewish world; this was Antiochus Epiphanes and "the abomination of desolation" all over again. Petronius marched south, but when he arrived at Ptolemaïs he was met by deputations of Jews who besieged him and protested that the whole nation would die as one man sooner than tolerate this outrage. Petronius, however, told them that he had no option; his duty was to execute the imperial decree.

At this critical moment Jewish Christians in Palestine called to mind some words of their Master which seemed to bear directly on this situation. Speaking of troubles in days to come which would lead up to the destruction of the Jerusalem temple and the desolation of the city, Jesus warned His disciples to flee from Judaea when they saw "the abomination of desolation standing where he ought not to be".[1] It is quite likely that this warning, together with other sayings of Jesus to the same effect, was committed to writing at this time and circulated as a broadsheet among the faithful.

In the event, it turned out that this crisis was not the fulfilment of these words of Jesus; the danger was averted. Thirty more years were to pass before the desolation overwhelmed the city and temple. But the crisis left a deep mark on the thought of the early church, and the broadsheet circulated at that time provided a form of words which we can trace in Christian writings later in the century – in the book of Revelation for example, and also in the Pauline correspondence. For example, in his second letter to the Thessalonians (written in A.D. 50), Paul tells his readers that the second advent of Christ will be preceded by a widespread revolt against the divine government, when "the man of lawlessness is revealed, the son of perdition who opposes and exalts himself against every so-called god or object of worship, going so far as to take his seat in the temple of God, proclaiming himself to be God".[2] He reminds them that he told them this when he was with them a few months before. And there is a clear connexion between his picture of lawlessness incarnate enthroned in the temple of God and the earlier reference to "the abomination of desolation standing where he ought not."

In A.D. 40, however, Petronius temporized, being genuinely unwilling to execute the emperor's mad command. While he procrastinated, urgent representations were made to Gaius himself by Agrippa. So great was Gaius's friendship for Agrippa that he gave in to him to the extent of writing to Petronius to say that, if the statue had already been erected, it must remain, but if not he was to take no further action.

But Petronius had by this time written to the emperor to say that it was impossible to carry out his order except by exterminating the Jewish people. Gaius, therefore, sent him a second letter ordering him to commit suicide as the penalty for his insubordination. Before Petronius received this second letter, however, news came that Gaius had been assassinated (January, A.D. 41).

Gaius was assassinated in a palace revolt because there was no constitutional means of removing an emperor who had become intolerable. The Roman senate thought of restoring republican government after his death, but the praetorian guards proclaimed his uncle Claudius emperor; and their decision was perforce accepted.

---

[1] Mark 13:14; the "abomination of desolation" is personal here, and could well have been taken to refer to the emperor, represented by his image.
[2] II Thess. 2:3 f.

When Claudius became emperor, he issued two edicts confirming the Jews in their traditional privileges in Alexandria (and indeed throughout the Roman Empire). The Alexandrian citizens were forbidden to renew their attacks on the Jews; the Alexandrian Jews were warned not to aim at further privileges than those which they already possessed, nor to exacerbate relations with their Gentile neighbours by encouraging illegal Jewish immigration into the city either from Palestine or from other parts of Egypt. If the two parties could not learn to live at peace, they would experience the just indignation of a benevolent prince, he told them. When further trouble between the two communities threatened to break out in A.D. 53, he proved himself as good as his word by the prompt severity with which he suppressed it.[1]

Agrippa, who was in Rome at the time of Gaius's death, was a long-standing friend of Claudius as well as of Gaius; and Claudius, at the outset of his principate, not only confirmed him in the kingdom which he had received from Gaius, but augmented it by the addition of Judaea and Samaria. For the remaining three years of his life (41–44) Agrippa ruled over a realm about coextensive with that of his grandfather Herod. Like many members of the house of Herod, Agrippa bore the family name Herod in addition to his more distinctive name. He is the ruler called "Herod the king" in Acts 12:1 ff., where his attack on the leaders of the Jerusalem church is described.

This narrative of Acts reveals Agrippa's eagerness to please the Jews of Jerusalem, and this eagerness is amply attested by our other sources of information. He sedulously courted the good will of his Jewish subjects, observing their customs and showing preference for their company, so that even the Pharisees thought well of him. They looked upon him rather as a Hasmonaean king (through his grandmother Mariamne) than as a member of the Edomite stock of Herod. This is indicated in a story preserved in the Mishnah, according to which it fell to his lot, as a Jewish king, to read the lesson Deuteronomy 17:14–20 ("the law of kingship") at the Feast of Tabernacles in a sabbatical year (probably A.D. 40–41). When he came to the words of verse 15, "One from among your brethren you shall set as king over you; you may not put a foreigner over you, who is not your brother", he burst into tears, as he bethought himself of his Edomite ancestry. But the people encouraged him by calling out repeatedly: "Be not dismayed: you are indeed our brother!"[2]

Even so close a friend of the emperor, however, had to regulate his actions in accordance with imperial policy. There were two occasions on which the Romans vetoed projects on which Agrippa had

---

[1] See F. F. Bruce, "Christianity under Claudius", *BJRL* 44 (1961–62), pp. 309 ff.
[2] Mishnah, *Sota* vii. 8.

embarked. One was the building of a third wall, north of Jerusalem, to bring the so-called "New City" (Bezetha) within the fortified area; the other was a conference of client-rulers like himself which he had called together at Tiberias.

Agrippa died suddenly in the spring of 44, having taken ill five days previously, during a festival which he had inaugurated at Caesarea in honour of the emperor. The picturesque details of the occasion are related both by Josephus[1] and by Luke.[2] He left a young family, the eldest of whom, also called Agrippa, was seventeen years old. Claudius considered appointing the younger Agrippa to succeed his father; but his advisers assured him that the control of Judaea was too serious and delicate a responsibility to be entrusted to a youth. Judaea accordingly reverted to government by procurators. But some years later Claudius gave the younger Agrippa the kingdom of Chalcis, at the foot of the Lebanon range, in succession to his father's full brother Herod, who had ruled there until his death in 48. In 53 Agrippa exchanged Chalcis for the territories north-east of the Lake of Galilee over which his father had been made king by Gaius in 37: and when Nero became emperor in 54 he augmented this kingdom by giving Agrippa the cities of Tiberias, Tarichaea, and Bethsaida Julias, with the surrounding districts and villages. As a compliment to Nero, Agrippa changed the name of his capital city from Caesarea Philippi to Neronias.

[1] *Antiquities* xix. 343 ff.   [2] Acts 12:21-23.

CHAPTER XXVII

TROUBLES MULTIPLY IN JUDAEA
(A.D. 44—66)

THE JEWS OF JUDAEA RECEIVED THE REIMPOSITION OF PROCURATORS with an ill grace, after the happy years they had spent under a Jewish king. Even good and considerate governors would have found their task an invidious one; as it was, the procurators from 44 onwards were no better than Pilate had been.

FADUS

The first procurator to be appointed after the death of the elder Agrippa was Cuspius Fadus (44–46). He claimed that, like the former procurators, he should have the right of appointing Jewish high priests, together with the custody of the high-priestly robes of office. This twofold right had been exercised by Agrippa, and the Jews did not relish the idea of its reverting to pagan officials. So they petitioned the emperor, who conciliated them by giving the privilege to Agrippa's brother Herod, who ruled the small principality of Chalcis in the Lebanon. After his death in 48 the privilege was given to the younger Agrippa, who retained it till the outbreak of the Jewish war in 66.

Early in Fadus's period of office, a pretended wonder-worker named Theudas[1] gathered a large band of followers and led them to the river Jordan, claiming that at his word of command the waters would divide, so that they might cross it dryshod. This suggests that he represented himself either as a second Joshua, who would wrest the Holy Land from the heathen,[2] or else as a second Elijah, precursor of the Messiah.[3] Fadus sent a body of cavalry against him and his followers; the multitude was dispersed and the head of Theudas brought to Jerusalem. Such "messianic" movements (as they may loosely be called) were to become increasingly frequent in these years.

ALEXANDER

Fadus was succeeded as procurator in 46 by Tiberius Julius Alexander, member of an eminent Jewish family of Alexandria. His father, Alexander, was head of the Jewish community of that city; his uncle was

---

[1] Not the Theudas of Acts 5:36, who probably led one of the revolts which followed Herod's death in 4 B.C.
[2] Cf. Josh. 2:13 ff.   [3] Cf. II Kings 2:8.

the philosopher Philo. But he himself had apostatized from the faith of his fathers, and therefore – in spite of his Jewish ancestry – could not be an acceptable figure in the eyes of religious Jews.

He, too, found it necessary to put down a revolt, which has special interest in that it was led by two sons of Judas the Galilaean, who had himself led the Zealot rising at the time of the census in A.D. 6. This new rising was put down, and the sons of Judas (James and Simon by name) were crucified. The crucifixion of two patriotic Jews by a renegade Jew did nothing to increase Alexander's popularity in Judaea.

The end of Fadus's procuratorship and the beginning of Alexander's coincided with a severe famine in Palestine. Luke tells how the Church of Antioch at this time sent a relief-mission, headed by Barnabas and Paul, to their fellow-Christians in Jerusalem;[1] Josephus tells how Helena, the Jewish queen-mother of Adiabene (a district east of the Tigris) bought corn in Egypt and figs in Cyprus and brought them to Jerusalem for distribution to its famine-stricken populace.[2]

The Jewish adherence of the royal house of Adiabene throws an interesting light on the extent and character of Jewish proselytization in those days. A Jewish merchant named Ananias, in the course of commercial dealings with ladies of the royal family, discussed religious questions with them and encouraged them to worship God according to the Jewish way. About the same time Helena, the queen of Adiabene, was similarly persuaded by another Jew. Under their influence Izates, the crown-prince, also embraced the Jewish faith, and soon afterwards succeeded to the throne (c. A.D. 40). Ananias assured him that it was not necessary for him to be circumcised, as this might be resented by his subjects. But a Galilæan Jew named Eleazar, who paid a visit to Adiabene, persuaded the king that unless he was circumcised he could not hope to win divine approval, and the king accordingly submitted to the rite. Other members of his family were also circumcised, including his brother Monobazus, who succeeded him as king about A.D. 64. Monobazus had a magnificent tomb built in Jerusalem for his mother and brother. Some of his relatives fought on the Jewish side against the Romans in the war of A.D. 66—70.

The rulers of Adiabene acknowledged the Parthian king as their overlord, but they were sufficiently powerful for the Parthian king on occasion to be very grateful for their support. There were large Jewish colonies in the western part of the Parthian Empire, and for some fifteen years (c. A.D. 25—40) a Jewish soldier of fortune named Asinaeus served the Parthian king as governor of his Babylonian province. This period of Jewish ascendancy was followed by anti-Jewish riots, especially in Seleucia on the Tigris, chief city of the province, where several thousand Jews were massacred by their Gentile neighbours.

[1] Acts 11:29 f.   [2] *Antiquities* xx. 51 f., 101.

Cumanus

Alexander was followed as procurator of Judaea in 48 by Ventidius Cumanus, whose four years of office were marked by constant tumults. The popular temper was such that the slightest incident might cause offence and start a serious riot. For example, during the passover celebrations in one of the years of Cumanus's procuratorship a Roman soldier from the fortress of Antonia so greatly angered the crowd of pilgrims in the Temple court by an insulting gesture that the ensuing tumult could not be quelled without bloodshed.

More provocative was the action of another Roman soldier during a punitive raid in Western Judaea. This soldier tore up a scroll of the law in a synagogue. This act of sacrilege was an attack on the Jewish religion, which enjoyed the express protection of Roman law. A Jewish deputation went to Caesarea and refused to be satisfied until Cumanus had the offending soldier executed. But the fact that the soldier *was* executed shows how scrupulous Roman law was to avoid giving unnecessary offence to Jewish religious susceptibilities.

Towards the end of Cumanus's procuratorship a frontier dispute broke out between the Samaritans and Jews. Some Galilaeans were murdered in a Samaritan village, but Cumanus took no steps to have the offenders brought to justice. Two Jews therefore (Alexander and Eleazar by name), put themselves at the head of a Zealot band and made a reprisal attack on the Samaritans. Although Cumanus had not taken steps against the Samaritan murderers, he was quick to take military action against this Zealot band. The Jewish leaders accused him of partiality, and lodged an appeal with Quadratus, the legate of Syria. Quadratus ordered leading representatives of the Jewish and Samaritan communities, together with Cumanus himself, to go to Rome and have the dispute heard there by the emperor. In the imperial court the Jews found a powerful advocate in the younger Agrippa. So effective was his advocacy that Claudius acquitted the Jews, sentenced the hapless Samaritan delegates to death, and removed Cumanus from his procuratorship.

Felix

Cumanus was succeeded as procurator by Antonius Felix, who appears to have held a subordinate post in Samaria under Cumanus.[1]

Felix was not a member of the equestrian order, as the other procurators of Judaea were: be belonged to the humble rank of freedman. With his brother Pallas he had once been a slave in the household of Claudius's mother Antonia. After they were emancipated Pallas attained a position of great influence in the imperial household as head

[1] *Cf.* Tacitus, *Annals* xii. 54.

of the civil service, and it was through his influence that Felix was given the extraordinary honour (for a freedman) of governing a province.

In spite of his low birth, Felix married into the highest circles. He had three wives in succession, all of royal birth: one of them was a grand-daughter of Antony and Cleopatra; the third and last was Drusilla, daughter of the elder Agrippa, who left her former husband – Azizus, king of Emesa – to come and live with Felix as his wife (A.D. 54). They had a son, Agrippa, who met his death in the eruption of Vesuvius in A.D. 79.

Felix set himself energetically to rid his province of the insurgent bands which were increasing in strength and activity. His severe measures against them were attended by temporary success, but they alienated large numbers of the population, in whose eyes the insurgents were not bandits but patriots.

One device which began to be widely adopted by some disaffected Jews was assassination. They mingled with the crowds at festivals and similar occasions, and stabbed their opponents (especially Jews who were suspected of being pro-Roman) unawares with the daggers which they carried concealed in their garments. From the Latin word for dagger (*sica*) they came to be known as *sicarii* ("dagger-men"). One of their earliest victims was an ex-high priest, Jonathan the son of Annas, a man of moderation, who on that account was specially obnoxious to extremists.

One of the rebel-leaders who created a stir about A.D. 54 was an Egyptian who claimed to be a prophet, and led a following of some four thousand men out to the Mount of Olives, east of Jerusalem, promising that at a given signal the walls of Jerusalem would fall down flat (as the walls of Jericho had done in Joshua's day), so that they might march in and seize control of the city. But Felix sent troops against him, who killed 400, captured 200, and scattered the rest. The Egyptian disappeared. Two or three years later, when the military tribune commanding the garrison in the fortress of Antonia rescued a man from being lynched by an angry crowd in the Outer Court of the temple, he imagined somehow that it was this Egyptian, on whom the populace were venting their anger for the way he had left his followers in the lurch. But he discovered that he was mistaken: this man was no Egyptian but a Jew of Tarsus, Paul by name.[1]

The Egyptian, however, was but one among many impostors who in those days led people out into the wilderness of Judaea, promising to perform miracles which would repeat the wonders of the days of Moses and Joshua, and signal a new deliverance from Israel's oppressors.

Meanwhile the official leaders of the Jewish nation were rapidly

[1] Acts 21:38, where "Assassins" (R.V., R.S.V.) represents *sicarii*.

losing the respect to which their office might have entitled them in the eyes of the Jews. The high-priesthood had become the prize of a few wealthy Sadducean families, whose high-handed arrogance won them the hearty dislike of the common people.

But of all the high priests, none exposed himself to greater obloquy than Ananias the son of Nedebaeus (A.D. 47—58). He appears on one occasion in the New Testament, when as president of a judicial meeting of the Sanhedrin he acted with disgraceful lack of impartiality.[1] He is commemorated in Jewish tradition mainly for his greed, which led him to seize and sell those portions of the temple sacrifices which were the rightful perquisities of the ordinary priests, who were faced with starvation in consequence.[2]

The closing years of Felix's procuratorship were marked by fierce rioting between the Jewish and Gentile citizens of Caesarea. The Jews of the city claimed special privileges because its founder was a Jewish king (Herod). When civil strife broke out between the Jewish and Gentile populations, Felix intervened on behalf of the Gentiles, and sent the leaders of both parties to Rome. But Nero, the stepson of Claudius, was now emperor, and Felix himself was recalled to Rome. Realizing that he had gone too far in offending the Jews, he tried at his departure to win their good will by leaving their *bête noire*, Paul of Tarsus, in prison at Caesarea, instead of setting him at liberty. Felix could no longer count upon his brother Pallas to maintain him in office. Soon after Nero's accession in 54 Pallas had been removed from his post as head of the imperial civil service; but he still retained sufficient influence to ensure that Felix suffered no other penalty than removal from his procuratorship.

FESTUS

The next procurator of Judaea was Porcius Festus (c. 59—62). Soon after Festus's arrival in the province, the dispute at Caesarea was decided in favour of the Gentiles by an imperial rescript. According to the Jewish account, the Gentile Caesareans procured this favourable verdict by bribing Beryllus, Nero's secretary. Far from receiving the special privileges which they desired, the Caesarean Jews were reduced to the level of second-class citizens. This decision, in view of the embitterment which resulted from it, must be numbered among the causes of the Jewish revolt of A.D. 66.

Short as Festus's term of office was, it gave him time to take energetic action against a number of militant insurgents. A less serious

---

[1] Acts 23:1-5.
[2] TB *Pesachim* 57a. He plays a more commendable part in Josephus's narrative (see pp. 220 f. below).

incident of his procuratorship arose from a dispute between the temple officials and the younger Agrippa. Agrippa had a town-house in Jerusalem, to which he added a tower from which he had a convenient view of the temple courts and could watch the priests performing their sacrificial duties. The priests did not like this supervision by a layman, even if he was the "secular head of the Jewish church".[1] So they built a high wall to block his view. Agrippa protested to Festus, who ordered the wall to be demolished. But the chief priests appealed to Caesar. They sent an embassy to Rome, where they now had a powerful friend at court in Poppaea, Nero's new wife and empress. Through her mediation they obtained permission to maintain the wall which they had built to block Agrippa's view.

Festus died suddenly in office about the year 62, and a three months' interregnum ensued before his successor Albinus arrived. During this interregnum the high priest, Annas II, seized the opportunity to pay off a number of old scores. He brought a number of men before the Sanhedrin and procured their condemnation to death. Among these the most notable person was James the Just, leader of the large Christian – or more accurately Nazarene – community in Jerusalem. This judicial murder shocked many of the Jerusalemites who were not themselves Nazarenes, for James's asceticism and piety had won him widespread veneration, and when Jerusalem was besieged a few years later there were not wanting those who declared that the disaster had befallen them because James's continual intercession for the city had been so violently cut short.

Annas's high-handed behaviour was quickly terminated by Agrippa, who deposed him from the high priesthood and replaced him by a rival, Jesus the son of Damnaeus. Street fighting ensued between the partisans of the two rivals.

ALBINUS

Albinus, the next procurator, is represented by Josephus as being even more scandalously venal than most procurators were. He arrested a large number of *sicarii*, and also those partisans of Annas II who were stirring up riots in Jerusalem in resentment at their master's deposition from the high-priesthood; but set them free when he was offered a sufficiently handsome bribe.

At the Feast of Tabernacles in the autumn of 62 an uncanny impression was made in Jerusalem by the appearance of a peasant, Jesus the son of Ananias, who incessantly proclaimed the imminent doom of the city:

[1] Because of his right to appoint the high priest (see p. 211.).

> A voice from the east,
> A voice from the west,
> A voice from the four winds;
> A voice against Jerusalem and the sanctuary,
> A voice against bridegrooms and brides,
> A voice against this whole people.[1]

Like the ominous pronouncements of Solomon Eagle before the Great Fire of London, this peasant's utterances seemed prophetic in retrospect, when disaster overtook the city and temple.

Albinus was recalled after three years in office. According to Josephus, before he left the province he executed convicted criminals, but set free those who were awaiting trial for less serious offences, thus filling the land with robbers.

It must be kept in mind that Josephus is interested in giving an unfavourable picture of the last procurators of Judaea, in order to minimize the blameworthiness of the Jews in rebelling against Rome in 66.

FLORUS

The last procurator of Judaea was Gessius Florus, who owed his appointment (as rumour alleged) to his wife's friendship with the Empress Poppaea. His appetite for bribery and extortion was such, Josephus says,[2] that he made his predecessor Albinus appear a public benefactor in comparison with him; for he plundered whole towns and gave brigands a free hand in return for bribes.

Even if Josephus exaggerates Florus's wickedness, there can be no doubt that his incapacity and his insensitiveness to the state of feeling in Judaea contributed greatly to the outbreak of war in A.D. 66.

---

[1] Josephus, *War* vi. 300 ff.   [2] *Antiquities* xx. 253.

CHAPTER XXVIII

THE WAR WITH ROME AND
THE END OF THE SECOND TEMPLE

(A.D. 66—73)

AFTER THE SEVENTY OR EIGHTY YEARS OF INDEPENDENCE WHICH THEY
had enjoyed under the Hasmonaeans, the Jews did not take
kindly to the fresh imposition of an alien yoke. The late Hasmonaeans had been oppressive enough to many of their subjects, but in
retrospect their evil deeds were forgotten, and only the fact that they
were a native dynasty which had freed Israel from foreign domination
was remembered.

So long as a Hasmonaean retained the high-priesthood, however, the
situation was not intolerable. Even Herod was technically a Jew,
although he was of Edomite stock and the creature of Rome. While
he reigned, he absorbed much of the odium which was directed
against Rome when Judaea was governed by imperial procurators.
Although the national leaders who petitioned for the removal of
Archelaus in A.D. 6 hoped that internal autonomy under a Roman
governor would be preferable to his tyranny, the event was to prove
them wrong. There were, of course, those who, like Judas the Galilaean
and his Zealot disciples, found the mere fact of being directly tributary
to a pagan ruler outrageous. But others might have been content
had the administration been equitable and understanding. Unfortunately, the extortionate and brutal behaviour of procurators like
Pilate played into the hands of the extremists. The situation was even
more intolerable after the brief Indian summer which they enjoyed
under Herod Agrippa I. Administrative injustice increased the disaffection against Rome; and when disaffected bands took up arms,
the ruthlessness with which they were crushed increased popular
sympathy with them and antagonism to Rome.

It is plain, too, that what may loosely be called the "messianic"
spirit was in the air. Rome began to replace the Seleucid Empire in the
minds of interpreters of Daniel's vision as the final Gentile power which
was to be pulverized by the "stone cut out without hands."[1] When the

---

[1] Dan. 2:34 f., 44 f.; cf. Josephus, *Antiquities* x. 210.

Hasmonaean dynasty lost its independence, the expectation began to revive of a champion of David's line who would crush Israel's enemies and establish dominion for his people. Even the pious, near-Essene community of Qumran cherished the hope of a final warfare against Rome in which, when God gave the signal, they would play a decisive part.[1] The Zealots did not believe that they should wait for a signal: the fact that they were under heathen domination was signal enough for them: they knew their duty and believed that God must prosper their cause and give them victory in their fight for Israel's freedom.

To a nation which was so convinced of its divinely-appointed destiny the temptation to co-operate with destiny was great, especially when the situation in Judaea was so intolerable as it became under the governorship of Florus.

The Gentiles of Caesarea, after being awarded by Nero superior civic privileges to the Caesarean Jews, who had opposed their request, lost no opportunity of rubbing salt into the wound, and annoyed the Jews in a great variety of ways. On one occasion they sacrificed a bird outside the synagogue door, thus not only defiling its precincts, but also hinting delicately at the common Gentile report that the Jews were a leprous nation (for the sacrifice of a bird was part of the Levitical ritual for the removal of leprosy). This was a breach of the privileges which imperial law secured to Jewish religion, apart from being a breach of good taste and good manners; and the Jews appealed to Florus for redress. Knowing that it was useless to appeal to Florus without bribing him, they paid him eight talents of silver. Florus took the money, but paid no further heed to their complaint.

Florus's rapacity, however, passed the limits of endurance when he proceeded to raid the temple treasury and seize seventeen talents of the sacred funds. Pilate had levied a tax on the treasury, it is true, but he had taken the money for what he considered a perfectly justified purpose.[2] Florus had no such excuse. The people of Jerusalem were unable to prevent the procurator from perpetrating this sacrilege, but two city wags relieved their feelings by taking up a mock-collection in public for a governor who was evidently reduced to such desperate straits. Florus, infuriated by this insult, sent his troops against the populace. There was much bloodshed and looting, and several citizens, including some who even belonged to the Roman equestrian order, were seized at random and crucified. The people's reaction was violent; they cut the communications between the fortress of Antonia and the temple courts, to prevent a sudden incursion by members of the Roman garrison in the fortress to seize and occupy the temple area.

1 See my *Second Thoughts on the Dead Sea Scrolls*[2] (1961), pp. 74 ff., 85 ff.
2 See p. 201.

The legate of Syria, Cestius Gallus, sent a military tribune, Neapolitanus, to Jerusalem to investigate the disturbances. During his visit the citizens remained calm, and the younger Agrippa did his best to dissuade them from the idea of revolt. Rebellion would be futile, he urged; the wise and safe course was to remain obedient to Rome. But when his hearers asked him if obedience to Rome involved submission to Florus, he had to admit that it did, and they refused to listen to his further pleas.

The leader of the party in Jerusalem which was for war with Rome was a priest named Eleazar, captain of the temple and son of the former high priest Ananias son of Nedebaeus. It was at his instance that the first overt act of rebellion against Rome took place. This was the cessation of the daily sacrifice which for decades had been offered in the temple on behalf of the emperor's welfare. This was tantamount to a deliberate renunciation of the emperor's authority; it was in effect a declaration of war.

There were, however, some moderate leaders in Jerusalem who contemplated with horror the turn that events had taken, and tried to check them. Chief among these were Ananias, son of Nedebaeus (father of the Eleazar just mentioned), and his brother Hezekiah. They appealed to Florus and to Agrippa for co-operation in preventing the revolt from spreading. Florus did nothing; it looked as if he had no desire to prevent war from breaking out.[1] Agrippa sent reinforcements to the peace party; together they were able to maintain themselves for a time in the western (upper) quarter of the city, but they were insufficient to take effective action against the insurgents in the temple area. On September 5, A.D. 66, the latter captured the fortress of Antonia which overlooked the temple precincts, wiped out the Roman garrison and manned it with their own forces.

The Zealot party naturally viewed this situation as one which called for their leadership; the day of national revolt against Rome was the day for which they had waited and fought and suffered. Their leader at this time was Menahem, last surviving son of that Judas the Galilaean who led the abortive revolt of sixty years before. Menahem and his followers had already seized the fortress of Masada, built by Herod on the south-western shore of the Dead Sea, and massacred the Roman garrison which occupied it. Now, arming themselves with the weapons which they found in the arsenal there, they marched to Jerusalem. They took charge of the attack on the western quarter of the city, and soon gained control of it. The soldiers of the peace party, along with the reinforcements sent by Agrippa, were compelled to sur-

[1] In estimating the measure of Florus's responsibility, we should consider that Josephus's account of him is no more objective than an Eoka account of Field-Marshal Lord Harding's actions in Cyprus in 1955–56 would be.

render but were allowed to leave the city unharmed. The Roman forces were shut up in the three towers of Herod's palace on the western wall.

But Menahem's evident ambition to be sole leader, if not indeed king, of an independent Jewish state, brought him into rivalry with the priestly insurgents. Moreover, he and his followers had incurred the deadly enmity of Eleazar, captain of the temple, because on September 25 they had killed his father, the former high priest Ananias, during mopping-up operations in the upper city. Ananias was as closely associated with the peace party as his son was with the insurgents, but Eleazar felt himself none the less obliged to avenge his father's death. His followers therefore attacked Menahem while he was worshipping in the temple; Menahem tried to escape but was caught and tortured to death, together with his chief lieutenants. One of his lieutenants, however – a kinsman of his own, Eleazar son of Jair – got away safely to Masada with a number of followers, and they remained in occupation of that stronghold until the spring of A.D. 73.

Soon after Menahem's death the remnants of the Roman forces in Jerusalem were reduced. They surrendered on condition that their lives should be spared, but as soon as they laid down their arms they were massacred almost to the last man.

Florus now found himself faced with a situation completely beyond his control. The forces at his disposal were insufficient to check the revolt; it was necessary for the legate of Syria to intervene. The legate, Cestius Gallus, marched south with the Twelfth Legion and additional forces to recapture Jerusalem. He occupied the northern suburb, Bezetha, but concluded that the troops he had brought with him were not numerous enough for the task of reducing the remainder of the city and temple area. He therefore withdrew, and as his army was marching north it was ambushed by Jewish insurgents in the pass of Beth-horon and suffered heavy losses (November 25, A.D. 66).

The fact that even Cestius Gallus (as it appeared) did not dare to invest Jerusalem and had suffered a serious reverse on his retreat added great prestige to the insurgent cause. The moderates who had hoped that he would restore order were discredited. Most of the Jews of Palestine were now united for a war of liberation. Joseph ben Gorion and the former high priest Annas II were put in charge of the defence of Jerusalem; Jesus the son of Sapphias and Eleazar, captain of the temple, commanded the army in Idumaea. Another Eleazar – a Zealot leader, Eleazar the son of Simon – although he was given no command, nevertheless enjoyed considerable power through gaining possession of the wealth captured from the Romans and a large part of the public treasure of Jerusalem. Among the commanding officers of the insurgent forces in Galilee was Josephus, son of the priest Mattathiah (and future historian of the war). Josephus had a rival for his Galilaean command in one John of Gischala, whom he charges with constantly plotting to undermine his position. (It is quite likely that John had no great confidence in Josephus's zeal for the insurgent cause.)

Since Cestius Gallus had proved unable to deal with the revolt, Nero sent Vespasian, a veteran soldier who had held successful commands in Gaul and Britain, to Judaea with an independent command. He arrived in the province in the spring of A.D. 67 with three legions of auxiliary forces (about 60,000 men in all). In his first campaign he reduced Galilee, and incidentally won a strange adherent in the insurgent leader Josephus, whose life was spared on his surrender because he predicted Vespasian's elevation to the imperial dignity. (Josephus concluded that his fellow-Jews had been misguided in expecting the messianic prophecies to be fulfilled in a Jew: the world-ruler who was to arise from Judaea was none other than the commander of the Roman forces in Judaea.)

Josephus's rival, John of Gischala, avoided capture when Galilee was conquered and escaped to Jerusalem. There he aimed at establishing his own supremacy, and played off the priestly group against the Zealots, whose leader in Jerusalem was Eleazar the son of Simon. After a winter of civil strife and intrigue, he became master of the city in the spring of A.D. 68. Soon afterwards the last high priest of Jerusalem entered into office – a country priest named Phinehas, son of Samuel. Unlike his predecessors he was not selected from one of the leading chief-priestly families but chosen by lot from the priestly rank and file. The last survivor of the former high priests, Annas II, was killed about the same time on suspicion of being willing to negotiate with the Romans.

By the end of spring, A.D. 68, Vespasian's forces had reduced Peraea, western Judaea and Idumaea. All was now set for the siege of Jerusalem. But in June of that year a revolt against Nero broke out in the west. Nero committed suicide to avoid a worse fate, and civil war raged in and around Rome as one military leader after another tried to gain control of the city and empire. Vespasian suspended military operations to see how events would turn out.

The unexpected respite thus granted to the defenders of Jerusalem seemed to them to be a last-minute divine intervention in their defence. Rome, it appeared, was on the verge of destruction by internecine slaughter: the Empire was on the brink of dissolution: surely the hour for which they had waited so long, the establishment of Israel as an empire ruling "from sea to sea, and from the River to the ends of the earth",[1] was about to strike. The holy city would not fall: on the contrary, the time of its redemption was at hand.

1 Ps. 72:8.

By June of A.D. 69, however, Vespasian had resumed activity and was master of all Palestine except Jerusalem and the three strongholds of Herodion (south-east of Bethlehem), Masada, and Machaerus (in Peræa). Meanwhile further civil strife had broken out in Jerusalem. During Vespasian's inactivity one Simon bar Giora, an ally of the Zealots entrenched at Masada, had become master of Idumaea. Driven from Idumaea by the resumption of military action, he entered Jerusalem and led a faction hostile to the leadership of John of Gischala. Simon established control over Jerusalem and its surroundings, but John retained control of the outer court of the temple, while the Zealot leader, Eleazar the son of Simon, held the inner court with the bulk of the temple treasure. While civil strife between these three party leaders and their followers was warming up in Jerusalem, Vespasian was proclaimed emperor at Alexandria in July (by Tiberius Julius Alexander, former procurator of Judaea, who was now prefect of Egypt). Caesarea and Antioch soon followed suit, and before long Vespasian had the support of the armies in all the eastern provinces. When his partisans had seized Rome for him, he left Judaea for Rome in order to restore order there, and left his elder son Titus to finish the war in Judaea.

Accordingly, in April of A.D. 70 Titus invested Jerusalem. But so confident were the Jewish people of the invincibility of the city that on the very eve of its investment large numbers of Jewish pilgrims went up there as usual for the Passover festival. Their presence in the city once it was closely besieged added to the difficulties of the defence. The defence was already embarrassed by the rivalry between the three factions mentioned above. But the Zealot leader Eleazar was overcome by John at the Passover season; and thereafter John and Simon were united in defence of the city and temple.

As the siege wore on, the horrors of famine, and even cannibalism, were added to the hazards of war, but the defenders had no thought of capitulating, least of all when Titus, using Josephus as his interpreter, urged the advantages of timely surrender upon them. On July 24 the Romans captured the fortress of Antonia. Twelve days later the daily sacrifice in the temple was discontinued. On August 27 the temple gates were burnt; two days later, on the anniversary of the destruction of the First Temple by the Babylonians in 587 B.C.,[1] the sanctuary itself was set on fire and destroyed. By September 26 the whole city was in Titus's hands. It was razed to the ground, only three towers of Herod's palace on the western wall being left standing, with part of the western wall itself.

According to Josephus, Titus wished to save the temple, but was

[1] See p. 92.

unable to prevent his soldiery from venting their vengeful wrath on the structure which had been the core of the resistance during the siege. This was no doubt the account which Titus wished to be believed in the cooler reflection of later years, and Josephus, the grateful client of the Flavian dynasty, gave it the required publicity.

But an interesting variant has come down to us in a historical fragment preserved by Sulpicius Severus (c. A.D. 400):[1]

> Titus first took counsel and considered whether he should destroy so magnificent a work as the temple. Many thought that a building which excelled all mortal works in sacredness ought not to be destroyed, for if it were saved, it would serve as a token of Roman moderation, whereas its destruction would display an eternal mark of savagery. But others, on the contrary, *including Titus himself*, expressed the opinion that the temple ought most certainly to be razed, in order that the Jewish and Christian religions might more completely be abolished; for although these religions were mutually hostile, they had nevertheless sprung from the same founders; the Christians were an offshoot of the Jews, and if the root were taken away the stock would easily perish.

Whatever Titus himself thought, there were no doubt many who cherished this hope. But they were doomed to disappointment. The temple had outlived its usefulness. Christianity, of course, was essentially free from the trammels of the old sacrificial system; but so was all that was best in Judaism.

When the temple area was taken by the Romans, and the sanctuary itself was still burning, the soldiers brought their legionary standards into the sacred precincts, set them up opposite the eastern gate, and offered sacrifice to them there, acclaiming Titus as *imperator* (victorious commander) as they did so. The Roman custom of offering sacrifice to their standards had already been commented on by a Jewish writer as a symptom of their pagan arrogance,[2] but the offering of such sacrifice in the temple court was the supreme insult to the God of Israel. This action, following as it did the cessation of the daily sacrifice three weeks earlier, must have seemed to many Jews, as it evidently did to Josephus, a new and final fulfilment of Daniel's vision of a time when the continual burnt offering would be taken away and the abomination of desolation set up.[3]

The capture and sacking of the city was accompanied by indiscriminate slaughter; large numbers of the population were enslaved, others were destined for gladiatorial games, while seven hundred were reserved for Titus's triumphal procession.

[1] Frequently thought to be a fragment of Tacitus's *Histories*; but see H. W. Montefiore, "Sulpicius Severus and Titus' Council of War," *Historia* 11 (1962), pp. 156 ff.
[2] The Qumran commentator on Habakkuk 1:16.
[3] Daniel 8:11 ff.; 9:27; 11:31; 12:11. Josephus evidently recognizes the fulfilment of these prophecies in the events of A.D. 70 (*War* vi. 94, 311, 316).

View of the enclosure of the
shrine of Abraham's tomb at
Hebron. The outer wall, except
for the uppermost part, is of
Herod the Great's building.
(Courtesy, Stephen Baldock.)

Side arch below the Damascus
Gate, Jerusalem. The upper part
is Roman (Hadrian or later) the
footings and incomplete pillars
are probably the work of Herod
Agrippa. See p. 210.
(Courtesy, Howard Peskett.)

PLATE XII

Stone sarcophagus from a tomb north of Jerusalem, bearing the name of Queen
Saddah in Aramaic and Hebrew, probably Helen of Adiabene, see p. 212.
(Musée du Louvre, Paris.)

The fortress of Masada, last stronghold of the Jewish Revolt. Aerial view of the north end looking west after excavations had laid bare Herod's palace at the tip, storehouses in the centre, and the enclosing walls in which the defenders lived. In the upper right corner are two Roman siege camps.
(Courtesy, Prof. Y. Yadin, the Masada Expedition.)

Silver shekel of the Jewish Revolt depicting three pomegranates with the words 'Jerusalem the holy' and a chalice with the words 'Shekel of Israel' and date above, 'Year 5' (the last year of the revolt). Actual size.
(Dept. of Coins and Medals, British Museum.)

Sculptured panel in the Arch of Titus at Rome showing the golden candlestick, table, and trumpets from the Temple being carried in triumph through Rome.
(Courtesy, A. R. Millard.)

The three remaining Jewish strongholds were reduced within the following three years – Herodion with relative ease, Machaerus with greater difficulty, and lastly the almost impregnable Masada, which fell on April 21, A.D. 73, after the mass suicide of its defenders.

Titus did not remain in Judaea for these mopping-up operations. After a victorious progress from Caesarea to Antioch, followed by a visit to Alexandria, he returned to Rome, in the summer of A.D. 71, and there he was accorded a magnificent triumph, in which his father and brother also participated. In the procession were carried spoils of war, including sacred trophies from the temple, together with tableaux depicting events from the siege and capture of the city. The prisoners of war who were led in the procession were headed by Simon bar Giora and John of Gischala; Simon was executed when the procession finished while John was condemned to life imprisonment. Scenes from the triumphal procession have been preserved in Rome to the present day in panels on the Arch of Titus, which was erected as a memorial to him shortly after his death in A.D. 81.

With the fall of the temple and the abolition of the sacrificial ritual, the Second Commonwealth of Israel, with its priestly constitution, came to an end. No doubt many thought at the time that the national life of Israel itself had come to an end. But the event proved them wrong. The disappearance of the temple order marked the beginning of a new and glorious chapter in Israel's story, which does not come within the scope of this book.

GENEALOGICAL
AND CHRONOLOGICAL
TABLES

THE HOUSE OF DAVID

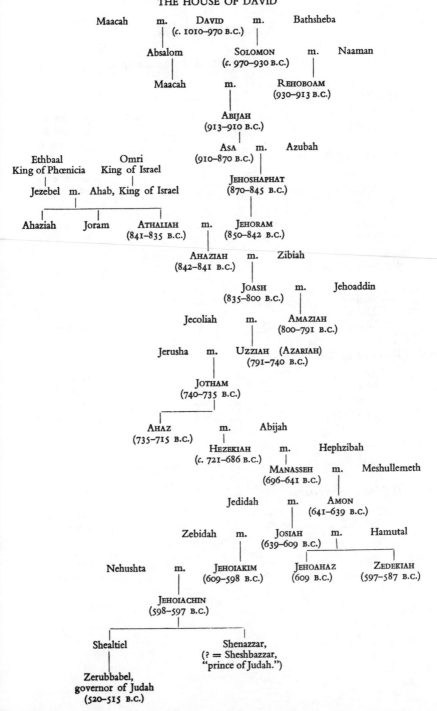

KINGS OF ISRAEL

After the disruption of the monarchy.

DYNASTY OF JEROBOAM

Jeroboam I ... ...   *c.* 930–909 B.C.
Nadab ... ... 909–908 B.C.

DYNASTY OF BAASHA

Baasha ... ... 908–885 B.C.
Elah ... ... 885–884 B.C.

Zimri ... ... 884 B.C.
Tibni ... ... 884–881 B.C.

DYNASTY OF OMRI

Omri ... ... 881–873 B.C.
Ahab ... ... 873–852 B.C.
Ahaziah ... ... 852–851 B.C.
Joram ... ... 851–841 B.C.

DYNASTY OF JEHU

Jehu ... ... 841–814 B.C.
Jehoahaz ... ... 814–798 B.C.
Jehoash ... ... 798–782 B.C.
Jeroboam II ... ... 782–745 B.C.
Zechariah ... ... 745 B.C.

Shallum ... ... 745 B.C.

DYNASTY OF MENAHEM

Menahem ... ... 745–736 B.C.
Pekahiah... ... ... 736–735 B.C.

Pekah ... ... 735–732 B.C.
Hoshea ... ... 732–724 B.C.

KINGS OF ASSYRIA

883—610 B.C.

Ashurnasirpal II	... ...	883-859 B.C.
Shalmaneser III	... ...	859-823 B.C.
Shamshiadad IV	... ...	823-810 B.C.
Adadnirari III	... ...	810-781 B.C.
Shalmaneser IV	... ...	781-771 B.C.
Ashurdan III	... ...	771-753 B.C.
Ashurnirari V	... ...	753-745 B.C.
Tiglathpileser III	... ...	745-726 B.C.
Shalmaneser V	... ...	726-721 B.C.
Sargon II	... ...	721-705 B.C.
Sennacherib ...	... ...	705-681 B.C.
Esarhaddon ...	... ...	681-669 B.C.
Ashurbanipal	... ...	669-c.627 B.C.
Ashuretililani	... ...	c.627-620 B.C.
Sinshariskun ...	... ...	c.620-612 B.C.
Ashuruballit II	... ...	612-610 B.C.

THE CHALDAEAN DYNASTY OF BABYLON

Nabopolassar	... ...	626-605 B.C.
Nebuchadrezzar II	... ...	605-562 B.C.
Evil-merodach	... ...	562-560 B.C.
Neriglissar ...	... ...	560-556 B.C.
Labashi-marduk	... ...	556 B.C.
Nabonidus ...	... ...	556-539 B.C.

KINGS OF PERSIA

Cyrus II	... ...	559-530 B.C.
Cambyses	... ...	530-522 B.C.
Pseudo-Smerdis ...	... ...	522-521 B.C.
Darius I (Hystaspis)	... ...	521-486 B.C.
Xerxes I	... ...	486-465 B.C.
Artaxerxes I (Longimanus) ...	... ...	465-423 B.C.
Xerxes II	... ...	423 B.C.
Sekydianos (Sogdianos)	... ...	423 B.C.
Darius II (Nothos) ...	... ...	423-404 B.C.
Artaxerxes II (Mnemon)	... ...	404-359 B.C.
Artaxerxes III (Ochos)	... ...	359-338 B.C.
Arses	... ...	338-336 B.C.
Darius III (Codomannus)	... ...	336-331 B.C.

THE PTOLEMIES OF EGYPT

Ptolemy I Soter	satrap of Egypt	323-305 B.C.
	king	305-285 B.C.[1]
Ptolemy II Philadelphus		285-245 B.C.
Ptolemy III Euergetes I		247-221 B.C.
Ptolemy IV Philopator		221-203 B.C.
Ptolemy V Epiphanes		203-181 B.C.
Ptolemy VI Philometor		181-145 B.C.
(Ptolemy VII Neos Philopator		145 B.C.)
Ptolemy VIII Euergetes II (Physcon)	169-164 and	145-116 B.C.
Cleopatra III and Ptolemy IX Soter II (Lathyrus)		116-107 B.C.
Cleopatra III and Ptolemy X Alexander I		107-101 B.C.
Ptolemy X Alexander I and Cleopatra Berenice		101-88 B.C.
Ptolemy IX Soter II (Lathyrus), restored		88-80 B.C.
Ptolemy XI Alexander II		80 B.C.
Ptolemy XII (Auletes)		80-51 B.C.
Cleopatra VII (associated successively with her brothers Ptolemy XIII and Ptolemy XIV and with her son by Julius Caesar, Ptolemy XV Caesar)		51-30 B.C.

---

[1] Abdicated 285, died 283 B.C.

THE HOUSE OF
SELEUCUS

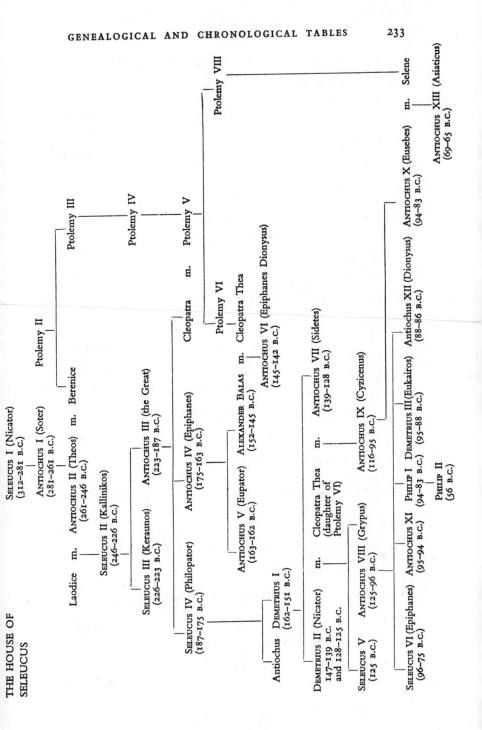

SELEUCUS I (Nicator)
(312–281 B.C.)

ANTIOCHUS I (Soter)
(281–261 B.C.)

ANTIOCHUS II (Theos)   m.   Berenice
(261–246 B.C.)

Laodice   m.   SELEUCUS II (Kallinikos)
(246–226 B.C.)

SELEUCUS III (Keraunos)
(226–223 B.C.)

ANTIOCHUS III (the Great)
(223–187 B.C.)

SELEUCUS IV (Philopator)
(187–175 B.C.)

ANTIOCHUS IV (Epiphanes)
(175–163 B.C.)

Cleopatra   m.   Ptolemy V

Ptolemy II

Ptolemy III

Ptolemy IV

Ptolemy VI   Ptolemy VIII

ANTIOCHUS V (Eupator)
(163–162 B.C.)

ALEXANDER BALAS   m.   Cleopatra Thea
(152–145 B.C.)

ANTIOCHUS VI (Epiphanes Dionysus)
(145–142 B.C.)

Antiochus   DEMETRIUS I
(162–151 B.C.)

DEMETRIUS II (Nicator)   m.   Cleopatra Thea   m.   ANTIOCHUS VII (Sidetes)
147–139 B.C.   (daughter of   (139–128 B.C.)
and 128–125 B.C.   Ptolemy VI)

ANTIOCHUS VIII (Grypus)
(125–96 B.C.)

ANTIOCHUS IX (Cyzicenus)
(116–95 B.C.)

SELEUCUS V
(125 B.C.)

SELEUCUS VI (Epiphanes)
(96–75 B.C.)

ANTIOCHUS XI
(95–94 B.C.)

PHILIP I
(94–83 B.C.)

DEMETRIUS III (Eukairos)
(95–88 B.C.)

Antiochus XII (Dionysus)
(88–86 B.C.)

ANTIOCHUS X (Eusebes)
(94–83 B.C.)

PHILIP II
(56 B.C.)

Selene   m.   ANTIOCHUS XIII (Asiaticus)
(69–65 B.C.)

JEWISH HIGH PRIESTS IN GRAECO-ROMAN TIMES

The House of Zadok

Jaddua	*c.*350–320 B.C.
Onias I	*c.*320–290 B.C.
Simon I	*c.*290–275 B.C.
Eleazar	*c.*275–260 B.C.
Manasseh	*c.*260–245 B.C.
Onias II	*c.*245–220 B.C.
Simon II	*c.*220–198 B.C.
Onias III	*c.*198–174 B.C.

Appointed by Seleucid Kings or Pretenders

Jason (brother of Onias III)	174–171 B.C.
Menelaus	171–161 B.C.
Alcimus	161–159 B.C.
Interregnum	159–152 B.C.
Jonathan the Hasmonaean	152–143 B.C.
Simon the Hasmonaean	143–140 B.C.

Appointed by Popular Decree: The Hasmonaean Dynasty

Simon	140–134 B.C.
John Hyrcanus	134–104 B.C.
Aristobulus I	104–103 B.C.
Alexander Jannaeus	103– 76 B.C.
Hyrcanus II	76–67 B.C.
Aristobulus II	67–63 B.C.
Hyrcanus II	63–40 B.C.
Antigonus	40–37 B.C.

Appointed by Herod the Great (37–4 B.C.)

Hananel	37–36 B.C.
Aristobulus, last of the Hasmonaeans ...	Spring–Autumn 36 B.C.
Hananel (restored)	*c.* 36–30 B.C.
Jesus son of Phabes	*c.* 30–23 B.C.
Simon son of Boëthus	*c.* 23–5 B.C.
Matthew son of Theophilus	*c.* 5 B.C.
Joseph son of Ellem	*c.* 5–4 B.C.
Joazar son of Boëthus	*c.* 4 B.C.

Appointed by Archelaus, ethnarch of Judaea (4 B.C.–A.D. 6)

Eleazar son of Boëthus	*c.* 4–3 B.C.
Jesus son of Seë	*c.* 3 B.C.–A.D. 6
Joazar son of Boëthus (second time)	A.D. 6

Appointed by Quirinius, Legate of Syria (A.D. 6–9)

Annas son of Seth	A.D. 6–15

APPOINTED BY VALERIUS GRATUS, PROCURATOR OF JUDAEA (15-26)

Ishmael son of Phabi	A.D. 15-16
Eleazar son of Annas	A.D. 16-17
Simon son of Kami	A.D. 17-18
Joseph Caiaphas, son-in-law of Annas	A.D. 18-36

APPOINTED BY VITELLIUS, LEGATE OF SYRIA (35-39)

Jonathan son of Annas	A.D. 36-37
Theophilus son of Annas	A.D. 37-41

APPOINTED BY HEROD AGRIPPA I, KING OF JUDAEA (41-44)

Simon Cantheras, son of Boëthus	A.D. 41-42
Matthias son of Annas	A.D. 42-43
Elioenai son of Cantheras	A.D. 43-44

APPOINTED BY HEROD OF CHALCIS (44-48)

Joseph son of Kami	c. A.D. 44-47
Ananias son of Nedebaeus	c. A.D. 47-58

APPOINTED BY HEROD AGRIPPA II (50-100)

Ishmael son of Phabi	c. A.D. 58-60
Joseph Kabi son of Simon	A.D. 60-62
Annas II (Ananus) son of Annas	A.D. 62
Jesus son of Damnaeus	c. A.D. 62-63
Jesus son of Gamaliel	c. A.D. 63-65
Matthias son of Theophilus son of Annas...	c. A.D. 65-68

APPOINTED BY THE PEOPLE DURING THE WAR

Phinehas son of Samuel	A.D. 68-70

THE HASMONAEAN FAMILY

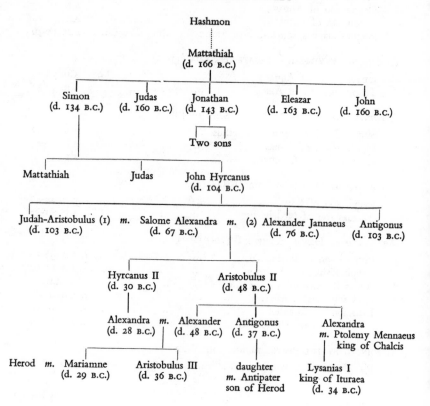

HEROD'S ANCESTRY AND KIN

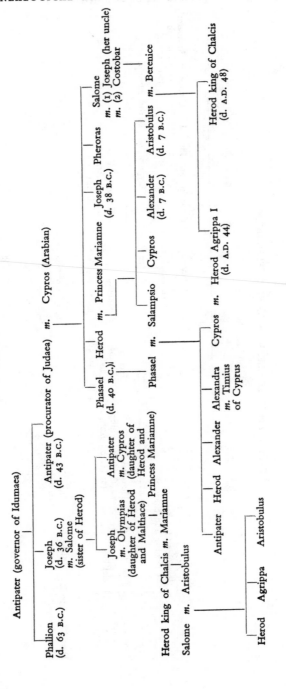

DESCENDANTS OF HEROD AND PRINCESS MARIAMNE

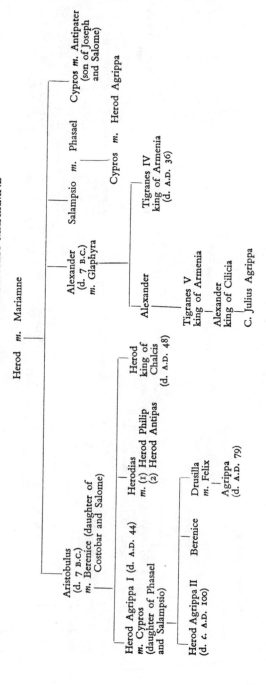

SOME DESCENDANTS OF HEROD BY OTHER WIVES

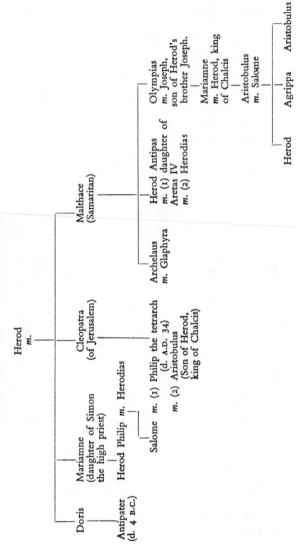

RULERS OF JUDAEA

Herod (king)	...	...	...	...	37–4 B.C.
Archelaus (tetrarch)	...	...	...	...	4 B.C.–A.D. 6

PROCURATORS

Coponius	...	...	...	...	A.D. 6–9
Marcus Ambivius	...	...	...	...	A.D. 9–12
Annius Rufus ...	...	...	...	...	A.D. 12–15
Valerius Gratus	...	...	...	...	A.D. 15–26
Pontius Pilatus ...	...	...	...	...	A.D. 26–36
Marcellus	...	...	...	...	A.D. 37
Marullus	...	...	...	...	A.D. 37–41

Herod Agrippa I (king)	...	...	...	A.D. 41–44

PROCURATORS

Cuspius Fadus	...	...	...	...	A.D. 44–46
Tiberius Julius Alexander	...	...	...	A.D. 46–48
Ventidius Cumanus	...	...	...	...	A.D. 48–52
Antonius Felix ...	...	...	...	...	A.D. 52–59
Porcius Festus ...	...	...	...	...	A.D. 59–62
Albinus ...	...	...	...	...	A.D. 62–65
Gessius Florus ...	...	...	...	...	A.D. 65–66

ROMAN EMPERORS OF THE FIRST CENTURY A.D.

THE JULIO-CLAUDIAN DYNASTY

Augustus (Octavian) ...	...	...	31 B.C.–A.D. 14
Tiberius ...	...	...	...	...	A.D. 14–37
Gaius (Caligula)	...	...	...	...	A.D. 37–41
Claudius	...	...	...	...	A.D. 41–54
Nero	...	...	...	...	A.D. 54–68

Galba	...	...	...	...	A.D. 68–69
Otho	...	...	...	...	A.D. 69
Vitellius	...	...	...	...	A.D. 69

THE FLAVIAN DYNASTY

Vespasian	...	..	...	...	A.D. 69–79
Titus	...	...	...	...	A.D. 79–81
Domitian	...	...	...	...	A.D. 81–96

Nerva	...	...	...	...	...	A.D. 96–98

BIBLIOGRAPHY

I. PRIMARY SOURCES

The primary sources for the history of Israel and the neighbouring peoples during the period covered by this survey are these:—

The books of the Old Testament. A convenient English edition is the Revised Standard Version (1952).

The Apocrypha. A convenient English edition is the Revised Standard Version (1957).

Contemporary inscriptions and other documents from Egypt, Palestine and Mesopotamia. For the English reader convenient selections are accessible in :

J. B. Pritchard (ed.), *Ancient Near Eastern Texts relating to the Old Testament* (Princeton, 1950).

J. B. Pritchard (ed.), *The Ancient Near East in Pictures relating to the Old Testament* (Princeton, 1954).

J. B. Pritchard, *The Ancient Near East: An Anthology of Texts and Pictures* (Princeton, 1959). An abridged edition of the two preceding volumes.

D. W. Thomas (ed.), *Documents from Old Testament Times* (London, 1958).

D. J. Wiseman, *Chronicles of Chaldaean Kings* (London, 1956).

Especially for the Persian and Graeco-Roman periods, the works of ancient historians: notably Herodotus, Thucydides, Xenophon, Polybius, Diodorus, Livy, Tacitus and Josephus. (Their most important works are available for the English reader in the Loeb Classical Library or the Penguin Classics.) For the last two or three hundred years of our survey the works of the Jewish historian Josephus (c. A.D. 37—103) – his *Jewish War*, *Jewish Antiquities*, *Autobiography*, and *Treatise against Apion* – are of the greatest value.

II. FOR FURTHER READING

W. F. Albright, *From the Stone Age to Christianity* (2nd edn., Baltimore, 1957).

W. F. Albright, *Archaeology and the Religion of Israel* (3rd edn., Baltimore, 1953).

W. F. Albright, *The Archaeology of Palestine* (Pelican Books, revised edn., 1960).

E. R. Bevan, *Jerusalem under the High Priests* (London, 1904).

J. Bright, *A History of Israel* (London, 1960).

L. E. Browne, *Early Judaism* (Cambridge, 1920).

R. de Vaux, *Ancient Israel: its Life and Institutions* (London, 1961).

C. H. Gordon, *The World of the Old Testament* (New York, 1958).

C. H. Gordon, *Before the Bible* (London, 1962).

J. Gray, *Archaeology and the Old Testament* (London, 1962).

L. Grollenberg, *Atlas of the Bible* (London, 1956).

A. H. M. Jones, *The Herods of Judaea* (Cambridge, 1938).

K. M. Kenyon, *Archaeology in the Holy Land* (London, 1960).

M. Noth, *The History of Israel* (2nd edn., London, 1960).

W. O. E. Oesterley, *The Jews and Judaism during the Greek Period* (London, 1941).

W. O. E. Oesterley and T. H. Robinson, *A History of Israel* (2 vols., Oxford, 1932).

H. M. Orlinsky, *Ancient Israel* (Ithaca, 1954).

S. Perowne, *The Life and Times of Herod the Great* (London, 1956).

S. Perowne, *The Later Herods* (London, 1958).

C. F. Pfeiffer, *The Patriarchal Age* (Grand Rapids, 1961).

C. F. Pfeiffer, *Between the Testaments* (Grand Rapids, 1959).

R. H. Pfeiffer, *History of New Testament Times with an Introduction to the Apocrypha* (New York, 1949).

G. Ricciotti, *The History of Israel* (2 vols., Milwaukee, 1955).

H. H. Rowley, *The Faith of Israel* (London, 1956).

D. S. Russell, *Between the Testaments* (London, 1960).

E. Schürer, *History of the Jewish People in the Time of Jesus Christ* (5 vols., Edinburgh, 1892-1901). Abridged paperback edn. in one vol., edited by N. N. Glatzer (New York, 1961).

V. Tcherikover, *Hellenistic Civilization and the Jews* (Philadelphia, 1959).

J. A. Thompson, *The Bible and Archaeology* (Grand Rapids, 1962).

M. F. Unger, *Israel and the Aramaeans of Damascus* (London, 1957).

A. H. van Zyl, *The Moabites* (Leiden, 1960).

C. F. Whitley, *The Exilic Age* (London, 1957).

Much valuable material will be found in the historical and archaeological articles in *The New Bible Dictionary*, edited by J. D. Douglas (London, 1962).

ABBREVIATIONS

ANET	..	*Ancient Near Eastern Texts relating to the Old Testament* (ed. Pritchard).
BA	..	*The Biblical Archaeologist.*
BJRL	..	*Bulletin of the John Rylands Library* (Manchester).
CAH	..	*Cambridge Ancient History.*
DOTT	..	*Documents from Old Testament Times* (ed. Thomas).
IEJ	..	*Israel Exploration Journal.*
JBL	..	*Journal of Biblical Literature.*
JTS	..	*Journal of Theological Studies.*
PEQ	..	*Palestine Exploration Quarterly.*
R.S.V.	..	Revised Standard Version.
R.V.	..	Revised Version.
TB	..	Babylonian Talmud.

INDEX

245